America Through the Looking Glass

America Through the Looking Glass

A Constitutionalist Critique of the 1992 Election

Roger M. Barrus
Editor

John H. Eastby
Associate Editor

ROWMAN & LITTLEFIELD PUBLISHERS, INC.

ROWMAN & LITTLEFIELD PUBLISHERS, INC.

Published in the United States of America
by Rowman & Littlefield Publishers, Inc.
4720 Boston Way, Lanham, Maryland 20706

3 Henrietta Street
London WC2E 8LU, England

British Cataloging in Publication Information Available

Library of Congress Cataloging-in-Publication Data

America through the looking glass : a constitutionalist
critique of the 1992 election / Roger M. Barrus, editor; John H.
Eastby, associate editor.
p.   cm.
1. Presidents—United States—Election—1992. I. Barrus, Roger
Milton. II. Eastby, John,   .
JK5261992j   324.9730928—dc20   94-14609   CIP

0-8476-7967-5 (cloth: alk. paper)
0-8476-7968-3 (pbk: alk. paper)

Printed in the United States of America

♾ ™ The paper used in this publication meets the minimum requirements of
American National Standard for Information Sciences—Permanence
of Paper for Printed Library Materials, ANSI Z39.48–1984.

Contents

Preface

This book was born on the night of October 15, 1992. That was the date of the Richmond presidential debate. The Richmond debate, with its talk-show format, represented something new in presidential politics. On the basis of overnight polls, which demonstrated the popularity of the new format with voters, the event was proclaimed an immense success.

The Richmond debate was significant not only for itself, as an important innovation in presidential politics, but also for what it represented. Its audience participation format was but one of many innovations in methods and practices introduced in the course of the 1992 campaign. The number of such novelties was remarkable but not in itself particularly troubling. What *was* troubling was the uncritical way that they were accepted by politicians, journalists, political scientists, and the people.

During the campaign, discussion of the many political innovations was limited to the immediately practical issue of their effectiveness or utility. Completely forgotten, in the uncritical acceptance of the new campaign methods, was the question of their lasting effects on American government and politics. Presidential campaigns, after all, do more than elect a president. They shape the way that the people think about their government—in particular, what they understand as its purposes and essential problems.

The essays in this book attempt to do what was never done during the 1992 election: think through the implications of the methods and rhetoric of the campaign for the fundamental political opinions of the American people, what might be called the "unwritten constitution" of the American polity. For this reason, the essays are primarily concerned with the public events of the campaign, rather than the behind-the-scenes decisions that are the staple of so many presidential election postmortems. The essays consider the new campaign methods introduced by the candidates, along with the candidates' rhetorical treatment of the institutions of government and the issues of politics. Taken together, they demonstrate how the presidential election of 1992 was, for better or worse, something of a watershed for the American political community.

This book never would have seen the light of day if it had not been for the unstinting efforts of a number of individuals. Particular mention should be made of Jane Mahne, Mary Buchanan, and Rondi Arlton for help in manuscript preparation, Diane Barrus for work on the index, and Lynn Gemmell and Dianne Marion for editorial assistance. Preparation of the book was supported by a grant from Hampden-Sydney College.

Introduction

Change, Change, Change

Harvey C. Mansfield Jr.

The American election on November 3, 1992, was a resounding vote for change—in the presidency. Congress was to have many new faces, but almost entirely through retirements, because incumbents who ran for reelection were almost all returned. The vote for change, fed by a passion against all government, spent itself on the unfortunate President Bush, who manfully and gracefully took the onus for all. He watched his popularity fall from the highest rating ever to the lowest and his prospect change from a sure winner to a sure loser without his having done anything except be himself. Not even delighted Democrats, wondering at his fall, wished him ill.

At the end of the campaign all one heard from the Democrats was change, change, change; from the Republicans, trust, trust, trust. What this meant was—would you rather change to a man you don't quite trust, or trust a man you would rather change? Americans chose to do the former, putting their trust in change. One poll found 80 percent of the respondents in favor of "fundamental change," as if they were in a revolutionary mood.

No one speaks now of "progress." Change is the postmodern equivalent, assuming change for the better without having to admit the assumption, much less justify it. Americans were angry—not so much that things were bad, but that they were not getting better fast enough. So, in keeping with their general, unforgiving, and unchanging demand for change for the better, it was time for a change of party. No competition between democratic impatience and the trust or distrust of individuals will be won by the latter. What people want, fundamentally, is an agent of change rather than a trustworthy person. Bill Clinton understood that; George Bush did not.

The vote, which went 43 percent for Clinton, 38 percent for Bush,

1

and 19 percent for Ross Perot, was directed mostly (62 percent) against Bush, since both Clinton and Perot campaigned against him. What went wrong for Bush, all agree, was the stalled economy, technically no longer in recession but growing feebly. Curiously, none of the candidates addressed the recession as such, preferring instead to offer long-term measures that they would have favored at any time. Clinton attacked the excesses (i.e., the prosperity) of the Reagan years for having brought stagnation under the Bush administration; Bush, in reply, had nothing to offer in defense and tried to distract criticism by making more promises for the future. But does the criticism make sense?

Recessions are bound to occur, and only if economists knew how to prevent them should politicians be blamed for them. This one was Bush's bad luck, coming when it did and unaccountably lasting so long. The common assumption on all sides is that government is responsible for assuring an uninterrupted rise in prosperity for all. Virtually all democratic politicians today believe, they say, in a free market, but they do not accept the business cycle which, with its fluctuations of mood and behavior, seems to be the necessary accompaniment of a free market. In this they reflect the opinion of the voters. A successful politician must appear to "take action" against the recession, and this Bush did not achieve. He was blamed for the bad numbers on growth and employment and got no credit for the good ones on inflation and interest rates. Lack of improvement in the trends hurt him perhaps as much as worse performance would have done, and the inexorable rise in health costs made everyone feel insecure. But, according to the models of economistic political scientists, who make electoral predictions based on economic trends, he still should have won. It is no surprise that Democrats exaggerated the pain, but why did people believe them?

Bush is afflicted with a constitutional inability to explain himself. It is not just lack of eloquence, though that is part of it, and it is not that he cannot make up his mind or register the result, because he makes his views known well enough. But he cannot fit them into a whole or supply an argument. Two general laws of change exist for modern democracies: the first for a rising standard of living and the second toward more democracy. These are what they mean by "change." Both desires are insatiable, having no resting point, and they are in large part incompatible, since getting rich tends to make the rich proportionately richer. The two motions are irrational, and it is the task of democratic politicians both to express and to contain them, explaining them as reasonable so that the people can see what they want and a majority can be formed.

Ronald Reagan excelled in this ability; Bush lacked it. Although he had eight years as vice president in which to watch Reagan work his magic, he apparently learned neither how to explain by himself nor how to repeat Reagan's explanations. He did not really appreciate that he was elected in 1988 not for his own qualities but because of Reagan. When the Democrats denounced Bush for "trickle-down economics"—an old accusation dating from the New Deal—he had no defense but a lame retort against "trickle-down government." In a time when socialism has become disreputable, Bush could find nothing to say against Clinton's various economic "plans" except that they would raise taxes. But why are taxes bad and why is less government better? In the campaign Bush could not offer a picture of America in which all would prosper freely, that is, on their own: a democratic defense of capitalism.

Likewise in governing, Bush lacked such a picture and so could not sustain himself, as was necessary, against a Democratic Congress. Reagan, having a principle, knew how to retreat when he was compelled to and he had security in hard times; in his recession in 1982 he could say "stay the course." But Bush had no course, and so he was unable to make his retreats distinct from his advances. He confused his supporters and emboldened his critics. It is harsh to call his term a failed presidency, because nothing really failed at home and he enjoyed great success abroad. Any disappointments could have been blamed on a failed Congress, but Bush was unable to get that point across. If his presidency failed, it is because he failed to explain it.

Yet perhaps something more is required to understand the rejection of Bush. Unexpected triumph in the Cold War has caused Americans to look inward in unhealthy fashion or with disappointing results. What exactly have we gained, now that we have won? We are already rich, and we are democratic. Is all we want to become more so? Where is America's greatness? Bush was not prepared to say.

The situation is epitomized in dissatisfaction with the Gulf War, than which no better military success could be imagined. But the war left Saddam Hussein in power, much enfeebled but now after the election chortling at the overthrow of his enemy, George Bush. Saddam is a reminder of the survivability of evil and a symbol of frustration. Here was decisive action by Bush and little credit for it. He could not turn his victory to account, and the Democrats, who had mostly opposed the war, profited from Bush's decision—reasonable if unlucky—not to try to depose Saddam. Whether Bush acted (as in the war) or not (as with the economy), he was damned for inaction. So the people acted, making a change, thereby purging the desire for change and renewing their trust in government. This is the alchemy of a democratic election.

Clinton began his campaign for change by changing his own party. After the Democrats' 1984 defeat at the hands of Reagan, he had helped to found the Democratic Leadership Council in order to take control of the party from the left and to reconstruct a winning coalition. Unlike Bush, Clinton studied Reagan and learned from him. In his campaign he disarmed the Republicans by occupying their ground, for example with regard to welfare, for which he proposed the addition, in some cases, of a requirement to work. He spoke more of inducing responsibility in the poor than of compassion for them. He declared he would raise taxes only on the rich and promised actually to reduce them for the middle class. Animus against taxes appears to be a lasting Reagan legacy. And he rebaptized government spending as investment, on job retraining for example, which as opposed to the entitlements of the welfare state, is supposed to improve productivity.

Clinton worried in Republican terms about the consequences of Republican policies. The deficit has mortgaged the future of America's children, leaving them liable to the fate of living no better than their parents. These were the New Democrats he was leading, not susceptible to the charge of being liberals (the notorious "L-word" Bush used so effectively in his 1988 campaign). It is true that Clinton had a "plan" for everything, but this was not government planning in the hoary socialist sense because the plan would rely on the manipulation of market incentives.

Two excellent strokes of policy helped Clinton in the campaign. He used an invitation from the ever-carping black leader Jesse Jackson to denounce a black racist singer, Sister Souljah, whom Jackson had praised. This brutal reproof put Jackson on his best behavior during the campaign (he had been a noisy bother to Walter Mondale in 1984 and Michael Dukakis in 1988), and it did not prevent Clinton from gaining 90 percent of the black vote in the election. The other was his choice of Albert Gore for vice president, a moderate Southerner like himself. Clinton avoided the usual ticket-balancing, and thus confirmed rather than confused his message. With all these moves Clinton brought back the Reagan Democrats in droves and appealed successfully to suburban voters.

In the campaign Clinton kept the message simple in the Reagan manner; "the economy, stupid!" was the slogan of his principal adviser. The Republican attempt to divert voters from the economy by raising the cultural question—"family values"—was effectually countered with sincere confessionals. In several installments all America was frankly told the Clinton family history. Clinton easily but remarkably survived the charges that he consorted with a floozy and dodged the draft. His trouble with the draft revealed him, in 1969, to be indecisive under pressure and notably concerned for his political future. Since he is known as "slick," it must be concluded that he speaks too fluently to speak well, but he has an impressive command of fact, argues coherently, and confidently addresses his listeners. In facility of rhetoric he is everything Bush is not. To learn the difference between personality and character, one could look at Clinton and Bush. Clinton has personality without character; Bush character without personality.

Clinton's victory brought an end to "divided government," and now both the president and Congress are Democratic. In their campaigns, Clinton and Perot attacked divided government as "gridlock." Bush did not attack Congress and defensively allowed "change" to be understood as changing him, not Congress. In fact, during his administration, divided government produced opposition, not gridlock, between the two branches. Compromise was effected between Bush and Congress in the debatable budget agreement of 1990 (in which Bush abandoned his pledge of no new taxes), a new Clean Air Act, and another Civil Rights Act. Bush also narrowly won authorization of the Gulf War from Congress.

If there was gridlock, it was in the minds of the electorate who had voted for a Republican president and a Democratic Congress. That indecision was overcome through the success of Clinton's coalition-making. The Democratic party, as Perot said on withdrawing from the race in July, 1992, has been revitalized. Nonetheless, an obvious possibility of tension, if not gridlock, between the two branches lies in the liberalism of Democrats in Congress versus the centrism of Clinton's administration.

Clinton is too ambitious not to want reelection and too prudent to allow his liberal supporters to take full advantage of a victory due to him, not them. Therefore tension can be anticipated. Whether the Democrats return to their status under the New Deal as the majority party, or Republicans stage a comeback, is now in Clinton's power to effect more than in any other person's. He must get the economy moving, satisfy the demand for health care reform which he adopted, reduce the deficit, and not raise taxes on the middle class. And he must do all this coherently, with a view to his Democratic party. At least during the first months of his presidency, his ambition for liberal reform was more evident than his desire to change the Democratic party.

Apart from the partisan opposition between liberals and conservatives, one senses the creeping advance of libertarianism, composed of free-market economics and choice on social issues, in the center of both parties. As a party libertarians are a tiny minority, but when diluted and combined with the two major parties, their principles become more persuasive. An example might be the growth of pro-abortion sentiment among Republican women, many of whom apparently deserted to Clinton. The number of women taking the side of Anita Hill in her accusations against Clarence Thomas seems to have increased since the original confrontation in 1991. This change to an opinion less caring than liberalism and less judgmental than conservatism may affect both parties under Clinton. How it is to be judged depends on whether it represents deliverance from subjection or flight from responsibility.

No account of the election would be complete without discussion of Perot, the "temperamental tycoon" (as Vice President Dan Quayle called him) from Texas, who got 19 percent of the vote. Perot is an American, all-too-American character full of moxie (combative independence), arrogance, and paranoia—in the order of acquaintance as you get to know him. He brings to mind Henry Ford, a man of similar qualities and habits who also made plenty of money. Perot was the last in a series of outsiders who appeared in or near the 1992 presidential primaries: David Duke, Patrick Buchanan, Jerry Brown, and Paul Tsongas—all appealing to disaffection in the major parties. But Perot did them one better by condemning the parties as such and avoiding the primaries altogether, thus effectually nominating himself. He announced his readiness to run on the *Larry King* show, a television program that invites guests who answer callers. (The talk show was a new feature of this campaign, adopted in response to the lack of straight reporting and increasingly intrusive analysis from regular journalists. It was a way for the candidates to say what they, not the media, wanted.) Then, using his paid volunteers to gather signatures for nomination, he got himself on the ballot without the trouble of being opposed.

Perot presented himself as Mr. Fixit. Others could talk, he would act. His analysis of the country's predicament was that of the classic demagogue (and that is what he is): the sole cause of difficulty is corruption in government. We must, he said with unconscious irony, do away with government by "ego-driven, power-hungry people." The Constitution, based on the principle of making ambition counteract ambition, earned his contempt. It's too old. He would gladly replace it with a more responsive system using modern technology to register popular mandates. Those who want to fix things, he meant, cannot be choosy as to how they fix them. The most direct way is best.

But the idea of a constitution is opposed to such disregard of niceties and formalities. A constitution specifies the how by constructing proprieties all must obey in whatever actions they take to fix things. Change presupposes something unchanged which is the subject of change, and that is the constitution. The U.S. Constitution is the how that answers the question, what is America's politics?

That 19 percent of the voters were willing to accept Perot's casual dismissal of constitutionalism was the most disturbing aspect of the election. (His lowest totals were in the South, apart from Texas, where people know his type.) Despite his concern for education, Perot showed little deference to intellectuals. In a funny joke he repeated several times, he said that he had learned about life as a youth by hitchhiking; this made him a "roads scholar" equal to Clinton. But Perot's bottom-line managerialism is encouraged, if not promoted, by the anticonstitutional philosophy of pragmatism, now resurgent among American intellectuals. Pragmatism means doing what works, and the trouble with it—ask George Bush!—is that it works only when it works.

The election of 1992 was about the economy, it was said by all. But "the economy" describes dignity as much as money: the loss of a job, the relative status of rich and poor, the fear of decline. Clinton seemed to sense the political and cultural nature of economic questions, again in the fashion of Reagan but as a Democrat (of some kind). He had little to say about two issues that ought to have decided the election— the low quality of American education and foreign policy in the postcommunist world. Republicans said that his entire experience in foreign affairs consisted of his once having had breakfast at the International House of Pancakes. But perhaps he will deal with Saddam Hussein as smartly as he handled Jesse Jackson. In his usual campaign stump speech Clinton asserted that "change is the law of life." In accordance with this truth, we can be sure he will not be repeating it in 1996.

In a more reflective mode, we can wonder what has brought us to so mindless a word as "change" to describe our political goal. Change from what to what? And why? The American Constitution was written in the context of change—the great democratic revolution of which Alexis de Tocqueville spoke fifty years later. That revolution toward ever greater equality among men he thought to be irresistible, but it could be controlled. The Framers of the Constitution, working before the French Revolution, spoke more optimistically about man's capacity for self-government. They hoped for progress and would not have settled for change. The Constitution they made was supposed to set in motion a tendency toward progress, if not guarantee its achievement. Progress, for them, would be not so much the replacement of myth by scientific understanding or a rise in the standard of living—though both were included in its meaning—as the success of self-government. With self-government we are not merely subject to change, nor simply desirous of change. Human control, while accepting its limitations, takes over the management of human affairs from fate.

In neglecting the mindless or fateful in change, Clinton reflects a general loss of understanding today among intellectuals whose avid support of democracy often does not extend to ideas that support democracy. One of these is the idea of intended progress as opposed to drifting along with mere change. A constitution in the extended sense comprises everything not directly or apparently political that affects—supports or undermines—a certain way of rule. The written constitution, of which the American Constitution is almost the first and certainly the most successful example, depends on ideas and practices not contained in itself; it depends on an unwritten constitution. A certain spirit of democracy is needed to nourish a democratic government.

Both the written and the unwritten constitutions need to be renewed periodically, which is done (among other ways) in the elections required under the written constitution. Elections teach the people about their government, for good or ill, at the same time that they are passing judgment on it. What was taught to the American people in the election of 1992? Clearly the people meant to correct the drift they felt in the Bush administraton, particularly with respect to the economy. But where is the improvement in replacing passive, unreactive drift with conformity to unspecified change that comes and goes mysteriously? Somehow Bush and Clinton were not the same thing, but it cannot be said that the candidates made the difference clear.

An earlier version of this chapter appeared as "Change and Bill Clinton," in the *Times Literary Supplement,* November 13, 1992. Reprinted here by permission of the publisher and author.

Part One

Campaign Methods

Politics as Theater: The Presidential Debates

Roger M. Barrus

The 1992 election probably marked the final establishment of presidential debates as a permanent feature of American politics. It is now, after five elections in row in which debates have played a part, simply expected that the major party candidates will meet each other in debate. So strong is this expectation that it has become a great political liability to be seen as avoiding debates. The 1992 campaign demonstrated the potential of debates for influencing the outcome of presidential elections. Exit polls indicated that a majority of the electorate tuned into one or more of the debates, and that a substantial minority based their final decisions on what they saw and heard in them. This contrasted with earlier campaigns, in which debates seemed to have served more to confirm voters' prior decisions on the candidates than to actually determine how they would cast their ballots. The effect of the debates was all the more remarkable because they involved no major gaffes, such as Gerald Ford's rhetorical liberation of Poland from the Soviet empire, in 1976, or Jimmy Carter's maudlin tale of bedtime discussions of nuclear weapons policy with daughter Amy, in 1980. Nor were there any memorable knockout lines, such as Ronald Reagan's "There you go again" to Carter's insinuations that he could not be trusted with his finger on the nuclear button, also in 1980.

It was the Richmond debate, with its unique talk-show format, that accounted for the influence of presidential debates in the 1992 election. Indeed it might be argued that if there was one decisive event of the campaign, it was the Richmond debate. The talk-show format—candidates in a setting of utmost informality responding to questions posed by members of the studio audience, the whole affair presided over by a media-star moderator—showcased the very different personalities of President George Bush, Governor Bill Clinton, and billionaire businessman Ross Perot. And personality, even more than the economy, was the crucial issue on which the election ultimately turned. Voters were motivated more by the desire to remove Bush from the Oval Office than to put Clinton in it. Clinton was able to carry only about two-thirds of the total anti-Bush vote. Bush was rejected because he was perceived as being too far removed from the concerns of ordinary people. The problem was that Bush did not—perhaps could not, because of his aristocratic upbringing—feel the pain of the people, beset by fears of unemployment and financial ruin because of the lingering recession. Clinton's basic strategy was to exploit this perception, contrasting the president's aloofness with his own empathy and compassion. This was the essential theme of the Democratic National Convention and the immensely successful bus tour that Clinton scheduled immediately after it. The Richmond debate was crucial because it seemed to make clear just how far Bush was from the people. It featured what soon became indelible images of Bush's aloofness, in particular his fumbling for a response to a question on how the economic problems of the nation affected him personally.

The Richmond debate, which was hailed by newspaper and television commentators as a triumph, seemed to fulfill the promise of presidential debates to energize American politics. This is something that the "joint press conferences" of previous campaigns, with candidates responding to questions from panels of journalists, clearly had not accomplished. What made the Richmond debate so effective was its theater or drama. It was not more informative than other debates. The audience of average citizens did not ask more thoughtful or probing questions than the professional journalists. The candidates were not more revealing of their plans for the nation. In substance, the Richmond debate was similar to the many so-called "town meetings" held during the campaign: questions were typically nonconfrontational, dealing with how the candidates would handle some specific problem of concern to the questioner; responses were typically equivocal, taking the form of expressions of sympathy by the candidates, along with promises of programs to solve the problem under consideration. It demonstrated what led one commentator to call the campaign's town meetings exercises in "the blind leading the evasive."[1] While lacking in information and argument, the Richmond debate was fairly bursting with drama. There was real pathos in the scene enacted: average citizens laying their fears and hopes before the candidates for the highest office in the land; the candidates identifying themselves with the aspirations of the citizens and assuring them that all would be well with only the right changes in political leadership. Bush, Clinton, and Perot were actors in a nationally televised drama, or melodrama, and were judged in large part by how well they played their parts in it.

It appears from the Richmond debate that the institutionalization of presidential debates has introduced a new element of theater in American politics. The "theatricalization" of politics is, of course, nothing new. There is much that is theatrical in the operation of government. Election campaigns are essentially theatrical events. What is novel about debates, as a new form of political theater, is their dramatic form. In theater, however, dramatic form is the essence of meaning. Everything depends on the context within which the speeches and deeds of the drama take place. The Richmond debate in particular, with its talk-show format, had a message about the nature of American government and politics. What was never considered, in the general celebration of the Richmond debate, was whether the message of the new political theater was consistent with the requirements of the American system of constitutional, representative democracy.

The Institutionalization of Debates

The institutionalization of debates was a long time coming, indicating something problematic about them as means for deciding the presidency. While the technology for broadcast debates was available from the 1930s, first with radio and then with television, the first debates were not held until 1960. In that year, Vice President Richard Nixon squared off against Senator John Kennedy in a series of four encounters. In what should have been taken as a warning about debates, Kennedy emerged as the overall winner, as much on image as on argument. Those who heard the debates on radio generally picked Nixon as the winner. Kennedy came across better on television because of his appearance of youth and vitality. Nixon, in contrast, looked old and tired. He showed up for one of the debates without makeup and needing a shave. There was no immediate follow-up to the Nixon-Kennedy debates. No debates were held during the 1964, 1968, and 1972 campaigns. The next debates were in 1976, and they have been a feature of every campaign since then.

The emergence of debates as an instituition of American politics has been the result of weakness, and a certain degree of absentmindedness, in the presidency. With one exception, all presidential debates have occurred in situations in which there was no incumbent, as in 1960 and 1988, or in which the incumbent was politically vulnerable, as in 1976, 1980, and 1992. The first incumbent to agree to debate was Ford, in 1976. His willingness to debate was related to his anomalous position as an unelected president, the only occupant of the Oval Office never to have faced the national electorate. Ford had been named to replace Spiro Agnew when he was forced to resign the vice presidency, and then had succeeded to the presidency on the resignation of Nixon. In addition, Ford had taken the politically unpopular step of pardoning Nixon for all crimes committed in the Watergate affair. Similarly, it was political weakness that led Carter in 1980 to debate. Carter was politically vulnerable because of the combination of high unemployment and record high interest rates at home, and the embarrassing Iranian hostage crisis abroad. He was assailed not only from the right wing by Reagan and the Republicans, but also from the left by liberal Democrats led by Senator Edward Kennedy, who challenged him for the Democratic nomination.

Political vulnerability accounted at least in part for Bush's decision to debate in 1992. Bush at first was cool to debates. He rejected the proposal of the independent Commission on Presidential Debates—the formation of which in 1987 was a milestone in the institutionalization of debates—for a series of three meetings, all to be conducted by a single moderator. Bush and his strategists were concerned that Clinton would come across better in the direct give-and-take between candidates that the commission's proposed format was designed to facilitate. The result of Bush's rejection was a "debate about debates" that for some weeks dominated news of the campaign. Bush was heckled by Clinton supporters dressed in chicken costumes, mocking him as "Chicken George." Eventually, trailing in the polls and with no hope of catching up as long as public attention was focused on the debates issue, Bush agreed to meet Clinton in three debates, as recommended by the commission, but with different formats from the one proposed by it. Two would be in the traditional "joint news conference" format, while the other, the debate to be held in Richmond, would be in a new talk-show style. The talk-show format was Clinton's idea, as he was proud to declare.

The only incumbent not politically vulnerable ever to agree to debate was Reagan, in 1984. Reagan's decision to debate was perhaps a matter of political calculation. He had come off the winner in his 1980 encounter with Carter. His easy-going manner seemed to have reassured many who were inclined to vote for him but were concerned whether he was tempermentally fit for the presidency, with its responsibilities in foreign and especially military affairs. It is possible, however, that the decision to debate was due to nothing more than a general inattentiveness to the institutitonal interests of the presidency. Reagan, it has been argued by a number of commentators, was timid about using the powers of his office and his popularity with the public to defend the presidency as an institiution.[2] He responded weakly to invasions of presidential authority by Congress, for example in the passage of the Special Prosecutor Law. The most egregious example of this inattentiveness was Reagan's handling of the Iran-Contra affair. Confronted by allegations of administration wrongdoing in the conduct of U.S. policy in Central America, instead of challenging Congress on the issue of the constitutionality of the Boland Amendments' restrictions on presidential foreign policy-making, he took the safer and easier course of simply denying all knowledge of illegal activity. Rather than risk a showdown with Congress, he conceded to it the right to set the ground rules of American foreign policy. Reagan showed the same kind of disregard for the institutional interests of the presidency in the 1984 campaign, when rather than risk his popularity he agreed to meet Walter Mondale in debate. As things turned out, Reagan's decision to debate was a bad one: his poor performance in the debates with Mondale was the cause of the only anxious moments for him during the campaign.

Other strong presidents—Lyndon Johnson in 1964, Nixon in 1972—have avoided debates, for a number of very practical reasons. The president is a known quantity to voters; as such, he gets nothing from the public exposure. He is not likely to be able to persuade hostile or even undecided voters, his actions in his years in office speaking much more loudly than anything he might have to say in the snippets of time allowed him in debate. The president runs the risk of committing a verbal slip, making him look stupid and unfit for his office. This danger is compounded by the necessity of weighing every word that he utters, especially in matters relating to foreign affairs. Time limits will force the president to simplify, to and even beyond the point of parody, the rationale for his programs and policies. He will be compelled to defend his past record, while his opponent will be free to make promises for a better future. Finally, there is the problem for the president that by simply meeting his challenger in debate, he gives him stature and credibility in public opinion. This is really the converse of a much more fundamental problem. Perhaps the greatest political advantage of incumbency for the president is the aura that comes from standing alone at the pinnacle of government power. Meeting an opponent in debate, arguing issues back and forth, on a level of equality, the president gives up that aura of being one alone at the top.

All of this, given the institutionalization of debates, represents more than a problem of incumbents. The presidency is such a personal office that what is bad for the incumbent is—within limits—bad for the institution. James Madison had the presidency primarily in mind when he described the constitutional system of government as connecting "the interest of the man" with the "rights of the place."[3] In no other office is there such a close identification between individual and institution. The Constitution provides for the personalized presidency by endowing the president with only a few broadly defined powers, leaving it to him to make what he will of them, given the circumstances confronting him during his tenure in office. It does this in order to make possible the energetic exercise of executive authority, in situations requiring it, without inviting such assertiveness on the part of the president, as it would if it too clearly delineated his extraordinary powers. The presidency is a trust or stewardship, more than a legally defined office. The president, who is clearly visible to the people, standing alone at the pinnacle of government power, is held politically responsible by them for the exercise of his stewardship. The personalized presidency is the Constitution's means of weaving together power and responsibility in the executive. The aura or mystique—really the gravity—of the presidency is the result of this conjunction of power and responsibility.

The institutionalization of debates affects what from this point of view appears as the principal institutional interest of the presidency. Debates are essentially means for demystifying the president, and the presidency. This was most clearly manifested in the Richmond debate, which placed the President of the United States of America, along with the other major candidates for the presidency, in the same setting as the physically and emotionally afflicted that are the staple of *Donahue* and *Oprah*. The Richmond debate had nothing even of what might be called the "official unofficial" look of other debates, with their panels of journalists questioning the candidates, reminiscent of presidential news conferences or appearances on *Face the Nation*. Debates developed as an institution during a time when, because of the perceived excesses of the "Imperial Presidency" in the Vietnam War and the Watergate scandal, a demystified, diminished presidency fit the national mood. The aura of the presidency, however, is one of the most potent weapons at the president's disposal in pursuing his political agenda before Congress and the nation. It is the basis of the president's power to persuade—and the power to persuade, as has been argued, is the fundamental power of the presidency.[4] The president, by virtue of his position alone at the top of government, combining power and responsibility in a way that no other official does, commands a hearing whenever he speaks. This power to command a hearing is diminished with the demystification of the presidency. Given the experience of presidents since Vietnam and Watergate—every incumbent except one popularly deemed a failure and defeated for reelection—it is at least questionable whether such a demystified presidency—of which the institutionalization of debates is both a cause and a consequence—can really work.

The Purpose of Debates

Apart from their theatrical quality, debates would appear to be of little value in choosing a president. They reveal little or nothing about the natural capacity or practical preparation of individuals for the presidency. The intellectual ability required of a president is very different from that demonstrated in debating, which basically reduces to the delivery of canned answers to anticipated questions, spiced by occasional snappy rejoinders to an opponent's comments. The preparation required of a president is not so much that of public confrontation, as of private persuasion. Debates correspond to no political requirement for the presidency. Presidents do not debate, particularly in public, members of Congress, Cabinet officers, or foreign leaders. Finally, debates do little to clarify the issues of politics. Issues that would require long discussion to be even minimally covered are in such events compressed into one- or two-minute sound bites. Against all of this, it is argued that debates are useful because they focus public attention. In contrast with other campaign events—in particular the national party conventions, which have such poor television ratings that the major networks have dropped gavel-to-gavel coverage—people actually tune in to watch debates. They tune in because debates, featuring direct confrontation between the candidates, promise to be entertaining. Debates are intended as a corrective to what appears as a serious, if not fatal, defect of American government—its inability to hold the interest and concern of the people on whose behalf it claims to rule.

There is, to be sure, something profoundly alienating about American government. This is a consequence of the constitutional system of representative democracy, which makes the individual citizen into both the source of government power and its largely voiceless subject. Government has its origin in the consent of the people; once it is brought into being, however, the people have little direct say in its operation. To be an American citizen is to be aware simultaneously of one's de jure sovereignty and one's de facto subjugation. On the one side, there are the ringing affirmations of the Declaration of Independence; on the other side, there are the imposing political forms of the Constitution. The contradiction at the heart of the American political system is a constant source of popular dissatisfaction. This dissatisfaction has shown itself in the form of passionate reform movements—populism in the 1880s, progressivism in the 1910s, new left radicalism in the 1960s. It is the root of what has been called the "paranoid style" of American politics, the tendency to attribute social and political problems to the activities of evil conspiracies.[5] For many people, lacking real understanding of the complex institutions of representative democracy, it is difficult to trace the problems of the existing order back through the operation of those institutions to the exercise of popular sovereignty. It is much easier to ascribe those problems to the schemes of the power elite, whether identified as the railroads, the trusts, the military-industrial complex, or—in the rhetoric of the 1992 campaign—Washington insiders. This alienation can also express itself in more benign forms, including the political apathy that is at present so widespread.

To this democratic dissatisfaction with representative government, the Framers of the Constitution would perhaps reply that alienation is the price that must be paid to make democracy work. The Framers elaborated their new system of government with a view to the problems of ancient direct democracy, articulated by the classical political philosophers, and the possible correctives to those problems, invented by the modern political philosophers. Democracy, in the classical analysis, has its characteristic problems, deriving from the nature of its ruling class, the *demos* or the many. The many are the poor, or at least the relatively less well-off. The many poor are more immediately subject to the vicissitudes of fortune than the few rich. They are thus more fearful of what the future might bring. The many further lack the wealth and leisure necessary for the more noble pursuits of life. They are therefore in need of reassurance of their own worth. This makes the many subject to manipulation by those who offer them what they most crave: security and honor. Demagoguery is the great danger of democratic government. The pandering of the demagogues corrupts the people, who eventually come to identify justice with whatever they happen to desire, no matter how evil, corrupt, or dangerous their desires might be. In this way, democracy degenerates into mob rule. Mob rule in turn leads either to the disintegration of society or to the acceptance of despotic rule for the sake of public order—anarchy or Caesarism.[6]

The problem of democracy, for the Framers, was represented by the tragic fates of Athens and Rome. The history of the ancient democracies, according to Alexander Hamilton, was one of continuous "distractions" and a "rapid succession of revolutions" keeping them in a "state of perpetual vibration between the extremes of tyranny and anarchy." All of which had brought democracy, and indeed the "very principles of civil liberty," into disrepute. It is only because of the "improvement" of the "science of politics" in modern times, Hamilton argues, which has led to the invention of "powerful means, by which the excellencies of republican government may be retained and its imperfections lessened or avoided," that there is any hope at all for democracy. The improvements Hamilton refers to include all the devices incorporated in the Constitution: separation of powers, checks and balances, life tenure for judges, etc. The most important of these devices is "the representation of the people in the legislature by deputies of their own election."[7] Representation is the principal corrective for the defects of democratic rule. The Framers understood that the people can safely rule themselves only if they do so indirectly, through institutions created with their consent and by means of government officials at least ultimately chosen by them. The temptations involved in direct democracy, of the people using their political power to fill their immediate physical and psychological needs, mean that it is inevitably susceptible to the wiles of the demagogues.

The forms of representative government established in the Constitution are not intended to thwart the rule of the people—contrary to the claims of populists, progressives, and radicals—but rather to dignify it by refining the popular will. Popular passion is to be filtered through the institutions of government, with their various structures, modes of operation, and political constituencies. To rationalize democratic rule, the Constitution institutionally separates governors and governed. More fundamentally, it separates the people understood as the source of government power and the people understood as the subjects of government power. The institutions of government help the people to look at themselves and their needs objectively, and hence to govern themselves rationally. This is the deepest meaning of the alienation in American government and politics. The forms of the Constitution alienate the people from themselves. The great temptation in American politics, providing much of its impetus, is to overcome the alienation inherent in the constitutional system of representative government. In practice, this translates into the urge to "take power back to the people" by breaking down the formal distinctions between governors and governed.

Taking power back to the people has been, of course, a recurring theme of American politics, almost from the very beginning. It was the war cry of Thomas Jefferson in 1800, Andrew Jackson in 1828, Woodrow Wilson in 1912, and Franklin Roosevelt in 1932. Since the 1960s, however, with the turmoil of Vietnam and Watergate, it has become a staple of presidential politics, the campaign theme of both liberal Democrats and conservative Republicans. This has been reflected in changing campaign practices. It is no accident that debates have emerged as the principal public events of presidential campaigns in this period, for they answer to a deeply felt need in the American people. Debates have as their dramatic motif the overcoming of the sense of distance between governor and governed. The candidates appear without any of the trappings of power or office. They address the people directly, rather than through their party leaders or elected representatives, as in the candidates' convention speeches or the president's State of the Union address. Their tone is conversational rather than oratorical. This, in passing, accounts for the popularity of the Richmond debate: in other debates, journalists have acted as mediators between the people and their would-be governors, leaving the underlying problem dramatically unresolved. The Richmond debate, with its informal setting and immediate interchange between candidates and audience, completely abolished the separation between governors and governed created by constitutional political forms. The debate was "direct democracy" in action, rather than the "representative democracy" of the Constitution.

The theme of the reconciliation of governor and governed, sovereign and subject, was displayed for all to see in what by all accounts was the dramatic highpoint of the Richmond debate. This came in a question to Bush, who was asked: "How can you honestly find a cure for the economic problems of the common people if you have no experience in what's ailing them?" The question was an invitation to the candidates to establish their claim to office on nothing but their feeling for the people. Empathy—fellow feeling—was to be the qualification for rule, not prudence, wisdom, or judgment. Bush was briefly taken aback by the question, but eventually said something. This was taken as conclusive proof of his removal from the people and their problems. There was no such hesitancy on the part of Perot or Clinton. Perot claimed that he had been compelled to interrupt his successful business career in order to rescue the American people from the morass of deficit spending, into which they had been innocently led by corrupt politicians. Clinton, fairly radiating compassion, moved caringly toward the questioner. "You know people who've lost their jobs and lost their homes?" he asked. He went on to claim that, as governor of a small state, "When people lose their jobs, there's a good chance I'll know them by their names. When a factory closes, I know the people who ran it."[8] All but lost in the drama of the moment was what was really remarkable about this interchange: none of the candidates objected to the question itself, for what it implied about the nature of government or the requirements for public office.

From the point of view of the problem of political alienation, it might be argued that presidential debates serve a very important purpose. Debates allow for the release of powerful passions generated in the body politic by the operation of the system of representative government. The problem with this argument is that the release afforded by presidential debates does not purge these passions, but rather excites them. In Richmond, the candidates themselves led the charge in attacking the evil elite responsible for the ills of the nation, whether it was Republicans in the White House (Clinton), the Democratic majority in Congress (Bush), or Washington insiders of both parties (Perot). What the American people most desperately need is to understand the cause of their political frustrations, in the processes of the constitutional system of representative government, in order to learn to put up with them. What the people get in presidential debates, however, is the illusion of direct democracy. This exercise in direct democracy can only have the effect of delegitimizing the forms of representative democracy. The necessity of the elaborate system of representation established in the Constitution is totally obscured. The formalities of representative government must appear as austere and even cold, in comparison with the personal warmth of the "electronic town meeting" held in Richmond. While the problem that presidential debates— as a kind of political theater—are intended to address is a real one, their effect—as reflected in the extraordinarily theatrical Richmond debate—is rather to exacerbate than to remedy the problem.

Debates as Political Education

Debates, as a new and popular form of political theater, are more than an arena of presidential politics. They are, willy nilly, elements in the political education of the American people. Every form of government needs a civic education appropriate to its specific character. This is a delicate problem for the American system of representative democracy. Claiming to represent the people, it cannot impose itself excessively on them. This means that, in its civic education, it must confine itself to inculcating only the most essential principles of political morality. This kind of education is sufficient because it demands relatively little from its citizens—basically obedience to the law. This is easy, however, because the law is made for the purpose of protecting the citizens in the enjoyment of their rights. It is in their self-interest to obey the law. Real sacrifice is demanded in only the most extreme circumstances, and is elicited by appeals to the private interests of home and family. For this kind of citizenship, only a minimal civic education is necessary, one that establishes the connection between individual rights and obedience to law, while instilling a degree of patriotic love of country. The principal means for this political education are the theatrical elements or occasions of American government. These are designed to impress on the citizens the democratic nature of the law, as originating in the will of the people, and the dignity of the law, as the work of institutions embodying reason and deliberation. This theatrical education fits not only the practical needs but also the moral limits of American government. The crucial question concerning the institution of presidential debates, the new political theater, is whether it supports the civic education that is the purpose of the old.

The theater—the pomp and ceremony—of American government is by no means mere useless display. It is essential to the functioning, and even the survival, of the political system. Public displays by government institutions give meaning to what otherwise would be utterly incomprehensible. Only a relatively few individuals ever hold public office. For most of the rest, lacking real political experience, what they understand of government comes from what they see in its pageantry. They get at least an image of the relationship between popular sovereignty and the organization and operation of government. It is a fundamental problem of representative democracy that the most basic power of government—lawmaking—must be exercised by institutions—legislative assemblies—that because of the size and diversity of their membership must function in a complicated system of structures and processes that will forever remain baffling to most outsiders, and perhaps many insiders as well. This problem is reflected in the American public's perennial low opinion of Congress as an institution. Because it derives its "just Powers from the Consent of the Governed," American government requires trust between rulers and ruled. Human beings cannot trust, however, what they cannot understand. The theatricalization of government gives the people some basis of understanding, and hence trusting, the complicated and remote institutions of the American political system. In the real world of representative democracy—where the limitations of the *demos*, the many, set the parameters of politics—the theatricalization of government is necessary for its very existence.[9]

The political theater of American government is the dramatic representation of the relationship between popular sovereignty and constitutionalism or the rule of law. This relationship is a complex one: the Constitution limits the exercise of the people's sovereign power; it does so, however, in order to actualize the sovereignty of the people, in the form of the rule of law. One way the Constitution limits popular sovereignty is the institutionalization of political power. The only means it provides for the implementation of the will of the people are the established institutions of government. There is no provision in the federal Constitution, as there is in many state constitutions, for the direct expression of the people's will, through referendum, initiative, or recall. Another of the Constitution's limits on popular sovereignty is the system of checks and balances. It is crafted to give the officers of the various branches of government, in Madison's formulation, "the necessary constitutional means and personal motives to resist encroachments of the others."[10] The purpose is to keep any one branch of government, and the interests it serves, from becoming dominant. The Constitution limits the sovereignty of the people in order to make possible the effective rule of law. Without such limitations, popular sovereignty tends to degenerate into factionalism and tyranny of the majority, where the people are led by their passions to courses of action, again in the words of Madison, "adverse to the rights of other citizens, or to the permanent and aggregate interests of the community."[11] The essential purpose of the Constitution's limitations on popular sovereignty is to allow reason to rule by giving it the operative balance of power among the passions. This makes the rule of law into a kind of political representation of the rational self-legislation that modern philosophy identifies as the highest expression of the sovereignty of man.

The themes of popular sovereignty and constitutionalism are developed in the great ceremonial occasions of American government—the inauguration of the president, the meeting of Congress in joint session, the convening of the Supreme Court. These occasions mark the progress of the rule of law, under the aegis of the Constitution. They are dignified and even solemn in tone, as befits the solemn realities that must be confronted in the establishment of democratic self-rule. As Madison observes, it is a profound "reflection on human nature" that such constitutional devices as checks and balances "should be necessary to control the abuses of government." [12] The meaning of the "officially sponsored" political theater is most clearly manifested in the inauguration of the president, the most theatrical event in the cycle of American government and politics. The president, the most powerful officer of American government, in taking the oath of office to "preserve, protect, and defend the Constitution of the United States," proclaims before the whole nation his subservience to the Constitution. The presidential oath is both a promise and a warning to the people. As defender of the Constitution, the president appears both as protector of the sovereign rights of the people and as executor of the law against them. The effect is to present popular sovereignty and the rule of law as inextricably connected. Lest anyone miss the point, it is typically repeated by the president in his inaugural address. It is continued even in the traditional inaugural parade, which mixes symbols of government power—military marching units—with symbols of individual freedom—high school bands and private organization floats.

The fundamental difference between the new political theater of presidential debates and the old is in the treatment of the Constitution. In the debates, it is notable primarily by its absence. In Richmond, the candidates had literally nothing to say about the Constitution. There were no direct references to it. The only indirect references were in a few comments by Bush on the foreign affairs responsibilities of the president. The neglect of the Constitution is not attributable simply to thoughtlessness on the part of the candidates. It is, rather, a consequence of the dramatic context of debates. The focus in debates is on the problems of the nation, and how the candidates for the presidency will solve those problems. Any discussion of the nature, purposes, or limits of government power would be out of place. The Constitution, however, is concerned above all else with these very issues. In Richmond, the silence on the Constitution was a direct result of the talk-show format that made the debate so effective as theater. Presented by the audience of average citizens with a litany of economic, social, and political ills, it would have been politically suicidal for the candidates to even have raised questions about the competence of government to deal with them. It would have appeared insensitive in the extreme. Any discussion of constitutional issues would have appeared as pointless pedantry. As the debate turned out, Bush, Clinton, and Perot strove to outdo each other in promising solutions to every conceivable ill of the body politic—AIDS, crime in the streets, the deficit, the decline in educational standards, family disintegration, spiraling health care costs, lagging worker productivity, the recession, unfair trading practices, and unemployment. All the while they were loudly proclaiming their devotion to the American people—always referred to as "real people"—and their disgust for Washington politicians—presumably something other than "real people."

The dramatic meaning of the Richmond debate was distilled in one particular question. "How can we the people," the candidates were asked, "as symbolically the children of the future president, expect the three of you to meet our needs, as opposed to the wants of your political spin doctors and your political parties?" It was necessary for the candidates to "make a commitment to the citizens of the United States to meet our needs."[13] The premise of the question was that any political issue not immediately pertaining to the needs of the people was a ruse, concocted by political operators to mislead the public. This would include everything having to do with the Constitution. Issues of a constitutional character were nothing but obfuscations. Bush seemed to recognize that there was something wrong with the question. He pointed out that the president has certain general responsibilities to the nation, in particular in foreign affairs and national defense, and therefore his job is not reducible to care for the people's immediate needs. He then went on, however, to list programs he had pushed to deal with just such needs. There was apparently nothing in the question to bother Perot or Clinton. Perot gladly took the prescribed pledge. His whole campaign was focused on the need to solve the economic ills of the nation. He did not have any "spin doctors" working for him to make up campaign issues not related to the people's needs. Clinton claimed to be the victim of his opponents' spin doctors, who were continually bringing up irrelevant matters from his past, forcing him to defend his character and diverting him from discussion of the nation's pressing needs. With all matters beyond the needs of the people declared out of bounds as political "spin," it is not at all surprising that there was no discussion of the Constitution in the Richmond debate.

It is possible to question, of course, how much practical effect the new political theater of presidential debates will have on American government and politics. In the 1992 election, there was at least one indication of a fundamental change of public opinion, to which the new political theater might have contributed. This was the gridlock issue. Gridlock was Perot's main campaign theme. He promised to go to Washington, end the political wrangling, and implement the many plans to solve nation's ills that he insisted had already been developed. What Perot characterized as gridlock was at least as much the result of power struggles between the president and Congress as it was the result of policy disputes between Republicans and Democrats. That is to say, it was a consequence of the operation of the constitutional system of checks and balances. The popularity of Perot's gridlock theme represented a potentially momentous change of public opinion on the Constitution and its system of divided government. In passing, this indicates just how profoundly alienated Perot supporters are from conventional politics, and how difficult it is really going to be for traditional politicians to reclaim them. Now the most effective forum for Perot was the presidential debates. By all accounts he came off very well in the debates, with his homespun humor and down-to-business attitude. It was during the debates that, contrary to all expectations, his public support began to firm up. It might well be that the secret of Perot's success in 1992—he received an amazing 19 percent of the vote—was the perfect fit between medium and message in the new political theater of presidential debates.

Conclusion

The institutionalization of presidential debates might appear to be a small thing. It is simply a matter of the emergence of another new campaign practice, and these are always arising as a result of the development of new technologies, and new social circumstances. Debates, after all, fit the taste for entertainment of a people raised in front of the television set. As Aristotle—the first great student of democratic government and politics—teaches, however, political regimes frequently undergo profound changes because of the neglect of small things. Revolutions can occur one small step at a time. Alterations in election practices are a specific cause of fundamental political change. In particular, anything that affects the political education of the citizens is important, Aristotle argues, because government rests on a foundation of opinion. "There is no benefit in the most beneficial laws," he claims, if the citizens "are not going to be habituated and educated in the regime."[14] The new political theater of presidential debates affects in many ways the foundation of opinion on which rests the American system of representative democracy. It influences, and not for the better, the unwritten constitution that is the basis for the written constitution. While the institutionalization of presidential debates might be a small matter, it could have unpredictably large consequences.

Notes

1. Larry Sabato, quoted in *New York Times*, Aug. 15, 1992, p. L7.

2. See, for example, Terry Eastland, *Energy in the Executive: The Case for the Strong Presidency* (New York: Free Press, 1992).

3. *Federalist* 51, p. 322. Alexander Hamilton, James Madison, and John Jay, *The Federalist Papers*, ed. Clinton Rossiter (New York: Mentor Books, 1961).

4. See Richard Neustadt, *Presidential Power* (New York: Wiley, 1960).

5. See Richard Hofstadter, *The Paranoid Style in American Politics* (New York: Knopf, 1965).

6. See Aristotle, *Politics*, V. 5, on the causes of the degeneration of democratic regimes.

7. *Federalist* 9, pp. 71–73.

8. *New York Times*, Oct. 16, 1992, p. A10. Clinton's "body language" was specifically and repeatedly noted in the *Times* report of the debate.

9. On the argument for the necessity of the "theatrical" elements of government, see Walter Bagehot, *The English Constitution* (Ithaca: Cornell University Press, 1963), chaps. 2, 3, and 7.

10. *Federalist* 51, pp. 321–22.

11. *Federalist* 10, p. 78.

12. *Federalist* 51, p. 322.

13. Remarkably, given its astounding implications, this question and the candidates' responses to it were not reported in the press.

14. Aristotle, *Politics,* vol. 3, 9–11, in Lord Carnes, trans., *Aristotle: The Politics* (Chicago: University of Chicago Press, 1984), pp. 151–52.

2

Familiarizing Ourselves in the Television Age

John H. Eastby

The typical postmortem of the 1992 election portrayed the campaign and its media innovations as another step in America's progress toward democratic perfection. The model for that progress was bequeathed to us by Woodrow Wilson and the progressive movement which sought the elimination of artificial barriers, often sustained by corruption, between the people and the government. In a well-organized political community, according to progressive doctrine, the best ideas and the best people will be sorted out by a discriminating and mature public in the course of electing candidates to public office.

At first glance it appears that this campaign fit the Wilsonian model perfectly. Each candidate offered the nation his program and his leadership. Technology brought each message and leadership style into the living rooms, family rooms, kitchens, bathrooms, and bedrooms of America. A well-informed America made its choice. Moreover, this election made it established practice that national leaders will debate their way through the issues while the people will register the national opinion through the presidential vote.

Many people are understandably pleased by the triumph of the progressive campaign doctrine made evident by this election. But such popularity should not of necessity be considered proof of its wisdom. The progressives desired an unobstructed relationship among the people, the candidate, and policy. To establish this relationship, they willingly trumpeted the virtues of popular leadership. Yet the Founders seemed to think that ambition was sufficiently plentiful that the "popular arts" needed no encouragement. The proponents of the extended commercial republic intended to restrict, not to unleash, the "unworthy candidates" who "practice with success the vicious arts by which elections are too often carried." (*Federalist Papers* 10). Founders such as James Madison and Alexander Hamilton considered that demagogues, who rhetorically play on the people's fears and unrequitable hopes as their chief means of securing election, were among the primary causes of the failure of republican government.

The 1992 election should be seen as having intensified a trend toward demagoguery and, ultimately, Caesarism behind the guise of Wilsonian "leadership." Wilson believed that the maturity of the nation protected it from seductive promises. And so it might. Unfortunately, contemporary experience indicates that leadership appeals aim at the mood of Americans, not at their reason. Such indications are not proofs of a decaying political process, but practical proofs of such consequences are not always desirable. Moreover, Caesarism might be among the more benign forms of demagoguery. The fate of Athens and the internal bickering of the other Greek democracies remind us that demagoguery can be a life and death issue for political communities.

Whether demagogic or not, it is certainly the case that this campaign was a very personal one. The friendly exercise in expectation inflation became the staple of candidates themselves, not simply their supporters. There was a time in American government when the politician, at least formally, waited for others to make him president. Supporters, not the candidate himself, made outrageous claims about a candidate's abilities. But those days are gone. The transformation has been gradual, but this election, with its three candidates, finally broke what little partisan (party) capacity to define a campaign and its style remained in American politics. It entrenched the personal "leadership" campaign.

Now, curiously, the television set appears to be the perfect vehicle for progressive campaigning. Television is the primary news and information medium of the American public. Further, television discourages any sense of reserve, distance, or deliberation.[1] The lost reserve implies a corresponding need to establish familiarity between a candidate and the public. Consequently, the expectation of the Founders, that campaigns might be conducted with taste and dignity, is undermined by the need of candidates to be on familiar terms with as many American citizens as possible. While it is not clear that this familiarity is really what Wilson had in mind when he set about promoting popular leadership, it is certainly sufficiently similar to encourage easy identification. In short, the rise of the "rhetorical presidency" has been abetted by technological development.[2]

It even seems likely that, at this point in time, technological development leads the development of doctrine. In starkest terms, the political and nonpolitical use of the television and, increasingly, all media aims at numbers. Aiming at numbers, those who wish to offer political leadership appeal to the lowest common denominator. It was genuinely embarrassing to watch a sitting president, with a distinguished record of foreign policy deeds, reduced to calling his opponents bozos in public forums. But the president's response to his situation was merely uninventive, not beyond the campaign pale. Given the pervasive role of the electronic media, the modern presidential campaign, urged on by the Wilsonian doctrine of leadership, appears a polar opposite to constitutional expectations. Moreover, it is not likely that this situation can be changed—at least not under normal circumstances. Television is woven throughout the fabric of American life.

But is it really a problem that progressive campaigning and television are transforming what Americans can expect from political campaigns? The 1992 campaign appears to have set the stage for more, and more intense, demagoguery. Yet America's governing institutions do not at the moment appear ready to fall under the strain of populist demagoguery. It is possible that the "leader as demagogue" argument overlooks the corrective capacity of liberal institutions.

The Use of the Media in the 1992 Campaign

Why are the electronic media, particularly television, so thoroughly associated with the contemporary campaign? It is a commonplace to say that the media determine the type of candidate who can succeed in electoral politics. All the cosmetics which accompany a candidate's appearance on television make people compare campaigns to beauty contests. It is even likely that, in one or two cases, faces have provided the springboard to political careers. But the American experience shows that good looks have little to do with electoral success. Jimmy Carter was no more handsome than Gerald Ford. Ronald Reagan was not appreciably better looking, if better looking at all, than Carter or Walter Mondale. Bill Clinton was the slickest but not the best looking of the "Gang of Seven" candidates for the Democratic nomination (according to my thoroughly informal and anecdotal poll).

What the voters did seem to respond to in this election, in the Carter election, in the Reagan elections, and even in the first Bush election was a manner and mood of familiarity. This trend has been evident since John F. Kennedy came off better in the 1960 debates with Richard Nixon. Though Nixon was, notably, not a more familiar candidate than Hubert Humphrey, his discomfort in front of the camera at least earned a draw with the visually aloof manner, and one might say, condescending air, of George McGovern. Acknowledging these exceptions, it would seem that breeding a certain kind of familiarity is the name of the television game.

Breeding familiarity is not incidental to the medium. Television goes wherever we go. It substitutes entertainment for conversation. Our absorption into the concerns of television personalities reduces loneliness and makes real friendships unnecessary. We can have a real, live president talking to us in the most intimate and private places and occasions of the day. It does not even seem to matter that the communication flow is initially one way. If people do not like what they see, they change the channel or get a beer. Polls or ratings ultimately provide politicians with feedback.

This concern to be close and familiar can be seen in the 1992 campaigns of the three major contenders for the presidency. All three were ultimately caught up in innovations in presidential politics aimed at breaking down walls of distance between the candidate and the voter. Governor Clinton, Mr. H. Ross Perot and, ultimately, President George Bush made unprecedented use of talk- and entertainment-oriented programming offered to them by the network and cable television industry. They altered the structure of the nonprofit, nonpartisan national debates to reproduce a town meeting or talk-show format. Infomercials took on a new political life in the hands of Perot. In general, the candidates carved out new relationships between the candidate and the campaign and between the candidate and the American citizen. This relationship, of candidate manufacture, is mirrored by a new relationship between politics and entertainment that was carved out by television entertainment-division personnel.

The Media's Use of the 1992 Campaign

There is strong evidence that, in the age of television, the line between politics and entertainment has been decisively blurred. Stars have always let their preferences be known. We are all familiar with Charlton Heston's commercials for *National Review*. Arnold Schwarzenegger made clear his Republican sympathies. But something more than star power was brought to the campaign in 1992.

The most obvious example was the Murphy Brown–Dan Quayle confrontation. In a speech on the family, Vice President Quayle singled out the *Murphy Brown* show, whose title character took on the role of an unwed mother, as a negative example of the role models provided American television audiences by network programmers. Subsequently, the first fall program of *Murphy Brown* engaged in a special one-hour attack on the Quayle. Seemingly, fairness would have suggested that the network offer the vice president equal time and equal production help and facilities to make his point. Instead, network programmers opted to choose sides and paint Quayle as a cruel, narrow-minded elitist.

The well-publicized relationship between Bill and Hillary Clinton and Linda Bloodworth-Thomason and Harry Thomason is also notable—even though the essential possibilities of self-consciously using television entertainment to teach political lessons was scoped out years ago by *All in the Family*. The Bloodworth-Thomasons are simply more subtle about their education project than was Norman Lear. While there is good evidence that the news media preferred President Clinton to ex-President Bush, and while it is general opinion that Hollywood likes the Democratic party, the important influence of the media on this election was not its biases.[3] Rather such efforts to make entertainment a political lesson only dovetail well with the more important effort of this campaign to make a political lesson homey and entertaining. Politics has come to resemble entertainment and entertainment has become political education.

The Candidates and the Media

Though engaged in a losing effort, the most intriguing innovator was Perot, who engaged in a massive and interesting use of paid television advertising (in the form of infomercials) and unpaid advertising (in the form of talk shows). He used 800 numbers as a substitute for polls and he invented and paid for an organization of grass-roots supporters. He submitted himself very infrequently to news conferences, however, and granted only limited question and answer periods with the traditional television news correspondents.

Perot's campaign had no institutional connection to any other segment of American government. He had no preexisting party organization to satisfy. He had no primary to win. He made no plans to elect a Congress favorably disposed to his leadership. No one else in the entire government would have been beholden to a Perot victory. He bent every effort to assure that, to the extent possible, his relationship with the American people was mediated only by electromagnetic waves and that he controlled what the people saw on those waves turned into pictures. The nature of the Perot campaign and its use of the media can be perfectly captured in one vignette.

The night of the Richmond debate, a local news station ran a news conference in which Perot discussed his performance. Just as Bush and Clinton did, Perot seemed to be submitting himself to a televised question and answer period. What was startling, however, was that none of the typical newspaper, network television, or local television reporters was in attendance at the conference. Rather, Perot had released a tape of the "news conference." Who asked the questions? We were not told. What intentions lay behind the questions (news or propaganda)? We were not in a position to judge. Astonishingly, Perot was successful in airing his videotape and having reporters themselves, though self-conscious and flustered, categorize it as a news conference—even though they could not go!

Perot, as the vignette vividly testifies, sought to run a campaign as an "end run" around all the traditional mediators of American politics. The fundamental mediator of American government, the Congress, was ignored or, worse, dismissed. Perot maintained that he had only to sit down with the lot, look over any extant plans (for health, the economy, trade), and work something out. If Congress was recalcitrant, he seemed to suggest that the president could still proceed to solve the nation's problems.

The political parties, so far from being ignored, were reviled. Perot took a partial truth, that government institutions in the hands of different parties is an invitation to deadlock, and turned it into the entire explanation for the slow workings of the government. The parties were, he suggested, the problem with Washington. He ignored, for the most part, the more likely consideration that the separation of powers is the ultimate cause of deadlock. He simply did not appreciate the political benefits (deliberation, legislation with wide social support) which accompany the painstaking effort to establish and maintain working, governing coalitions (traditionally forced on parties and our governors proper by the separation of powers and checks and balances).

When not blaming parties for deadlock, Perot suggested that constitutional changes might be necessary to put American legislative process on a par with that of European countries. Yet European parliamentarism and executive confidence depend precisely and absolutely on parties. Thus he could not have been serious about parliamentarism. Rather, he was simplistically searching for ways to step around legislative obstacles in the same way a CEO can dig down into his company to get personnel, ideas, and action on a hunch. Institutions which restrict a president from using his office to achieve, directly, his interpretation of the will of the people were made to appear illegitimate.

In the same way, the traditional news media came away battered by their encounter with Perot. His end run around the "representatives" of the media was astounding in its scope and irony. The press covered Perot, sometimes to his great discomfiture. Television news did the same thing. But, for the most part, he was tactically so far out in front of the press and television that neither form of the news was the first to get to the American people with the new. By way of talk-show and infomercial Perot offered the nation news events that could only be reported—belatedly and after they had already been experienced by the politically active population.

The Perot discovery was precisely that he or his "people" can control, or better, *buy* the news agenda. Call-in talk-shows, infomercials, electronic town halls, all aimed at circumventing mediators of his words that were not subject to his will. In some ways political argumentation was even restored to the public by way of Perot's media events. He gained attention by constantly offering up something new. He met the democratic taste for the new without having to be mediated by the news. The information medium of television permitted him to speak to us face to face without, in fact, having to be face to face. The message he presented was, however, predominantly personal. He essentially said, "We have a problem and I am the man to solve it." He portrayed himself as Ward Cleaver helping the national family out of the pickle into which it had been led by Eddie Haskel politicians. The timing, the setting, the message were all under the control of Perot.

Perot demonstrated that the press, the party, the bureaucracy, and, ironically, the television news itself, can all be neutralized by a direct, interesting, and sincere performance over the airwaves. He further demonstrated that while policy can be the focus of the event, it is more likely that personality will be the real issue. Even as private an individual as Perot clearly was seduced by the opportunity to be loved as a father by the entire nation.

Shortly after being elected, Clinton gave an interview with *TV Guide*. In the interview, he argued that appearing on "*Arsenio* and MTV give me a chance to directly communicate with younger voters— who might or might not watch news shows or read newspapers." According to Clinton, his approach "suggests that since the President is hired by all the people he should perhaps go where the folks *are*. I don't think there's anything undignified about a President going on *Larry King,* or on the right kind of MTV program."⁴ Clinton further argued that he resorted to entertainment shows because "anyone who lets himself be interpreted to the American people through these intermediaries [the mainstream media] alone is nuts."

To avoid reliance on the mainstream media, Clinton, accordingly, used a variant of Perot's "end run" media strategy. He appealed directly to the voters, bypassing the news. But he went beyond merely direct appeals: he purposely clouded the distinction between the serious and the merely entertaining. This distinction is tenuous under any circumstances, and Clinton's behavior made it more so.

Nixon played piano for the *Grand Ole Opry*. Reagan made a gradual transformation from movie and television star to politician. On the reverse side of the coin, it is generally acknowledged that campaign stumping was a form of entertainment in the nineteenth century— though presidential candidates did not stump. Therefore Clinton's decision to play a saxophone for a television audience was not unprecedented, but it was innovative. He explicitly intended to appeal to people who previously had not had the interest or desire to watch the "news" (let alone read a paper). All previous political forays into the entertainment business cast the politician as acknowledging the lighter side of life. Clinton explicitly offered his saxophone playing and his appreciation of rock music as *reasons* to pay attention to him and, ultimately, to vote for him.

Why would a presidential candidate cast himself in the role of entertainer? Entertainment distracts people and improves, or at least helps to set, their mood. Clinton, in offering himself as entertainment, offered himself as the barometer and corrective for the nation's mood. But to know, to care about, and to direct the national mood on a daily basis, a politician must be, or at least seem to be, close to the people. He or she needs to appear to be the friend of, or even part of the family of, constituents. Clinton, apparently as a matter of personal idiosyncracy, wishes to be friends with everyone in the country.⁵ It seemed to be (and continues to be) his ambition to be loved by all and to have those in his presence comforted. To be comforting the governor needed to be approachable. To be approachable the president chooses to seem like our ever-present friend. Now, is good friend Clinton the real Clinton or, in order to catch the public, did the governor hide his political ambition behind the lure of entertainment and mood setting?

Once the hook was set, of course, Clinton was prepared to take questions from the "people" for hours. He set the mood appropriate to a "horse sense" discussion at the "Chatterbox Cafe" of *Prairie Home Companion* fame. Such talk appears to transpire among friends. Each American who watches can imagine that he or she might have been the one talking to the candidate and asking the questions. Perot showed Clinton that people will respond to such familiarity. Having received a media education from his opponent, the governor ultimately offered grateful approval for Perot's understanding of the properly mediated relationship between the candidate and the people. "Perot" he said, "got me into the kind of electronic town meeting that allows for more call in possibilities, the remote spots and so forth. We'll see more of that." Clinton had used the media similarly in state office but he learned from Perot that, even at the presidential level, seeming like a friend is more important to being elected than seeming presidential.

Bush's innovation in the use of the media was nonexistent. His campaign was purely imitative, and appropriated as strategy only after the campaign registered serious trouble. Not even his typical commercial carried the bite of the 1988 commercials. Nevertheless, once he began to appropriate the talk-show format, he did so with a vengeance, appearing on whatever network talk-show or morning wake-up show would have him. It is not surprising, perhaps, that a man who appreciates deeds, and excelled in deeds, over words would have had the least creative grasp of the media transformation.

Is the New Personalism Healthy?

The appeal to friendship, or worse, the family analogy, as a justification for rule arguably undermines the spirit and, ultimately, the letter of modern liberal democracy. Two hundred and fifty million Americans cannot be friends, either with each other or with their governors, unless the friendship is based on the lowest common denominator of human expectations. Even then it is impossible to do more than care for the abstract idea of one's fellow Americans.

The Progressives had encouraged the development of an organic American community. A part of the centralization of American politics which the Progressives desired was historically necessary. Industrialism was an important source of progressivism and was the great centralizer of twentieth-century politics. In the most important respects, to win wars in this century a nation needed to be industrial. But despite progressive rhetoric, until the advent of radio and television, American political diversity was expected. The most important politics was local politics because that was what could be readily seen. There was no way to overcome, psychologically, the reality of physical distance between parts of the republic. Only television and radio could accomplish that feat.[6]

It is useful to note what was lost with the centralization of American politics. State and local government used to provide the personal touch, the real sense of political community, in America. As communities which could see themselves acting, and in which the individual could see himself or herself acting, state and local governments were the incubators and schools of self-government.

But television has accentuated the general trend toward centralization and deeply personalized the progressive understanding of the proper relationship between president and people. Television nationalizes the arena for political concern and, absent vibrant local politics and community, the apparent, but not the real, arena for friendship. The voting, television-watching population has forced ambitious men to pretend, as never before, that they can make up for the lost vibrancy of local politics. They pretend they are chief friend to a huge nation of friends. Any barriers, any formal obstacles, to a direct friendship between the people and the candidate have become suspect. Clinton has shown that adopting the "politics as entertainment" model is one of the best ways to dismantle barriers.

For policy purposes, in fact, it makes no difference if the president is a friend (except that presidents may have the government do things for their real friends). Economically, I am better off with a president who knows (and for the sake of reelection responds appropriately to) the possibilities for, and limits of, government management of the economy than a friend who has not a clue. My security is better provided by the hands of an ambitious man who understands the realities of foreign policy than by the hands of a best friend who thinks PALs refer to international pen pal clubs. My meaningful friendship with a government officer is simply irrelevant to my policy interests and needs.

This tendency to judge all issues of personal satisfaction in national terms and, more importantly, as something for which a president can be held responsible is encouraged not only by the existence of the electronic media but also by those said to be the representatives of the national information media. In the search for a national community, television stations and the newspapers go so far as to manufacture opinion communities to which politicians are required to respond. They commission polls to differentiate between the decision of the government and the more legitimate mood or opinion of the people. The poll is reported as an event of sorts. It is presented as a mini-election. Though congressmen, senators, and presidents are empowered by the Constitution to represent the people who compose their constituencies, television and newspapers substitute poll results as the legitimate expression of the constituency's opinion. As the technology of polling becomes more precise and timely, it is becoming evident that the electronic media are best positioned to make use of polling. Newspapers must often publish results a full day after they are available on television.

Furthermore, in the continuous search for new events to cover, media executives use polls to manufacture public agendas where there were none before. The pollster may ask the nation if enough is being done by government to prevent cancer. Since everyone knows that he or she could get cancer, there are very few people who, when presented with such a question, will answer yes. A new cancer crisis is created by the legitimate wish of people that more could be done. If the representative does not meet the new demand for cancer protection, she is failing at her job. Representative democracy, with its possibilities for deliberation and sensitivity to public policy trade-offs, is made to seem uncaring, unresponsive, and distant. All the media engage in this critique, but television does so most effectively.

Nonincumbent candidates such as Perot and Clinton instinctively understand and use the fact that people feel distant from their government. Because everyone is, in relation to campaigns, now a "progressive" (I know of few people who would be content with a campaign conducted according to the Founders' expectations), challengers easily assert that the incumbent has simply been insufficiently caring or that the process was insufficiently democratic. They pretend that the politics of the nation can be conducted with the intimacy of Athenian democracy—apparently unaware that it was the predicament visited upon Athens by the demagogues that representative government was meant to correct.

But the form of decision-making remains representative. Policy remains dependent on bureaucratic pronouncement, judicial ruling, and legislative resolution. All the old avenues of "interest group" politics remain in play. Television makes it seem as though a government for 250 million people need not be distant and need not be bureaucratic. Television has since its inception seemed to fit perfectly with the Wilsonian-progressive view of the relation between candidate and nation. Unfortunately it does so only at the level of the campaign, not of governing. Television makes it easier to ask more from government and easier for governors to offer more. But it does not make actual delivery of services, or performance of necessary deeds, easier. Television campaigners may flatter, cajole, bribe, and attempt to set a mood for the people, but they cannot always dictate satisfaction—especially when the complex policies derived from representative processes are judged by the simplistic appeals of television democracy.

When the campaign world does not fit the real world, people become disillusioned. It is well known that Perot's supporters were disgruntled with and disaffected from politics as usual. The hard question is why? Except for the deficit, which is more moral than economic in its import, the national government has been doing its job reasonably well. The problem is that the politics of friendship and the politics of family made possible by progressive doctrine and television have exaggerated expectations from, and undermined the credibility of, our institutions.

Reagan's first term showed precisely how effective direct charismatic appeals to the people could be for governing. His second term showed how weak a president could become after the appeal wears off. The contemporary appeal to populism defines government as the problem, then promises to clean up the government. But the cleanup may, or likely will, never occur. Carter did not clean up the government. Reagan did not clean up the government. Bush did not clean up the government. Clinton promised to clean up the government by adding new tasks for the institutions and new expectations from the people. It is difficult to see how he will clean up the government by giving it new national responsibilities.

If the cynicism induced by leadership appeals which subsequently cannot be translated into policy, or if the cynicism induced by simplistic presentation and critique of complex policies, which take time and patience to reach fruition, gains strength, only very firm "leadership" will be able to regain authority. Such leadership may not be progressive. It could destroy the nation by masking the appearance of a truly competent demogogue. Television for this reason appears to be a positive evil for constitutional government.

Is Caesarism Inevitable?

But this is a concern to be faced only if media politics can undermine all respect for, and the geographic necessity of, using the nation's constitutional system. The electronic media have facilitated the triumph of a debased and debasing form of Wilsonian progressivism. The conditions of election have made it unattractive for the reserved individual of judgment to run for office. But that does not mean that the American experiment is about to fold. In some ways we find ourselves testing daily the proposition of the Founders that decent goverment is possible even when statesmen are not typically at the helm.

Perhaps, in fact, the need for important deeds is attenuated. Perhaps Caesars are simply old hat. Perhaps we are witnessing the emerging politics of postmodernism. The postmodern campaign, in addition to serving as the vehicle for incremental policy changes, might further, or even primarily, serve, as a technology for legitimizing and maintaining the modern welfare state. One might consider the campaign a kind of show. People who make few of their daily decisions unaided by the government would be given, in exciting circumstances, the opportunity to chose their guardians; following which, the administration would reassert itself with regard to policy.[7] The separation of powers and checks and balances would further contain the successful candidate. The campaign would be a mechanism for venting the political passions of an otherwise complacent population. In such a situation personalism and familiarity would at worst be harmless, at best an entertaining means of involving people in politics.

Political science speaks of retrospective voting. The postmodern campaign would depend on voters being retrospective. If they were reasonably benefited by the incumbent or if they found the incumbent an interesting character to have in the White House (Senate, House of Representatives, etc.), they would ferment for a time but, in the end, grant the incumbent four more years. If no substantial interest could be maintained, or if a recession were to overtake the incumbent, fresh blood would be the order of the day. This has always been an important function of elections under any circumstances. Future elections may merely make the situation more obvious.

In the postmodern election people would vote to tax a slightly higher percentage of Social Security benefits or to raise the age at which one is eligible. People would vote to subsidize the automobile industry by quotas or to assist agriculture through price supports. People would not either expect or desire that the federal government would get rid of Social Security (especially if the argument against Social Security condemned it for fostering an undue dependence on the national government). Nor would the majority vote for the nationalization of the commanding heights of the economy in manufacturing or of agricultural production on the argument that distribution needed to be thoroughly planned and rationalized by government.

Postmodern politicians would not really differ from those who engaged in previous modes of politics. They would still desire to receive recognition for performing meaningful deeds. But circumstances would not assist the postmodern politician. The nation might be titillated at the thought of meaningful deeds but it would not be prepared actually to countenance such action. The fate of the nation would no longer depend on electoral results. The economic and social engines of the republic would be the objects of fine-tuning by government bureaucrats while the political problem of foreign policy would essentially be attenuated. Campaigns could be terribly earnest and highly populist at the same time. The act of persuasion would be the only real act available to public life.

The 1992 campaign certainly seemed to engage in a new kind of politics. The American economy was in the midst of its fifth quarter of slow, but real, recovery. Furthermore, much evidence suggested that America was among the most efficient economies in the world. Certainly the United States had done better at adding jobs to the economy over the previous ten years than had the European nations. Yet the Clinton campaign had only to say "It's the economy, stupid" enough times, at sufficient volume, to sell its message to a simple and simplifying media. The economy, and empathy for those whom the economy was hurting, became the focus of all campaign events. Ultimately, unemployment of 7.2 percent was accepted as constituting a crisis of Great Depression proportions. A majority of Americans (the Clinton and Perot voters) were persuaded to consider themselves worse off than at any time in the past sixty years.

Old and shopworn ideas were repackaged and accepted as new by the nation and the media. The new idea of "growing the economy," for example, is not new. A segment of the Republican party has always put growth in front of deficit reduction. In fact they have argued that growth was the proper way to attain deficit reduction. Candidate Clinton wanted to have the government try to stimulate the growth directly. The Republicans wanted to grow the economy indirectly through favorable tax treatment of investment. The issue debate of the election was over the most effective way to grow the economy. More government spending or additional governmental tax benefits were offered as the means to the end. Neither the end nor the means were really new. Roses changed their names yet remained roses. There was no crisis to call forth great deeds—the nation simply pretended that there was.

In the postmodern political world, the television medium might be faulted for superficiality but not cast as an evil for the republic. It might simply be the case that the media are unable to distinguish, in the first instance, between deeds and speeches. They are further unable to distinguish on their own a hierarchy between the serious and the silly. Such distinctions belong to the "paying" people who tune in to the television or radio, or who buy the paper or weekly newsmagazine. If the public loses, or does not need, its interest in making elections a serious matter, television, the medium of choice, will not insist on such seriousness. In this sense entertainment and politics really can be fused.

Is There a Theory for Postmodern Politics?

In providing an opening to rule by direct persuasion, televised politics flirts with a kind of return to classical democracy or republicanism. Among academics the most popular exponent of classical republicanism of the generation was Hannah Arendt. According to Arendt, public life in the Greek city displayed mankind's freedom. Not for the Greek citizen to rest satisfied in his private affairs, with securing the means of existence. The typical Greek life was one of *showing* to the rest of the community. It was the putting on of a public personality through action, either in deeds or in speeches. There was a certain theater quality about the political life. One put oneself together by deeds or speeches before peers. Such action was performed as a means of distinguishing oneself in relation to the other members of the *polis*. To *do* was not just to force but rather to move the public by persuasion. To carry one's point, to offer the *mot juste*, displayed the political man at the point of his excellence. Rather than his "inner" self the Greek citizen was his publicly argued or held positions.[8]

One can see a concern to recapture such a public realm in Woodrow Wilson's call for a new relationship between the public and its representatives. He praised the representative who could speak or give form to public opinion and lead the nation to its mature interests. Despite the Founders' concern that such a personal relationship between the public and the representative would encourage dangerous demagoguery, Wilson wished to open more room for action on the part of a president.

Yet, while Wilson hoped to bring rhetoric into the heart of the American governing process, he ultimately understood that speeches led to, or in some cases from, deeds. Wilson, in a sense, sought to make action more acceptable in the American polity and to do it in such a way as to bring speeches and deeds harmoniously together. He admired, as the vehicle to action, the British practice of programmatic campaigning, which was further linked to his view in favor of cabinet, or presidential, responsibility. In bald terms this view may be stated as follows: One should make one's pitch to lead the nation in the way it should go and then put up, or shut up.

Wilson's project was, of course, already far removed from the constitutionalism of the Founders. The founders wished to restrict the need for action and to count on deeds if action became necessary. To the extent that the Founders' conception of the natural ground of politics teaches us that the purpose of politics is to secure our personal rights, deeds performed for the sake of *showing* ourselves or establishing a public face are discouraged by our formal institutions. Rhetoric as a form of action is even more deeply discouraged.

Yet it is Wilson's argument which has shaped our outlook on leadership. After Wilson, leadership became the American equivalent of action and took on a new prominence in our political self-understanding. But if Arendt's "classical republicanism" is in the process of replacing traditional Wilsonianism, a new twist has been added to the expectations from leadership. Arendt praised not just action but particularly the nonviolent character of action as speech-making. In fact she so strongly weighted the side of rhetoric that she abstracted from the questions the Athenians had to decide, just as many modern democrats judge the *democracy* of the political process not its *achievements*. But Athenian political life was never simply the equivalent of a debating society. Action as speech always led to action as deed—and the deeds often required violence as the means of acquiring and securing domination.

The evidence that comes to us by way of Thucydides is that the Athenians, whose politics Arendt so appreciated, talked about issues of the law court on the one hand, and when and how to attack their neighbors on the other: effecting domestic justice and war. The Athenians further engaged themselves over the way in which they should rule subject territory. To draw the issue differently, one need only think of the ultimate relation between speech and deed in the Melian dialogue to see Arendt's gloss on ancient practice. The submission of Melos was the Athenian concern. Speech, having proved to be unpersuasive, gave way to conquering deed. For Athens the deed was symbolic speech, but the symbol required a real deed. For Melos there was no second chance to recoup failed speech. Arendt wrote as though ancient deliberation could be divorced from the ensuing deeds. But can speeches that do not lead to specific kinds of deeds be considered action or leadership? In short, can the process of politics long be divorced from the substantive issues of politics? If it cannot, is not direct televised persuasion a dangerous evil for the republic?

Notes

1. See particularly Harvey C. Mansfield Jr., *America's Constitutional Soul* (Baltimore: Johns Hopkins University Press, 1991), on the reason for the superficiality of the media. The media, in general, must continually present something new to their audience—the news. The media create the world we live in by linking us across space to people, events, and problems of which we would otherwise be ignorant. We come to live in a community with those with whom we share feelings and knowledge. The media make this sharing possible across great distances. They break down barriers between people by treating their audience as individuals not as representatives of particular groups, nations, or cultures. The new that is presented can then be presented indifferently, as fact, to everyone. But it is, first and foremost, presented as the new. The search for the new is a defining characteristic of our age, insofar as the age is continuously self-critical, and the media are fully modern and technological representatives of the age. The media search out or create "events" which can then be presented, in homogeneous fashion, as the news. Any invitation to deliberation is lost in the scramble to present the "facts" and then to query "what happens next" (not, what should we do)? Thus the media inherently direct themselves to the numerical majority, composed of isolated individuals, apprising that majority of the new things that have happened in the world of the media's own creation. Since the media must present information of import to all humanity they cannot help their superficiality. They must concentrate on appealing to those characteristics shared by the most people, preeminently their feelings.

2. On the "rhetorical presidency" see James W. Ceaser et al., "The Rise of the Rhetorical Presidency," *Presidential Studies Quarterly*, Spring 1981.

3. See, for example, Larry J. Sabato, "During '92 Campaign, Media's Bias Showed More Than Ever," *Richmond Times-Dispatch*, Jan. 10, 1993, p. F7.

4. Barry Golson and Peter Ross Range, "Clinton on TV," *TV Guide*, Vol. 40, No. 47, Nov. 21, 1992, p. 15.

5. See, for example, Howard Fineman, "The New Age President," *Newsweek*, Jan. 25, 1993, pp. 22–23.

6. See in general the discussion of the effects of television on politics in

3

Polls in the 1992 Presidential Campaign

James F. Pontuso

Polls were everywhere in the election of 1992. Each of the television networks and most major newspapers conducted polls of the presidential race. Independent polling companies, such as Gallup, made detailed studies of the electorate. The candidates ran their own extensive polls to gauge the strengths and weaknesses of their campaign tactics. Trial-heat surveys compared voter support for candidates during the primary season and throughout the general election, tracking polls measured changes in public preference, opinion polls tallied the electorates' views on the various issues involved in the 1992 race, and exit polls told the voters why they voted as they did.

Although the surveys underrated Ross Perot's strength, probably because Perot energized citizens who do not usually vote, polls accurately predicted the outcome of the election and the size of the margin of victory for Bill Clinton. Pollsters were pleased. They could point to the 1992 election as evidence of the validity and merit of their profession. They could claim that the sophisticated techniques now used to do surveys put to rest the usual complaints made against polling. But why is the credibility of their profession in question? Why is a practice so widely used and reported in the media during elections the subject of such intense debate among those who study survey research? Perhaps a brief sketch of the weaknesses of polling is in order.

Problems of Survey Research

Most of the contention about polls has to do with their credibility. Polling is based on the same principle that cooks use to taste their soup. One need not devour the entire pot to discern the flavor; a

47

small spoonful of the contents, well stirred, will give an accurate representation of the dish's savor. Pollsters use this device to gauge popular opinion. The views of a small sample of the population can reflect those of the whole population (called the universe) if the sample is randomly drawn and each member of the universe has an equal chance of being chosen as a member of the sample.

But critics of polling insist that survey research is far from a rigorous science. They argue that it is difficult to ensure that the sample, those people polled, genuinely reflects the universe, those people who vote. First, there are mathematical problems, for the laws of statistics dictate that virtually every sample will deviate from the universe. This margin of error, as it is called, can make predictions about elections quite difficult because the deviation from the universe, even in well-constructed polls, can be plus or minus three or four percentage points. Polls are accurate only within a certain range, and a spread of eight percentage points is not a helpful tool in discovering the real sentiments of the voters. Moreover, the laws of statistics decree that every once in awhile a poll falls outside the margin of error. Most pollsters accept that one poll in twenty will deviate more than the range established by the margin of error.

These mathematical complexities, as difficult as they may be for pollsters, are far from their most dire problem. Although it is quite simple for a cook to judge his soup by tasting a spoonful, it is much more formidable for a pollster to draw an accurate sample from the population. How, after all, does one ensure that every single person has an equal chance of becoming part of the sample? There is no master list of the whereabouts of all American citizens. There is no national voter list. People move around constantly and it is not certain that the voter lists kept by localities will be accurate from year to year. The national census provides the most thoroughgoing picture of the makeup of the electorate, but because it is taken only at ten-year intervals, it too is only a snapshot of the population at a specific point in time. A truly random survey, therefore, is difficult to devise.

Even the best-planned polls are of no merit if they are not carried out correctly. Interviewers must question only those people indicated by the design of the survey. Oftentimes, this guideline is difficult to follow, in particular if the intended respondents are not at home, or if they live in high-crime areas where interviewers are afraid to go. An accurate survey takes not only a good design, but also a great deal of persistence. Moreover, the way in which questions are worded has an enormous effect on the outcome of a poll.[1] Even the arrangement or sequence of questions on a survey can influence the response that people give.

Critics of survey research argue that polling depends on the honesty and forthrightness of the respondents, but there is no guarantee that the answers people give to questions are the truth.[2] If that were not bad enough, studies have shown that greater numbers of people are refusing to take part in public opinion surveys.[3] Finally, even though respondents may be telling the truth to interviewers, their opinions may not be well reasoned or strongly held. After all, we live in a democracy and citizens are expected to have a view on every public issue. Often they do not, of course. But when asked by a pollster, they may be too embarrassed to take the "no opinion" choice, and may instead offer an impromptu judgment, one that is quickly liable to change.

Pollsters insist that they have been able to overcome all of the difficulties associated with survey research. Extensive experience over many years in academic surveys, in media polls, and perhaps most importantly in market research has taught pollsters which pitfalls to avoid. New technology and methodology have also combined to make it easier to achieve pure random samples. Since the vast majority of American households now have telephones, surveys taken over the telephone have replaced personal interviews. A two-staged, random-digit-dialed procedure (which was devised by Warren Mitofsky and later refined by Joseph Waksberg) has now become the standard method of election polling. Telephone polls have a number of advantages over the more traditional method of personal interviews. Telephone polls are easier to make random, less expensive, and faster. They also do away with the problems associated with live interviews, such as the pollster's reluctance to visit crime-ridden neighborhoods or to question "dangerous-looking" people directly.

Polls are pictures of the public's attitude. In the past, they have been poor predictors of elections because they are valid only for the day they are taken. Tracking polls, which take a daily read of the public preferences, are able to judge shifts in public opinion. They more accurately measure the candidates' standing over the long haul and are far better at forecasting election day results. Exit polls have also become a standard procedure during election years. These surveys ask voters why they cast their ballots as they did. Exit polls help pollsters decipher the motives of voters, including the issues that were decisive in deciding how they cast their ballots. Exit polls provide a benchmark which pollsters can use to judge the accuracy of preelection surveys.

Finally, the very number of polls now taken acts as a mechanism to corroborate polling results. With so many surveys, pollsters have a good basis of comparison for deciding how trustworthy their own tabulations are. Taken together, the various polls provide a large sample which has an increased likelihood of actually representing the public's position.[4]

Explaining the Increase in Polls

Polling has grown markedly over the past five presidential elections. This rise in the use of polls has occurred for a number of reasons. As mentioned earlier, telephone polls have made surveys faster, easier, and cheaper than the old door-to-door method. In order to take a survey, all that one really needs is a telephone and some people with questions. Of course, campaign organizations are forced to take polls in order to gather information on the mood of electorate, to gauge the public's response to their candidate's message, and to avoid giving the opposing camp a tactical advantage by failing to use the available technology. In other words, more polls means more polls.

The media take polls for different, but no less compelling, reasons. No news-gathering organization wants to come in second to its competition. This rivalry extends to stories about the public's perceptions of candidates. The public's reaction to a candidate's speech, or to his or her performance during a debate, is exactly the kind of feature that the media feel compelled to report for fear that someone else will report it first. As one of the people made famous by scooping his brethren argues, "The greatest felony in the news gathering business today is to be behind, or to miss, a major story; or more precisely, to seem behind, or seem in danger of missing, a major story. So speed and quantity substitute for thoroughness and quality, for accuracy and context."[5]

The media also report polls because stories about who is ahead and who is behind make for more interesting copy than the candidates' stand on the issues. Reporters covering a campaign have heard the candidate's stump speech repeatedly and position papers are hardly the stuff that makes for exciting journalism. Many commentators have chided the media for focusing on the horse-race aspects of the campaign.[6] As one of America's foremost media watchers argues, "The main problem with polling . . . is that it drives out all other forms of news. Polls have a higher priority in the newscast than most other forms of campaign reporting. And, of course, polls tend to be among the least substantive kinds of political journalism."[7] But who really cares about position papers? They are crafted by campaign organizations to make candidates look as if they understand the issues. They have more to do with the candidate's image than with what he or she might actually do once in office. Certainly politicians do not feel bound to follow them once the election has been won. To paraphrase Winston Churchill: position papers are much neglected and have much about them that commands neglect. Moreover, given the length of current campaigns, especially at the presidential level, it would be all but impossible for the media to concentrate solely on the issues. It might take two or three days, perhaps a week, to present a candidate's views on the various issues that face the nation. What would the media report for the next year and one half that it takes to run for president? The media cannot be expected to offer dry and often technical information over and over again to a public that would quickly lose interest in such stories.

The media are driven by an inner imperative to deliver the news, which means of course something that is new, as in novel, unexpected, and never before seen.[8] Polls are a way for media to introduce something new into reportage of the campaign when nothing new is actually happening. This is especially true of the run-up to the general election, for then there are no primary results or elections returns to report, only the daily grind of press releases, campaign rhetoric, and the ubiquitous position papers. Polls give the media an opportunity to create news, not merely report it. Polls make it possible for the media to offer interesting stories to the public when none exist. And since the public seems to have an appetite for stories about itself, polls are a "salable" commodity. The media report polls as news in order to justify its own existence—for if there is nothing new, there is no news. Of course, reportage of the news can generate a profit for the corporation that pays for the news-gathering organization.

The media do not take polls merely to judge the strength of candidates during the campaign. Even when there is no election, polls are a very important component of media stories. News organizations want to create news—something new—so they take surveys that may lead to new areas for the news to explore. They delve into the various "crises" that confront our society and then report on the public's perception of those issues. If there were no AIDS crisis, or medical care crisis, or homeless crisis, one wonders whether the media would not have to create some crisis about which to talk. By establishing these subjects as part of the public discourse, the media have a hand in controlling events, in establishing the national agenda, and ultimately in ruling the country.

Does the media really wish to rule? If asked directly, members of the media would never agree to the proposition. They would contend that they are the guardian of the people's rights. They are a conduit through which information flows about the people we chose to rule and the governmental actions they perform. The media are a watchdog, ensuring that those who hold the public trust or wish to be elected do not become arbitrary in their exercise of power. The media's task is to reveal falsehood, waste, fraud, corruption, inefficiency, ineptitude, bad preparation, bad tactics, bad character, and all the other foibles of all-too-human nature to the harsh light of public scrutiny. The full disclosure of all relevant information helps the public choose its rulers wisely and prevents the exercise of power beyond the point that public opinion will tolerate.

The media, however, go well beyond their role as the guardian of the people. The process works something like this: An event occurs. The media report the event. Once the initial fascination of the story dies down, the media take a poll about the public's attitude toward the event. The media confront the government with evidence from the polling numbers which indicates that the public wants something done about the event. The government is either forced to respond or, more likely, is unable to respond rapidly to solve the problem caused by the event. The media take a poll asking the public to make a judgment on the government's inability to solve the crisis that the event has created. The government is compelled to take action, or to respond more quickly than it would have, because of the pressure from the public as expressed through the media and their polls. Now the media are not really attempting to govern in all this. They are merely trying to find and report the news—the new. But by forcing the government to act, or by forcing it to act more quickly than it would have, the media are indirectly governing.

Polls and the Candidates of 1992

During the 1992 election, Bill Clinton suffered the greatest humiliation, but ultimately gained the most, from public opinion polls. Clinton's bid for the presidency was nearly derailed by revelations about his long-time affair with Gennifer Flowers, an Arkansas state employee.

Clinton also admitted that he had smoked, but not inhaled, marijuana during his college years. His explanations about how he avoided the draft cast even more doubt on his credibility. Just before the all-important New Hampshire primary, Clinton's standing in the polls had sunk so low that pundits counted him out of the race.[9] Yet it was exactly at this gloomy point that the polls turned in Clinton's favor. He finished second in the New Hampshire primary, receiving 25 percent of the vote. Former Massachusetts Senator Paul Tsongas won in his neighboring state with 33 percent of the ballots. Clinton shrewdly got to the television cameras first and put the appropriate spin on the results, declaring himself the real winner. He portrayed Tsongas as a regional candidate, unable to compete outside New England. He anointed himself the "comeback kid" because his actual vote count was higher than the percentages he had garnered in preelection tracking polls. The moniker stuck. Pundits began to treat Clinton as the Democratic front-runner and to put questions about Clinton's past into the background. After all, these stories were no longer news and had not stopped Clinton from his comeback.[10]

What is most startling about Clinton's comeback, of course, is that it was not a comeback at all. The candidates conceded the Iowa caucuses to Senator Tom Harkin of Iowa, making New Hampshire the initial test of the primary season. Clinton made a comeback in the first election of the year because poll numbers were counted the same as an election. That Clinton made a "comeback" by gaining 25 percent of the vote in the first presidential primary indicates just how important polls have become in our perceptions of the electoral process.

In the general election, Clinton's strategy rested on turning George Bush's strengths into weaknesses. Bush's major forte was in foreign affairs. James Carville, Clinton's campaign manager, discovered a chink in Bush's armor. During his stewardship of Harris Wofford's successful bid in 1991 to fill a vacant Senate seat in Pennsylvania, Carville realized that many Americans were tired of bearing the burden of world leadership. With the Cold War over and Iraq suitably humiliated, there was no longer any reason to make the kinds of sacrifices that were necessary in the past. It was time to turn the nation's attention away from foreign adventures and to "take care of our own." In this light, Bush's very prowess in foreign affairs was a sign of his neglect of domestic matters. He was perceived to be so busy flying all over the world in his expensive jet, Air Force One, that he was unaware of his own nation's difficulties.

Perhaps no president in history had as much experience in government as Bush. He had served as vice president, director of the CIA, ambassador to China, and member of the House. His resume counted for nothing during the campaign, however. Clinton painted Bush as a Washington insider. He was part of the business-as-usual crowd, who had gotten the country into debt and recession. Experience and know-how were not as important as the need for new ideas and for change.

In 1988 Bush had been able to capitalize on his association with one of the most popular politicians of the age, Ronald Reagan. Bush had sold the American people on staying the course. But in 1992 Clinton persuaded the electorate that twelve years of trickle-down economics had not worked. The 1980s were not a decade of prosperity and of renewed hope in America, as Reagan had portrayed the times, but rather, an unprecedented era of greed. The abundance of the 1980s was a fraud; it was based on borrowing against the future. Incumbency, experience, and tradition all were made to work against Bush.

And let us not forget "the economy, stupid." Clinton used what was in reality a short-term, cyclical economic slowdown to attack the "twelve years" of Republican rule and the "failure" of trickle-down economics. Had the economy turned around before the election, Clinton's attacks would surely have carried less sting. How then to ensure that the economy did not suddenly rebound before election day? Here Clinton used polls to great effect as part of his electoral strategy. He and everyone associated with his campaign repeated over and again that the economy was bad. When polls were taken asking people what they thought about the economy, not surprisingly, they responded that the economy was bad. Of course the economy was bad: it lacked consumer confidence. What the economy needed to get moving was a burst of spending. But when consumer confidence is low, people are reluctant to make new purchases. Polls reinforced people's fears, which, in turn, kept consumer confidence and spending low. Clinton used the polls to help create a pessimistic national mood and the economy did not rebound.

The state of the economy was no longer a campaign issue once the election was over, and Clinton stopped talking about it. Without the daily drumbeat of negative details about the sorry state of the economy, consumer confidence returned. Polls showed that people no longer believed that the economy was in such poor shape and were more willing to spend some money. Along with increased spending came a revived economy. Interestingly, the media gave credit to Clinton for restoring consumer confidence, and so he had, in a way, by not talking about how bad the economy was.

Clinton's tactics were not founded merely on political calculation. His promise of returning a sound economy to America touched a deep chord in the national spirit. When people's votes are determined primarily by economic concerns, they are, no doubt, voting for their own self-interest and their own economic well-being. Yet citizens do not want to see their votes as a mere expression of economic selfishness. Political scientists have noted that people's anxieties over the condition of the economy are not based solely on a concern for personal prosperity. Many voters whose finances are in good shape still cast their ballots with the economy on their minds. Americans see something more than personal security in the productive capacity of the country. Our national wealth is a source of pride. The power and prestige that it confers on the country is a point of national honor. We really want to be, in the words of Alexander Hamilton, "the envy of the world." While this combination of self-interest and concern for the public good may seem an odd one (for when the economy is strong, people will be more self-interested, more likely to pursue personal gain, and less worried about the common good), it is, nonetheless, traditionally American. That most perceptive visitor to America, Alexis de Tocqueville, who journeyed through the United States in the 1830s, observed that there was "something wonderful" in the "resourcefulness" with which an American sought his fortune, "a sort of heroism in his greed for gain." Yet the love of gain led not to selfish egoism but to an "irritable patriotism." "The common man in the United States has understood the influence of the general prosperity on his own happiness," Tocqueville explained, "he sees the public fortune as his own, and he works for the good of the state, not only from duty or from [personal] pride, but, I dare almost say, from greed."[11]

Clinton was able to connect concern over a sluggish economy with a desire to promote the common good in two ways. First, he traced the source of the nation's woes to the gridlock in Washington. For him, gridlock meant more than just a stalemate between a Republican president and a Democratic Congress. Gridlock was a symbol for what had gone wrong in Washington. It represented our seeming inability to solve our problems, such as lingering poverty, an anemic economy, an expensive health care system, and a spiraling national debt.

Second, Clinton was able to portray himself as the epitome of the American dream. He did not make the same mistake as had Michael Dukakis who, despite being the son of an immigrant, could not shake the image that somehow he was a limousine liberal. Although Clinton had gone to prestigious schools, including a bastion of liberal legal thinking, Yale Law School, he was able to present himself as a self-made man from a humble background. He was the man from "Hope"—Arkansas. Clinton's plebeian roots were held to make him more adept at relating to the plight of those hurting from the recession. He felt their pain because he had experienced hard times. Bush, on the other hand, was born into a wealthy family. He just could not understand the problems of the common man. The Clinton campaign successfully argued that the economy was bad because Bush did not care about people.

Bush initially gained the most from polls, but eventually suffered dearly at their hands. His management of foreign affairs, including his handling of the collapse of communism and the aborted coup against then Soviet leader Mikhail Gorbachev, earned him high approval ratings with the populace. But it was Bush's strong leadership during the war with Iraq that gained him the mother of all positive polls. He attained the highest performance ratings of any president since surveys have been taken. Strong polls influence potential opponents. They may scare off the other party's activists, forestall the entrance of political elites into a campaign, and hinder fund-raising. Polls carry a particular importance for what are called strategic politicians, those who enter a race only if they see a clear chance of winning.[12] Bush's historically high evaluations surely influenced such formidable Democratic politicians such as Governor Mario Cuomo, Senator Bill Bradley, and Congressman Richard Gephardt not to test the waters.

Bush's impressive polls led in part to his eventual downfall. Citizens contrasted his stellar accomplishments during foreign crises with his performance on the economy. Clearly, he could not live up to the lofty expectations which his own successes had created. He might have been able to recover from the unwarranted demands of his accomplishments if events had conspired to give him the opportunity. Despite all the excitement associated with a presidential election, however, nothing of real importance happened during the 1992 campaign. The greatest struggle of the twentieth century, the Cold War, was over. The battle in Iraq was won. By comparison with other presidential election years, there were really no crises that took place, as for example the war in Vietnam in 1968 or the hostages held in Iran and the Soviet invasion of Afghanistan during the 1980 campaign.

In the absence of real events, polls took on even more importance. No doubt, the major ingredients in Bush's drop in popularity were caused by people's disappointment with his lackluster leadership in domestic affairs and his apparent patrician indifference to the plight of the ordinary man. But polls too played a part in his decline. They took on a multiplier effect, making him look even worse than he was. Polls tend to consolidate the image of a candidate. A politician who is running ahead in the polls is more likely to be portrayed in the media as "strong, intelligent, thoughtful, and capable. When the candidate is languishing, he or she is characterized as weak, stiff, hesitant, and incompetent."[13] Whether poor poll ratings influence voters has been a matter of debate for some time.[14] It does seem clear, however, that Bush's unprecedented slide in popularity gained a momentum of its own. Polls added to the downward trend by making his responses to popular dissatisfaction look confused and desperate. Whatever he proposed was explained by media analysts to be "just a response to the polls."

Bush's theory of governance also hurt his chances for reelection. Except in times of crisis, he did not believe in an activist presidency, preferring to allow his subordinates, experts in their fields, to formulate and execute policy. Prior to his elevation to the presidency, he had been the consummate insider, a professional who disdained political rhetoric and favored letting expertise and performance speak for itself. He had neither the knack nor the inclination to duplicate Reagan's feats of rhetorical leadership. He was, by his own admission, uncomfortable with "the vision thing." Peggy Noonan, one of America's most able speech writers, summed up Bush's predicament: "Serious people in public life stand for things and fight for them. Mr. Bush seemed embarrassed to believe. It left those who felt sympathy for him embarrassed to support him."[15]

The poor economy put Bush's "performance" rule to the test. He followed the recommendations of his senior advisers who believed that a stimulus package would come too late to help the recovery, and might actually do long-term harm to financial stability. He hoped that the hands-off policy would succeed and then people would see the wisdom of the policy. In the meantime, popularity polls were not his ally. He had to govern, and to govern means to put distance between the judgment of the ruler and the wishes of the ruled. He was responsible for making decisions which he thought best for the nation, not for doing or saying things that made him popular. The strategy of waiting out the worst met with the same success it had when Pericles counseled the Athenians to ignore the Spartans burning their farms.[16] Indeed, Bush hardly defended his own policy, hoping instead that the promised turnaround would make explanations unnecessary. When the lift-off failed to take place, he took to defending the country's economic performance, claiming that things were not really that bad, especially when compared to other nations. Interest rates and inflation were low, and both these signaled the likelihood of an upswing. But these protestations could not compete with the daily reports of worker layoffs, nor the drumbeat of forceful criticism coming from his rivals.

In desperation, it seems, Bush turned to the character issue. For Bush, as perhaps distinct from many of his workers, the character issue was more than a matter of Clinton's alleged sexual antics. He believed that Clinton was untrustworthy exactly because he was not an experienced professional or an insider. Clinton had not paid his dues, especially in foreign affairs. In a year when the term "Washington insider" became something of an epithet, Bush's assessment of Clinton fell on many deaf ears. Moreover, Bush had character problems all his own. Every time he moved his lips it reminded voters that he had broken his promise not to impose new taxes. Election-eve leaks from the Special Prosecutor's office about Bush's involvement in the Iran-Contra affair further sullied his credibility. Finally, Bush's background, education, and elitist image became a character issue. It made him seem out of touch with the plight of most Americans.

H. Ross Perot was the first American politician to use public opinion polls as an integral part of his campaign strategy. Because he never actually ran in a primary election, and at times was not even in the race, polls provided a means for his candidacy to gain legitimacy. He argued that he was the candidate closest to the people. He represented all those citizens who believed that the national government had abandoned its responsibility. The political system was no longer able to respond to the needs of the people. It could not solve the debt crisis, the drug plight, the crime problem, or the competitiveness crunch. The people's representatives had sold out the public trust to special interests and foreign lobbyists. The system was broken. It needed a new kind of mechanic to make the repairs. America's problems could be solved only if someone acted exclusively for the common good. Perot claimed that he could "just do it!" His plan for how he would do it was not altogether clear. For the most part he offered more or less mainstream solutions, such as cutting spending, raising taxes on gasoline, and investing public money in research and technology. While the actual policy changes he proposed were quite moderate, the way he attempted to implement them was not. He denigrated the traditional means of running for office, of deciding how elections are won and lost, and of governing once power was gained.

If elected, Perot pledged to clean up politics by banishing corruption and self-interest, to rid the government of special interests and lobbyists who acted as agents for foreign powers, and to straighten out the gridlock in Washington by doing away with business as usual. A major component of the nation's problems, according to Perot, was its political institutions. Institutions stood in the way of the people's will, which for Perot was a pure expression of the common good. To put it more plainly, the problem was a lack of democracy and the cure was more democracy. Perot claimed to be the embodiment of the people's will. He was a servant of the common good with no personal ambition, a moth to the flame of his volunteers. But how could a person who had never actually run for office allege such a connection with the public? Clearly, polls were the only route by which Perot could assert the validity of his relationship to the American people. For much of the campaign, his positive ratings in the polls gave him the appearance of a real candidate, at times the aura of a front-runner.

The media played a crucial role in promoting the pseudo-candidacy of Perot.[17] Tracking polls, which showed the relative strength of candidates, were reported almost as if they were the results of primary elections. In some instances, exit polls were given more credence than actual elections. For example, despite Clinton's conclusive primary wins in California and Ohio, victories which sewed up the nomination, the Democratic front-runner had to share the headlines with Perot's exit polls. They revealed that if Perot had been on the ballot, he would have won both elections.[18]

Perot's bid for the presidency was based more than on just good numbers in the polls, of course. He tapped into something much deeper in the American electorate, a yearning for a more cohesive and meaningful national community. As Roy Teixeira has pointed out, for some time Americans have felt a certain rootlessness and a lack of connection with their political institutions. Political parties once served as vehicles for what political scientists call the solidarity motive for participation in public life. People of like minds and often similar economic or ethnic backgrounds were drawn together to work for a common cause. Parties acted almost as social clubs where important matters were considered with fellow citizens in a hospitable atmosphere that gave people a feeling of true community. But parties are now so weak that they can no longer support this function.[19]

Cohesiveness at the local level has also declined. The electronic media spend much more of their time and resources covering national and international events than they do with local issues. Because people receive most of their information from the electronic media, they actually know more about national politics than they do about what is going in their own communities. The kind of participation that went on in neighborhood associations and in town halls is no longer as strong as it was in the past.

Many Americans still feel the desire to take part in something greater than themselves and to share, with others, in the governing of their own destiny and that of the nation. Since the electronic media play such a crucial role in providing us with information about public events, it is little wonder that the electronic media have become the new channel through which community is expressed. Now that the more traditional patterns of solidarity are absent, radio and television call-in shows, talk shows, electronic town halls, infomercials, and call-in polls are important means of participation. The power of these new phenomena is evident in the extraordinary growth of public affairs talk shows, the market-share of television and radio talk shows, such as Larry King's and Rush Limbaugh's, and the numbers of people who attempt to participate through the electronic media. For example, when CBS offered a call-in program after Clinton's first address to a joint session of Congress on February 17, 1993, the telephone company reported that there were 24 million efforts to reach the 800 number. In exit polls taken on election day, a large proportion of the electorate said that the candidates' appearances on talk shows influenced how they voted. The increased voter turn-out in 1992 may be proof that electronic participation techniques actually did have an effect, giving citizens a greater interest in the election and stronger feeling of connectedness with the political process.

Perot was the first politician to understand clearly that for many people these forms of participation are the common good. Plebiscitary democracy is seen as the remedy for the nation's ills. If only politicians would stop listening to the special interests, give up their perks, and not lose touch with the rest of the population, the debt would be reduced, waste and fraud would disappear, and solutions to other problems would become apparent. Perot enlisted followers in common cause to straighten out the mess in Washington through the electronic media. He used it to great advantage. He announced, unannounced, and re-announced his bid for the presidency on talk shows. After one such announcement on Larry King's call-in talk show, which propelled Perot into the lead in the next day's poll, King went so far as to immodestly assert "I was his New Hampshire." He bought television time in which he presented his views in a public affairs format, so-called infomercials. He participated in electronic town halls in which viewers were encouraged to ask questions on the candidate's views. (The questions were screened by Perot's staff as they came in.) He conducted his own call-in polls which he used to give his campaign credibility. He developed a method which identified the names and addresses of callers to his 800 number polls. He used these data to develop demographic information about his followers.[20]

Judged fairly, the electronic media furnish the opportunity for no more than a kind of pseudo-participation. People actually think they are involved in politics when in fact they sit around and listen to the Rush Limbaugh talk show on radio. This is not real participation because people are not doing anything. They are not involved in making policy. They are not deliberating between policy alternatives. They do not even control the agenda of the program; the host does. They are truly not taking action, at least not to govern themselves.

Polls are not really a form of participation either. But, like the other modes of pseudo-participation, polls give people the feeling both that they are part of a mass movement and that they are in control. Surveys show the individual that his or her views are similar to those of a large segment of the population. Polls are taken to be democracy in action because they express the will of the people. Again democracy, as it manifests itself in survey results, is taken to be the common good, as is indicated by a Gallup national survey in which 76 percent of the respondents believed that polls were a good thing and only 12 percent thought that they were a bad thing.[21] Those who live by polls, die by polls. When the public learned that Perot had placed surveillance on his workers, on his business competitors, and even on Bush while he was vice president, the Perot campaign unraveled. Instead of the average citizen, intent on cleaning up the mess in Washington, Perot became the manipulative and power-hungry tycoon whose eccentricities far outweighed his straight talk about national problems. Lacking the high ratings that gave his candidacy credibility, Perot withdrew. He reentered the race only after he and his staff had resuscitated his image, in part, by instituting a sham poll that counted every call to an 800 number as a request for Perot to resume his bid. Despite receiving the largest number of votes of any third-party candidate since Theodore Roosevelt, Perot never recovered his earlier momentum and was not a serious contender to win the presidency on election day.

Assessing Polls

The events of 1992 indicate that polls are not good for American democracy. The usual arguments made against polls are that they create the atmosphere of a horse race, crowding out the issues from the news, and that they establish a bandwagon effect, steamrolling less popular but sometimes more thoughtful candidates. Each of these criticisms has a certain validity, but they are far from the whole story.

Polls are answers to questions which are presented on the spot, if you will. Oftentimes, there is no warning at all when a pollster calls to solicit one's opinion. No forethought is necessary because polls assume that people have opinions on every issue and that all opinions about issues are of equal merit. Polls do not distinguish between well-thought-out ideas and those that are formed at that very instant. Polls do not measure deliberation because there is no way to tally such a thing. On the other hand, voting is a solemn act of citizenship. Democracy works best in nations where the people understand the importance of choosing those who will govern over them. Many, if not most, Americans who vote try, as best they can, to deliberate about the competence, views, and vision of the candidates. One reason why presidential debates are watched so widely, despite the fact that many Americans claim to dislike politics and politicians, is that the debates offer the voters a means of deciding the most solemn question in a democracy: who should rule. As Perot's campaign shows, polls are beginning to take the place of elections as a legitimate expression of the popular will. But polls do not demand that people deliberate; they ask only that people answer. Democracy suffers as a result.

As greater and greater numbers of surveys are taken, they are given ever more serious weight by political commentators as the expression of the popular will. In part, polls are accorded so much importance because the media must report something new, and the shifting opinions of the public are always new. Furthermore, polls make pundits look intelligent. Commentators interpret the meaning of survey results, tell us what we are really thinking, and speculate on why we are thinking it. Polls are used as a kind of pop psychology which reveals the public's innermost secrets to itself. This exploration of the public psyche reached its zenith during the 1992 presidential debates when pollster and television commentator William Schneider had volunteers wired to meters which instantaneously registered their reactions to the statements and exchanges of the candidates. Schneider provided the audience with immediate insights about what the respondents were thinking and how this attitude would translate into votes on election day. Armed with this information about the public, he also hinted at how his audience should view the outcome of the debates. With interactive technology now becoming a reality, Schneider's poll may indicate what is to come: instant opinions followed by instant analysis.

While commentary about the current state of public opinion is, by itself, harmless enough, it does create the impression among viewers that the will of the public is never wrong. Polls engender the belief that there is no right or wrong, there is only what people think is right or wrong. For years, those who believe in absolute standards have attacked this doctrine, called positivism, as a principle devoid of moral content. But well-orchestrated mass media campaigns directed at consciousness-raising have helped establish the conclusion that moral guidelines can be changed by public pressure and that the people's opinions are the source of right. It is a matter of debate whether a democracy, which more than any other form of government depends on the virtue of the people, can survive if such a valueless outlook comes to predominate in the public's mind.

Consideration of the moral effects of positivism are surely worthy of our deepest reflections, but it is more in keeping with the present topic to reflect on the political consequences. There is a widespread belief, of which polls are one aspect, that the people are competent to conceive, evaluate, institute, and carry out public policy. In this view, political leaders are no more than errand boys who deliver every provision that the people order. According to this concept, government fails when politicians lose touch with the superior wisdom of the people. Polls are good things because they continually inform the people's representatives of what they should be doing. George Gallup, perhaps somewhat self-interestedly, has expressed this view most clearly. "In my opinion," he wrote,

> modern polls are the chief hope of lifting government to a higher level, by showing that the public supports the reforms that will make this possible, by providing a *modus operandi* for testing new ideas. . . . Polls can help make government more efficient and responsive; they can improve the quality of candidates for public office; they can make this a truer democracy.[22]

But only a sycophant would place absolute faith in the ability of the people to govern themselves without capable leadership. It is impossible in a direct democracy to consider complicated issues, especially in a country so large as the United States. There are too many voices for serious discussion. Electronic town halls and telepolling are not true deliberation. They are at best merely public reactions to the agenda set by the moderator of the program. But in an age of thirty-second sound bites and entertainment-based news, these efforts at participation flatter the public's perception of itself by creating the illusion that complex problems can be solved simply and quickly once the voice of the people is known.

The American Founders understood democracy far better. They argued that representative government was superior to democracy because representatives would be more knowledgeable about public affairs. The Founders' advocacy of the republican form of government has lent itself to the charge of elitism. But the Founders did not believe that government needed to be dominated by men from the better social classes. Their argument rested more on the view that competence in public affairs, as in other walks of life, is gained by experience. Representatives can spend their time investigating and deliberating on the issues of the day. The people are busy doing their own jobs and have little time left over for public policy analysis. "No man," Publius explained in *The Federalist Papers,*

> can be a competent legislator who does not [have] . . . knowledge of the subjects on which he will legislate. A part of the knowledge may be acquired by means of information which lie within the compass of men in private as well as public stations. Another part can only be attained, or at least thoroughly attained, by actual experience in the station which requires the use of it.[23]

Polls also lessen the distance between voters and rulers. They place undue pressure on representatives to follow the directives of their constituents. In a diverse society such as ours, there are many interests to satisfy since not all citizens have the same interests. There are many government programs and much government spending not because politicians are out of touch with the people, but exactly because they are in touch. The people make demands and politicians attempt to fulfill them. Advocates for the old, the young, the poor, the rich, the sick, those who care for the sick, business, labor, and the environment, to name just a few, each have their own lobbying groups and all push their own agenda. All of these programs are no doubt worthwhile. However, resources are not unlimited. Politicians respond to these often conflicting demands by trying to make everybody happy; hence the penchant to overspend. Contrary to the claims of Perot, the special interests have not stolen the government and squandered the people's money; the people are the special interests. Again the Founders seemed to have had a deeper grasp of the true nature of the democratic impulse. They knew that there would be too many burdens placed on government if the people's will was followed too closely. They wanted to give representatives a certain autonomy from the people so that they could make laws dispassionately and wisely:

> The republican principle demands that the deliberative sense of the community should govern the conduct of those to whom they entrust the management of their affairs; but it does not require an unqualified complaisance to every sudden breeze of passion, or to every transient impulse which the people may receive from the arts of men, who flatter their prejudices to betray their interests. It is a just observation that the people commonly *intend* the PUBLIC GOOD. This often applies to their very errors. But their good sense would despise the adulator who should pretend that they always *reason right* about the *means* of promoting it.[24]

Representative government has the added advantage of slowing down the political process. It forces us to follow certain formal rules—such as considering bills, passing them into law, and having them signed by the president—before we can act. This pause offers us the opportunity for deeper reflection about the merits of our proposals. It allows us the time to deliberate. Not all democracies have taken such steps to guard themselves against hasty judgments. The Founders attempted to learn from the past and to avoid the errors of those countries:

> What bitter anguish would not the people of Athens have often escaped if their government had contained so provident a safeguard against the tyranny of their own passions? Popular liberty might then have escaped the indelible reproach of decreeing to the same citizens the hemlock on one day and statues on the next.[25]

There is no time for thought or reflection if polls are the moving force behind legislation. We can only wonder if, having at some future date become fully a "pollocracy," we will not repeat the fatal mistakes of the Athenians.

The formal institutions of government are also necessary to ensure fairness and stability in our political system. Experience has taught us that elections must be regulated by law or else the rivals for power will attempt to cheat. In this regard, it is interesting to consider what occurred during the 1992 race. Perot used false polling techniques to inflate his standing with the public. Pollsters cried foul. But on what grounds did they have to complain? For years they had put forward the view that surveys were a legitimate means of expressing the public mind. Pollsters rejected the view that polls undermined the political process because they had little regard for the forms of government. With no forms there are no guarantees that the rules will be followed. The Perot example reminds us why forms are necessary: ambition can make people reckless. Even pollsters, it seems, are in need of forms to protect their trade from the encroachments of the ambitious.

Imagine if Perot had been elected. He would have arrived in Washington with high hopes and a good deal of popular fanfare. He would not have had any institutional support in Congress. Neither the leaders of Congress nor the members of political parties who make up the lawmaking branch would have felt any loyalty to him. Given that members of Congress are under intense political pressures to please their constituents, it is unlikely that they would have "just done it." What then would Perot have done? Would he have turned to his old ally, polls, in order to push forward his campaign promises? Would he have attempted to put into effect policies which surveys indicated were popular without congressional approval? Would he have tried to govern with polls, but without law? Speculating on these questions is perhaps unfair to Perot, who avowed himself to be no more than a steward of the common good, yet we ought to recall that the formal institutions were put in place to protect us from the grandiose schemes of flamboyant leaders, even those who contend to be the champions of our dearest desires. Harvey Mansfield Jr. seems to have anticipated the problems raised by the Perot campaign and thus the need for the formal institutions of government:

> As democracy becomes more democratic, it becomes more informal. Forms of election, in particular, disappear; for election, as Aristotle noted, is an aristocratic principle. It is also true that one does not get rid of leaders and "elites" simply by attacking, undermining, or ignoring the leaders who have been elected. Informal leaders spring up like weeds to replace the deposed formal leaders, and doubt remains whether democracy can survive if it rushes toward more democracy by neglect of the forms of democracy.[26]

Conclusion

Elections are about interest, competence, and vision. Ironically, each of the candidates in the 1992 presidential race based his claim to rule on one of these attributes, although all attempted to exhibit prowess in all three areas. Public opinion polls played a part in determining how the messages of the candidates played with the public. Clinton appealed primarily to people's interests. He cautioned them that their futures were in jeopardy because of the ill-health of the economy and informed them that Bush had no plan to fix it. Clinton consciously used political rhetoric as a means of keeping the economy from improving. Polls helped him in this strategy because the public's anxieties about the state of the economy, as registered in surveys, dampened consumer confidence and kept the economy in the doldrums.

Bush's claim to rule rested on his experience and accomplishments. But nothing of particular moment materialized during the last year of his tenure and he was unable to exhibit his abilities. His past achievements, although greatly admired, were soon forgotten. The public came to doubt his much-vaunted competence because he seemed unable to deal with the economic slowdown. Polls reinforced the image that Bush was helpless and that social forces were beyond his control.

Perot's vision was to restore America to its former role as the single economic power in the world. This could be done, he insisted, by making government more responsive to the desires of the American people, particularly their desires for personal security and national prominence. He understood that the public was suffering from the malaise about which President Jimmy Carter spoke. But Perot never mentioned this word. Instead, he chose the tactics employed so successfully by President Ronald Reagan. He did not give the people scoldings; he attempted to give them hope. Perot seems to have been aware that democracy itself can provide a national purpose. He asserted that policies which could solve our most pressing problems were within our grasp if only those in government would really listen to the voice of the people, roll up their sleeves, and do what the people demanded. Polls were most important to Perot because they were his connection with the will of the people and with a common national purpose.

Although voters insist that candidates act as courtesans for their votes, they are unhappy when politicians get caught pandering for their favors. If politicians become too obvious, it reminds the people of the unwelcome truth that they, not their leaders, have solicited the pleasures which government programs can provide. Therefore, talk of a higher national purpose is always necessary at election time. It is necessary because people want to convince themselves that they are not just the "Johns" of democracy, who force politicians to prostitute themselves before the public will. Most people in America believe that members of Congress are either corrupt or, at the very least, have lost touch with their constituents. This is given as the reason why the government does not work. But those same people return their own congressman or woman to office because that representative has brought benefits home to the district. The people do not want to see their own complicity in the faults of the nation, especially as regards the creation of institutional gridlock and the national debt. Perot held that he could solve the problems of democracy by sidestepping the formal political institutions and by making democracy more democratic. He wanted to give the people power unrestrained by institutional limits. His remedy is similar to administering venom to cure the antidote.

Polls are a menace to American democracy. They flatter the worst instincts of the people. They make us believe that we can do no wrong. They force politicians to adopt policies that, in their best judgment, they know to be unwise. Polls open the door to demagogic leaders whose ambition for glory might someday ruin our political system. In thinking about the place of polls within our regime, and in particular in the 1992 campaign, politicians, pollsters, pundits, and the people ought to consider carefully the argument of Publius that leaders often have good reason for ignoring the transient impulses of public opinion. Such action, he claims, has often saved the people from very fatal consequences of their own mistakes, and has procured lasting monuments of their gratitude to the men who had courage and magnanimity enough to serve them at the peril of their displeasure.[27]

Notes

1. There are numerous examples of leading questions influencing the results of polls. Opinion polls are especially vulnerable to this confusion, but even polls taken to measure candidate strength can be affected. For instance in May 1980 an NBC poll, which did not mention any candidates by name, asked voters who they would like to see elected president in the 1980 race.

Carter received 24 percent, Reagan 24 percent, Anderson 5 percent, and undecided 25 percent. A week later a Harris poll asked likely voters, "If you had to choose right now, would you vote for Reagan, Carter or Anderson?" The tally on this poll was Reagan 39 percent, Carter 34 percent, Anderson 24 percent, and only 5 percent undecided. Herbert Asher, *Polling and the Public: What Every Citizen Should Know* (Washington, D.C.: Congressional Quarterly Press, 1988), p. 43.

2. The most famous instance of lying to pollsters was the 1989 Virginia gubernatorial race. Exit polls indicated that Democratic candidate Douglas Wilder, who is black, won by a wide margin over his Republican challenger. Wilder won the governorship, but the final returns showed a much closer race. Evidently the exit polls were thrown off because voters did not want to admit that they voted against Wilder on account of race.

3. John Brehm, *The Phantom Respondents* (Ann Arbor: University of Michigan Press, 1993).

4. Kathleen A. Frankovic, "Technology and the Changing Landscape of Media Polls," in Thomas E. Mann and Gary R. Orren, eds., *Media Polls in American Politics* (Washington, D.C.: Brookings Institution, 1992), pp. 32–54.

5. Carl Berstein, "The Idiot Culture," *The New Republic*, June 8, 1992, p. 24.

6. Thomas E. Mann and Gary R. Orren, "To Poll or Not to Poll . . . and Other Questions," in Mann and Orren, *Media Polls in American Politics*, pp. 12–14.

7. Michael J. Robinson and Margaret A. Sheehan, *Over the Wire and on TV: CBS and UPI in Campaign '80* (New York: Russell Sage Foundation, 1983), p. 252.

8. On the roll of the media and the "new" see Harvey C. Mansfield Jr., *America's Constitutional Soul* (Baltimore: Johns Hopkins University Press, 1991), pp. 163–76.

9. Dan Balz and David S. Broder, "Democrats Talk of New Candidates," *Washington Post*, Feb. 14, 1992, p. A1.

10. Charles Peters, "The Media's Rush to Anointment," *Washington Post*, Mar. 15, 1992, p. C15.

11. Alexis de Tocqueville, *Democracy in America*, trans. George Lawrence (Garden City, N.Y.: Doubleday Anchor, 1968), pp. 237, 347. See also pp. 54, 161, 183, 205, 211, 283, 306, 402–4, 413.

12. Harrison Hickman, "Public Polls and Election Participants," in Paul J. Lavrakas and Jack K. Holley, eds., *Polling and Presidential Election Coverage* (Newbury Park, Calif.: Sage Publications, 1990), pp. 100–133.

13. Mann and Orren, "To Poll or Not to Poll," p. 12.

14. While not all voters are open to influence by polls, those who are undecided are more likely to be influenced by tides in public opinion as expressed in polls. There were an unusually high number of undecideds at the beginning of the 1992 race. For an analysis of polls on public perceptions see

Michael W. Traugott, "The Impact of Media Polls on the Public," in Mann and Orren, eds., *Media Polls in American Politics,* pp. 125–49.

15. Peggy Noonan, "Why Bush Failed," *New York Times,* Nov. 5, 1992, p. A35.

16. The Athenians probably would have given a death sentence to Pericles, but he died before they could vote.

17. For a delightful and perceptive discussion of Perot's candidacy as a pseudo-event, see James W. Ceaser and Andrew Busch, "Being and Perot: The Metaphysics of the Perot Phenomena," *Upside Down and Inside Out: The 1992 Elections and American Politics* (Lanham, Md.: Rowman & Littlefield, 1993), pp. 100–101.

18. *New York Times,* June 3, 1992, p. 1.

19. Roy Teixeira, *The Disappearing American Voter* (Washington, D.C.: Brookings Institution, 1992).

20. Tom Steinert-Threlkeld, "High-tech Tactics by Perot Could Reshape Politics, Experts Say," *Dallas Morning News,* May 3, 1992, pp. 1, 15.

21. Asher, *Polling and the Public,* p. 13.

22. George Gallup, "Polls and the Political Process—Past, Present, and Future," *Public Opinion Quarterly* 29 (Winter 1965–66): 549.

23. Alexander Hamilton, John Jay, and James Madison, *The Federalist Papers,* 53 (New York: Modern Library, n.d.), p. 349.

24. *Federalist* 71, p. 464, emphasis original.

25. *Federalist* 63, p. 410.

26. Mansfield, *America's Constitutional Soul,* p. 175.

27. *Federalist* 71, p. 465.

Part Two

Government Institutions

4

Energy, Inaction, and the Bush Presidency

John Agresto

"Well, he's no McKinley," as a pundit during the campaign said about George Bush. Though Bill Clinton was often damned through his own past sins of commission, Bush's failings were more destructive politically: he was weighed and measured for his sins of omission, for inactivity and failure of leadership. He lacked Ronald Reagan's sense of vision and principle, John Kennedy's charm, and Lyndon Johnson's ability. In lacking whatever it was that even Williiam McKinley presumptively had, Bush lacked being presidential. And because of that, he could not win.

Considered either abstractly or in the context of surrounding events, this is an exceedingly odd statement to make. Abstractly, because there is no apparent reason why "doing" is preferable to its opposite; why, among an electorate usually spoken of as more conservative than liberal, "action" in the abstract seems preferable to inaction. Nor is it obvious why, in the context of the incredible success of the West over international communism, that normalcy, placidity, lack of high vision, or lack of grand leadership would be so soundly disparaged.

No human event ever has only one cause, and the result of a national presidential election is surely no exception. Factors abound: Clinton's youth and exuberance, the stagnant economy, the poor planning of the Republican convention, press bias, Iran-Contra revelations, . . . even down to the presidential debates with Bush looking at his watch. But above all this stood one picture, buttressed by example upon example, of a presidency stalled in leadership and two opponents ready to recommence the task of leading.

Again, the very saying of that seems strange. The negatives connected with each opponent were so formidable, so glaring, that one would have thought that even somniferous inaction, bored quiescence,

73

would easily win out. One candidate, Ross Perot, had entered the race playing generally a single note—the deficit—dropped out of the campaign in a fit of pique and then returned. Unprepossessing in looks, narrowly focused in ideas, and by his actions hardly reassuring regarding his steadiness, he nonetheless knew exactly the image that needed to be painted: a person who has *done*, has built, has led, and could do so again. In large measure Perot knew that the last thing people want in a president is one who presides. They want constant and perpetual leadership. And his favorite image of rolling up one's sleeves and getting under the hood was perfectly calculated to effect that result.

Clinton's image of leadership was considerably more substantive and less rhetorical. Even if we grant the commentators the view that virtually no one actually read the endless array of items in the various white papers put out by the Clinton campaign, at least the overall effect was that, under Clinton, things would be attempted. What those "things" were might have been poorly grasped by the general voter. Nonetheless, there *were* things, and they would be attempted. What this means is that, faced with a seemingly do-nothing opponent, even empty phrases such as "We have to get the country moving again" and "We have to grow the economy" and "We have to do something about health care in this country" begin to speak with tolerable clarity to the voters. Even saying the supposedly unsayable—we have to raise taxes—no longer kills when coupled with a problem, such as the deficit, which needs to be tackled.

To see more fully the perhaps unanticipated power of the idea of democratic leadership, imagine yourself in the Bush campaign. During your administration, the nearly half-century desire of all Americans has arrived—the collapse and disintegration of Soviet power. Indeed, mirabile dictu, in areas of foreign policy our implacable enemy has become our helpful ally. The global danger to America's national survival is gone. Second, though we lack a monumental enemy, the interests of America still have nasty, smaller opponents. One of them, Iraq, is hobbled by American might in 100 hours, and on world TV to boot. The president's popularity is, in some polls, at nearly 90 percent. Domestically, there is, to be sure, a recession. But inflation is down, interest rates are good, the markets remain healthy, and unemployment, while not great, could be and has been considerably worse. Moreover, it might be that the worst things one could do in what is probably a cyclical economic slump are precipitous and artificial actions. Until otherwise proven, inaction is the preferable course over action; the better part of wisdom is to sit tight.

Given a nation not only at peace but in victory, with a slumping but hardly depressed economy, against a major opponent with a history (to put it in hyper-political terms) of draft-dodging, womanizing, drug use, and the promise of raising taxes, what would *you* do? You'd do nothing. And you'd be dead wrong.

I do not mean to imply that the decision to be quiet and lay low during the campaign was a calculation on the part of the Bush team. It was of a piece with the character of the whole four years and was, itself, the advertisement of what the next four would be like.

Not that *nothing* was done, if by "done" one means "things happened." Surely communism did fall "on his watch" as President Bush liked to say. But "watch" is, more or less, the operative word. The administration was a witness to unfolding events, albeit a witness with a front-row seat. Even when actions in the international arena needed to be taken, or were demanded by events, the administration took what seemed to be retardant rather than proactive decisions. Mikhail Gorbachev was promoted and propped up long after he should have been allowed to exit. Boris Yelsin was demeaned and belittled far beyond any intelligent policy considerations. The early pleas of the Balkan states were spurned in our desire not to destabilize the area. It is possible, of course, that all this and more were done for intelligent reasons of state and in the pursuit of high policy, but that seems to strain credulity. The same desire for stability over proper results seems to have governed the China policy during the abortive democratic revolution and Tiananmen Square massacre in 1989. The administration's hands-off policy saw (despite the policy, I believe, not because of it) good results in the Soviet Union and its client states. Inaction had no such good result in China.

Oddly enough, this desire for the retention of the status quo—or the desire that *others* do while we observe—is what turned the president's virtually guaranteed success in the Iraqi affair to failure. The desire to end the Persian Gulf war in some symbolic 100 hours rather than "finish the job," the impossibly silly desire to let the disgruntled generals handle Saddam Hussein rather than do it ourselves, contributed to the result that, today, Saddam is in power and Bush is not.

But the war remains instructive. Here was America doing something and doing something ostensibly good. Here was, at first, strong presidential leadership. It was leadership that not only overcame domestic opposition but managed to rally the forces of other nations collectively under the American flag. Here were decisions made and actions taken. There's why the president's popularity was, then, the greatest in modern history. But when retreat followed victory, and the job, as Perot would say, was left undone, then the president went back to his old ways—he was no McKinley.

In domestic matters, the Bush presidency seemed even less able to formulate and defend any coherent policies. In large measure, "family values" became a slogan of ridicule because no policies that meant anything were used to fill in the empty words. When the Los Angeles riots occurred, was there any course of action proposed by the administration other than the tired and uninteresting response of more federal spending? With education at all levels held hostage by thugs and violence, by political correctness, and by social and sexual schemes of dubious merit, why was "vouchers" the only solution trotted out by the administration—a small and partial solution that even Reagan was unable to sell?

Finally, and instructively, there was the fracas over the National Endowment for the Arts. John Frohnmayer, it seems, was appointed without the president having the slightest idea what he wanted Frohnmayer to do in the area of cultural policy, nor even any idea what the issues were. When the NEAs grants became a source of friction in the months before the election, the president still seemed to have no policies, much less principles, that he could articulate or defend. Nor did the president or his aides discuss the matter with the president's own appointees to the commission set up to investigate arts funding and make recommendations concerning its future. (I know; I was one of his appointees.) Never once did it appear that the president had even looked at the commission's report after it was finished. In fact, in the whole area of culture, Bush said less and made less sense than Tipper Gore. Even on issues that were of burning concern to a large part of his natural constituency, Bush seemed to have given no thought; he exercised no leadership. His guiding light seemed to be to all the world no more than "Don't know, don't care."

Why is it that we are a country that, from school days on, "rank" our presidents? Why is it that the most active domestic and international leaders are on top and the more lackluster at the bottom? Despite real or supposed policy differences with, say, Franklin D. Roosevelt, most Americans would say he belongs in the list of "great" presidents. How many Americans say that of Warren Harding or Calvin Coolidge, even if it would be shown that "the times" over which they presided hardly cried out for a George Washington or an

Abraham Lincoln? Why is inaction at the presidential level, in the mind of the general American voter, tantamount to failure? Why is inaction the clue to failed leadership?

Perhaps we can glimpse the answer by asking another question. How is it that Alexander Hamilton knew that this would be the case before we even had a presidency? In the eleven papers Hamilton wrote on the presidency, the words most often used are "vigor" and "energy." "Energy in the Executive" is not only, in Hamilton's words, desirable, it is "a leading character in the definition of good government" (*Federalist* 70). Feeble execution of the government is a synonym for "bad government" (*id*). "Decision, activity, secrecy and dispatch" are the qualities of good Presidential leadership (*id* and *Federalist* 75). Presidential failure is marked by "feebleness and irresolution" (*Federalist* 71). Above all, the president should be able "to dare to act his own opinion with vigor and decision" (*id*).

Excerpted in this fashion, Hamilton may well seem unreasonable, for vigor and energy hardly seem, of themselves, to be good or bad. They draw their character from the character of the ends pursued. Are not decision, activity, secrecy, and dispatch surely worse than bumbling and failing at achieving bad ends? Are not sins of commission almost always more serious than sins of omission? Doesn't this comport with our common, everyday sense? Maybe, contrary to Hamilton, inaction is to be *preferred* to action. After all, as John Adams once remarked, "In this world, Laziness alone has prevented more wicked actions than all the virtues put together."

In truth, however, this is *not* our common, everyday sense. We rarely find time to praise inactivity. We count sloth among the vices. We sense the truth of Edmund Burke's dictum that all that is necessary for evil to succeed is for good men to do nothing. Even the most conservative man, who desires only that the status quo be preserved, knows the truth of T. S. Eliot's comment that just to keep a white fence white, it needs to be painted every year. Sins of omission by the good encourage sins of commission by the not-so-good. While true leadership, real statesmanship, involves both knowledge of the good and knowledge of the best means of achieving it, on a simple level the ordinary American knows that nothing good is accomplished by not doing. Hamilton doesn't say "vigor in just causes" or "energy properly directed." In this country, vigor, energy, daring, and dispatch will, in themselves, tend toward the good. At least that's what most Americans seem to believe, and not without justification.

Still, Hamilton cannot simply be saying that activity is better than inactivity in the abstract. But, within this constitutional system—our constitutional system—presidential vigor is helpful, constructive, and praiseworthy, and presidential inactivity is not. By why should that be the case?

Well, on one level, while change is not the same as progress, in a free country comprised of decent citizens, change often *is* progress. But why do we, as Americans, seem so naturally and instinctively to look to *presidential* vigor and energy? Perhaps the following might help: First, activity in the execution of *America's* laws will be good because, given the structure of constitutional government in America, our laws will most likely be good. Second, given the care with which the president himself is selected—the one office whose election Americans in 1789 seem to have found well constructed (per *Federalist* 68)—there would be little to fear and much to gain from presidential independence. His election, the mode of his reelection, his probable character, his ability and virtues, should lead us toward rather than away from confidence. We have managed to find mechanical and institutional ways to have the benefit of kings without the danger of tyrants. Finally, given the whole system of checks and balances, including impeachments, wicked or even simply unpopular presidential actions are not without remedy.

For all these reasons, presidential activity is, to be honest, simply preferable to presidential inactivity. It is almost certain to be productive of greater good than presidential vacillation. Indeed, given the internal frictions and internal brakes put on legislative action in this country by the Constitution, the president is naturally the main locus of forward motion in this country. (Without that, the mantle, more often than not, might fall on the courts. And there, because the makers of the laws become their own executors and judges, the results are potentially less salutary. Presidential activism is desirable if for no other reason than it might preempt judicial activism.) Americans know this even without reading Hamilton. They sense that presidential action, especially in a hostile world, is, in almost every instance, surely better than no action. Poor or pernicious proposals by a president can be deflected or, at some point, overcome. Irresolution cannot.

5

The Constitutional Presidency of George Bush

Peter Augustine Lawler

The 1992 presidential election, as Bill Clinton predicted, was mostly a simple vote for change, for anyone but the incumbent. This "negative landslide" showed most clearly that George Bush had a woefully inadequate understanding of how one uses power in order to preserve it. His theory of presidential power was too constitutional. That is to say, it was not democratic enough. Bush seemed insufficiently devoted to the revolutionary principle that animates democratic government even under the Constitution. Bush did not understand that even constitutional government must be defended by principle.

Bush's theory of presidential power, of what the president can and ought to accomplish in his constitutional role, is a part of *The Federalist*'s defense of the Constitution against revolutionary innovation or disorder. This defense has been revived in recent years by constitutionalist scholars to criticize the emergence of the "rhetorical presidency," which the Framers clearly did not intend.[1] Without claiming to know whether Bush was influenced directly by this scholarship, I can say he shared its constitutionalist, antirhetorical convictions.

Bush meant his presidency to be a criticism and correction of the rhetorical and other excesses of the "Reagan revolution." He meant to routinize or constitutionalize that revolution. He aimed to replace personal, rhetorical, and ideological leadership with good (meaning effective and relatively uncontroversial) government. He hoped to be reelected on the basis of his solid accomplishments which would speak for themselves.

The Federalist's Anti-Leadership Presidency

President Bush seemed to follow *The Federalist* in hoping to reduce executive leadership largely to administration, to the perpetuation of the political forms established by others. He shared its antagonism to "leaders," defined by *The Federalist* as those who would impose their own forms or "vision" in place of the Constitution's. Ambitious leaders cannot help but attempt to arouse the people against the given order, while at the same time arousing them on behalf of their own new order.[2]

The Federalist's view of leaders is ambivalent. Their demagogic influence is beneficial when revolution is desirable. But such influence is pernicious when it opposes good government. The Constitution, as good government, must oppose the influence of leadership. Bush believed that his time in office could be particularly antirevolutionary, because he was well positioned to provide an especially good form of constitutional government.

The Federalist regards good government as stable government. Unstable government, because it threatens rights or person and property with revolution, is always bad government. A government that effectively secures people's rights will always tend to be stable. The extended, diverse republic created by the Constitution differed from previous democratic experiments by the likelihood of its long duration. The Constitution effectively freed democracy from its deserved bad reputation.

The Constitution, *The Federalist* says, strongly empowers the president so that he will be its partisan. The combination of a long fixed term with the possibility of indefinite reeligibility allows and inspires him to pursue projects in the people's, the Constitution's, and his own long-term interests. He is given the power and incentive to oppose popular "inclinations," "temporary delusions" often inflamed by the "arts" of "flattering leaders" (*Federalist* 71). *The Federalist*'s president looks beyond the unstable whimsy of rhetorically aroused opinions to the people's more enduring gratitude. He hopes, in the best case, to have "lasting monuments" erected to his "courage and magnanimity" (*Federalist* 71). In Bush's less lofty words, he hopes that his prudence and honor will win him a lasting place in history.

The president aims at reelection, which *The Federalist* holds he can deserve. The Constitution leads him to trust in the people's ability to make periodic judgments about their interests, while distrusting the more impulsive forms of public opinion. The people will judge well when they reflect on the results of policy. They judge badly on the basis of rhetorical appeals which replace deliberation on long-term interest with unreflective passion. The Constitution aims to lead people to judge deeds, not words.

The president will be able to use his constitutional power to protect himself from the destructiveness of leaders. They are most powerfully animated by an indiscriminate hatred of those in power. This hatred extends to the idea that the president can legitimately exercise his constitutional power. Leaders always aim to undermine the Constitution and executive firmness on its behalf.

The high probability that leaders will often succeed in temporarily misleading the people is one reason why executive firmness cannot be rooted reliably in public opinion. Such opinion cannot be counted on to give the president the energy he needs to govern effectively. Rhetorical leadership is usually more effective in opposition. Its legitimation, our time has shown, typically empowers the president's opponents more than the president himself. It is harder to defend plans and accomplishments in public debate than it is to attack them. A time dominated by leaders is one in which the voters are easily and repeatedly moved by indignant campaigns "against Washington." Bush did not share that anti-Washington hatred, and he believed he could minimize its influence. He believed that his presidency would change to some extent the character of his time.

Recent presidents have tended to believe that they can and must govern as rhetorical leaders. The expectation has also developed that they do so. They have become partisans of crisis. To find enough energy to govern, they attempt to arouse the people to an awareness of their critical situation.

This understanding of leadership opposes the constitutional formalities which promote deliberation. It aims at the simple imposition of presidential will. But this understanding has not really tended to strengthen the presidency. It has made the incumbent more vulnerable, because he is always expected to be extraordinary. People have come to expect too much from the president and too much from government. They become too open to leaders' indiscriminate hatred or contempt for what government does. Incumbents have been too easily swept aside by the perception of crisis.

Bush's Bipartisan Constitutionalism

Bush believed that the Reagan revolution could be stabilized, or protected from leadership, if it were purged of its controversy. He aimed to achieve this goal during a time of "divided government," when the opposition promoted by the separated powers is routinely inflamed by partisan animosity. Bush viewed divided government as promising a certain kind of stability through a mixture of the parties' overly contentious principles. Good government required both the president's and the Congress's constitutional acceptance of the legitimacy of that mixture.

Bush literally began his presidency by offering to make divided government good government. In his inaugural address, he called for "a new engagement . . . between the Executive and Congress." The time for "divisiveness" and "dissension," based on the memory of Vietnam, must come to an end. The "old bipartisanship" that existed prior to that war "must begin anew again."

The new president reached out in friendship to the "loyal opposition" of Democratic congressional leaders. He envisioned their hard but friendly negotiations as aiming at good government, a strong foreign policy, and a fiscally sound budget. The president said nothing about the principles—economic, cultural, or constitutional—that separated the parties. He said nothing moralistic that would inflame animosity.

This call for bipartisanship brought to mind the American foreign policy of the 1950s and early 1960s. Then there was general agreement between the branches and the parties concerning America's purpose and strategy in the world. Divided government during the Eisenhower administration did not produce contentious foreign policy. Bush made it seem that all policy in the 1990s could be based on such bipartisanship. All that was necessary was to forget Vietnam, the now irrelevant cause of national division.

Bush had no intention, even at the beginning, of repeating what he regarded as Ronald Reagan's error of wasting energy in futile battles with Congress over public opinion. He had no intention of attempting to impose his domestic agenda through rhetorical leadership. Instead, he designed a strategy to remove most domestic issues from controversy. He was especially interested in negotiating compromises on those issues which might be used by the Democrats to gain partisan advantage in public opinion. He sought the reputation for moderate activism on education, civil rights, the environment, and other contentious issues. He hoped to negotiate compromises that would give him a record of uncontroversial achievement. He wanted to restore *The Federalist*'s preference for policy made by coalition-building among a wide variety of interests. He hoped that this process would mute ideological commitment and partisan animosity.[3]

Bush also decided not to risk controversy by pushing for substantial budget cuts that would affect sizable constituencies. He called for cuts in general, knowing that the people in general would want them. But he thought that finding specific cuts was primarily the constitutional responsibility of Congress. He said he wished for a balanced budget amendment and a line-item veto, but he surely did not wish for the contention that their actual existence would cause. He used their nonexistence as an occasion for leadership or demagoguery, for explaining why he could not do what he was not inclined to do.

Bush believed that the contemporary expectation that the president pursue a legislative agenda through rhetorical leadership gives the president more policy-making responsibility than the Constitution ordinarily makes possible. This expectation is particularly unrealistic during a time of divided government, especially for a president with quite ordinary rhetorical gifts at best. This expectation readily leads to the perception of a failed presidency.

Bush also believed that domestic strife and rhetorical leadership actually sap energy from the presidency. He aimed to save that energy in order to distinguish himself through the pursuit of foreign policy goals most Americans hold in common. His inclination was to prepare the presidency for the unexpected challenges that his foreign policy responsibilities would inevitably provide. He believed that he could avoid domestic crises, but he was glad for the need to be ready for international ones. The latter sort of crisis, handled decisively and skillfully, could unite the nation without much need for rhetorical leadership. It would allow Bush to prove his worthiness to be president.

Bush's Use of Constitutional Power

Bush's decision to forgo rhetorical leadership and pursue legislative compromise meant that he intended to govern with his constitutional powers alone.[4] He had an unusually fine understanding of those powers. He knew that the restoration of interbranch comity depended on each branch's knowing and respecting the nature and limits of its own power and the power of the other branches. Bush had a deeper understanding than his immediate predecessors of the ways that the separation of powers permits the executive to act independently and decisively. He pursued a clear, constitutional definition of executive and legislative responsibilities because he saw that their confusion had been at the expense of executive power and responsibility. He consistently used his constitutional powers to protect his office from legislative usurpation.

This reliance on constitutional powers is the core of *The Federalist*'s presidency. Bush's adroit use of them really did make him in some respects more energetic than Reagan. He was strikingly successful in establishing precedents that made the president's primacy in foreign policy more secure than before the Vietnam War. He did so largely by showing that *The Federalist* is right in holding that the president's perspective is the clearest view from which to make judgments concerning the nation's interests. Bush saw, for example, more clearly than anyone else what had to be done in the Persian Gulf, made clear that he would do it, and through his decisive, effective action led Congress and the people to accept his judgment. He also led commentators to observe that skillfully deployed presidential power is more than sufficient to move a nation. Rhetorical power had been overrated.

Bush also made better use of the veto than any of his predecessors. He knew, as *The Federalist* says, that the power of the veto exists primarily "to enable" the executive "to defend himself . . . against an immediate attack on his constitutional rights" (*Federalist* 73). Bush's uncharacteristically clear explanations of his self-defense vetoes are accounts of the president's rights and responsibilities under the Constitution.

Bush also used the credible threat of the veto as a way of negotiating with Congress over policy. Much more reliably than Reagan, he used the veto when Congress would not bargain, when it showed no inclination to alter legislation in ways the president could accept. His skillful use of the veto became a cause for wonder. He demonstrated the extent to which the president could influence the character of legislation without resorting to popular appeals. For most of his term, these policy vetoes were not a source of presidential unpopularity or perceived as a show of weakness (all defense, no offense). They were admired as evidence of the alleged wimp's unexpected strength.

The president used all of these powers to aim at winning by deserving reelection. This fact has been interpreted to mean that Bush would have done anything to keep his job. But the 1992 campaign showed that not to be the case. The president pursued what he believed to be the best way to deserve reelection. He shared *The Federalist*'s view that the Constitution works best when an effective president is returned to office on the basis of the people's considered judgment about their interests. He hoped that his record would be solid enough that his critics on both the left and the right would seem merely quarrelsome, or out of touch with the facts. He would appear as a statesman; they would be merely leaders.

Bush's goal was a "normal" election in 1992, one similar to the one which returned Dwight Eisenhower to office in 1956 or Calvin Coolidge in 1924. This election would also be like 1984, insofar as it would be an approval of the incumbent's strength of character as a condition for national and personal prosperity. Such a victory would not require the rhetorical excesses which Bush believed characterized Reagan's campaigns or his own in 1988. He hoped that there would be little "negative" about his campaign. He would depend on a largely nonpartisan evaluation of his character, as reflected in his deeds. His assumption that the Democrats would continue to dominate Congress is one sign of the extent of this nonpartisanship.

The Extent of Bush's Success

Bush's use of presidential power to secure a deserved second term seemed to work quite well for most of his term. His approval ratings were much more consistently high than Reagan's, and sometimes amazingly high. His critics complained with little effect that he succeeded in reducing what people expected from the president. Both liberals and conservatives argued that his administration lacked purpose or "vision." But this perception was not rejected so much as it was dismissed as unimportant by most Americans. Bush's merely but firmly constitutional administration seemed to fit the times. His possibilities, in any case, were limited by divided government. In domestic policy, he was counted on only to limit Congress's taxing and spending excesses, and to appoint antiactivist judges and bureaucrats.

The president's prudence seemed to serve him well in managing the end of the Cold War. But his popular approval actually neared unanimity with the wonderfully easy and overwhelming military victory in the Gulf. For a while, the president's deeds really did overwhelm his critics' words. One reason the Democratic ticket in 1992 was Bill Clinton and Al Gore instead of Mario Cuomo and Sam Nunn is that the first two were not clearly on record as opposing the president's use of force in the Gulf.

Bush's foreign policy successes could reasonably be viewed as a stunning and rather unexpected vindication of the Reagan-Bush or firmly anticommunist approach to foreign policy. Both the victory in the Gulf, America's first substantial, unambiguous triumph on the battlefield in over four decades, and the disintegration of Soviet communism owe much to the Reagan-led military buildup. The defeat of communism in Nicaragua, El Salvador, Afghanistan, and elsewhere can also be attributed to often maligned but generally sound judgments of the Reagan administration. Under Bush, America achieved more completely than anyone could dare imagine the strategic objectives of forty years of a foreign policy that realistically aimed only at the containment of communism.

Bush's Vulnerability and His Failure

But this much more than solid foreign policy success made Bush far less invulnerable than his constitutional theory would suggest. Its result was to make Americans feel secure militarily, and so far less worried about international developments. Bush got almost all of the votes of those who chose primarily on the basis of foreign policy in 1992, but they were less than 10 percent of the electorate. The Republican president suffered from the fact that 1992 was the first post-Cold War election.

Bush tried to make an election issue out of his foreign policy success. He said that victory was not inevitable, and that it was not really bipartisan. It would not have occurred under a Democratic president, especially under the inexperienced, vacillating, and perhaps dishonorable governor of Arkansas. Probably most Americans concurred with these judgments. But they seemed to add that now that victory had occurred, leaving America militarily strong and safe, it was time to move on to the other sources of personal insecurity.

The president was influenced by advisers who believed that winning a war could win an election more than a year and a half later. They seemed ignorant of all American and modern, democratic experience. They also ignored readily discernible facts about human ingratitude and self-interest. The president may have been unlucky that the Cold War and the Gulf War ended as early as they did in his term. But he should have anticipated the results of these misfortunes much better than he did.

Bush also had the misfortune of having the campaign take place in the midst of an unexpectedly prolonged recession. People ordinarily vote mainly on the basis of economic self-interest, and they do vote, to some large extent, retrospectively. It is very difficult for an incumbent to be reelected when the economy is bad. The recession, of course, was global. With the exception of Britain's very lucky John Major, incumbents throughout the postindustrial world were defeated in 1992. Bush's theory of solid success assumed that the economy would not be bad during the election year. Yet he really could neither know nor control whether it would be good or bad.

But the portrayal of the president as the victim of a domestic misfortune beyond his control is misleading. For one thing, the voters, however unreasonably, held the president responsible, as *The Federalist* expected they would. For another, they seem to have perceived the economy as worse than it actually was. Almost none of the social scientists who predict election outcomes with economic data thought Bush's defeat likely. But they should have known that the voters' perception of these data can be more important than their reality.[5]

Clinton and Ross Perot, both fairly effective rhetorical leaders, greatly exaggerated the economy's problems. They said there was a crisis, "the worst economic mess since the Depression." They tried to get the people to feel their misery and, because that was probably not enough, to fear for their future. They also led them to blame Bush. They cannot be blamed for this leadership. They did what Reagan did to Jimmy Carter in 1980. But things were really worse in 1980, when interest rates and inflation were also extremely high. Why did Americans so readily believe Clinton and Perot? Why did their words overwhelm the effects of the incumbent's deeds, which easily could have been worse? Bush's electoral misfortune, contrary to his theory, was greater than he deserved.

When the voters judged Bush, they did not do so only retrospectively. They also looked to the future, to how they might be helped or hurt by a second Bush term. Their perception was that things "are on the wrong track," that the future would be worse than the present. That perception came not only from the president's critics, because he himself did not make it clear why things might get better. A view shared by many liberals and conservatives was that Bush's presidency was "spent," that there was no energy left for securing the nation's future.

Voters today are understandably more reluctant than *The Federalist* thought they would be to trust a president with a second term. Richard Nixon's was a disaster. Reagan's was in many respects embarrassing when compared with the promise and performance of the first. Since the Twenty-second Amendment, which limits the president to two terms, second terms have characteristically been unenergetic and irresponsible. The president cannot hope to complete long-term projects. His opponents know they can wait him out. He is irresponsible in the sense that he knows that the voters cannot hold him accountable. The Constitution now becomes the president's enemy in his second term.

It is reasonable to ask how Bush would have performed without the incentive of reelection to organize and energize his administration. His *Federalist*-type theory would have lost its relevance. It is easy to see why voters would have more confidence in a first-term Clinton than a second-term Bush.

Voters were generally most concerned not with what Bush had done, but with what he would do. They looked for signals concerning his domestic policy, but they were confused. His theory did not allow him to see clearly why he would have to explain clearly what he would do. *The Federalist* says nothing about presidential campaigns, suggesting that incumbents ordinarily would not have to campaign. In this respect, its presidency is unrealistically nonpartisan and undemocratic. It does not accord with the experience of American elections, even before the rise of the rhetorical presidency.

The President's Revolutionary Leadership

The Federalist hoped that the Constitution would more completely supplant the revolution than it did. Substantial political controversy remained a characteristic feature of the American regime. Presidential elections have usually had a revolutionary component. They have been, in part, disputes concerning the continuing relevance of revolutionary principle under constitutional government. They have been arguments over liberty, equality, and democracy.

Presidential elections have been as much about progress as political stability. When understood properly, the Constitution has not impeded but secured the conditions for American progress. The energy given to the presidency from electoral victories, as well as energy supplied by the presidents themselves, have been the chief engine of that progress. This aspect of presidential power, Bush did not see clearly enough, is necessarily dynamic and moral.

Successful American presidents have usually made it clear how their administrations have and will be informed by progressive principle. Because presidential elections have been democratic, progress must be toward democracy. There is no way simply to routinize or constitutionalize this continuation of revolutionary aspiration.

Bush never did understand that he was not elected to stabilize or depoliticize, but to continue the Reagan revolution. That revolution aimed to undo what Franklin Roosevelt and Lyndon Johnson had accomplished during their Democratic revolutions. For the Democrats, progress toward democracy and prosperity depended on equality and security increasingly being guaranteed by government. They spoke of a process by which government would become progressively more responsible for the solution of human problems. Government would make human existence more just or equal. This process was also presented as a movement toward liberty, or freedom from the fear and anxiety that characterize human individuality.

Part of Reagan's power as president was his successful identification of American progress with the "conservative" criticism of this Democratic liberalism. He said that the Democratic movement was actually toward equality in dependency and away from individual opportunity. It was also movement away from personal responsibility and toward the impersonal irresponsibility of bureaucratic regulation. It was toward the rule of a paternalistic elite composed of bureaucrats, judges, and intellectuals.

According to Reagan, material and moral progress both depend on the individual securing his prosperity and dignity independently of big, impersonal government. The individual comes into his own in the context of communities such as the family, neighborhood, church, and local government, where the rule of personal responsibility is possible. Reagan made it seem that the reactionaries in America were not the conservatives who dominated his administration. They were the liberals in Congress who would perpetuate and extend government dependency or entitlement in a time when freedom is progressing throughout the world. He called for progress through the restoration of the Constitution's original understanding of equality in liberty.

Reagan's policies, in his own mind, were always guided by this controversial articulation of constitutional principle.[6] He used the power of the presidency, broadly speaking, to deregulate. Employing rhetorical leadership, he sought and received a tax cut from Congress. He also sought, but did not really expect, corresponding budget cuts. Before Reagan, "responsible" Republicans mainly worried like accountants, thinking that spending must be cut before taxes. Reagan saw that the beginning of progress must be tax cuts and tax reform.

Progress must be away from government-sponsored redistribution and entitlement. Reagan's policy was that taxes should be cut for everyone, a democratic principle. Its result, combined with no great domestic cuts and the cost of the military buildup, was to increase the deficit. But the newly large deficit was not all bad. It made bigger government seem impossible. Progress became possible only on Reagan's, and not the Democrats', terms.[7]

Reagan knew that the existence of divided government meant that people only half or half-heartedly accepted his view of progress. They tended to want the Republicans' low taxes and the Democrats' high entitlements. They did not really mind that this mixture of principles is particularly irresponsible. But Reagan refused to accept the view of some Republicans and the Democrats that higher taxes could ever be responsible. He hoped that eventually the people could be convinced either by leadership or by a genuine crisis to choose against entitlements.

Reagan, contrary to his critics, also generally pursued in principle and policy social or cultural deregulation. He opposed bureaucratic and judicial intrusion on personal and family responsibility. He used his power to appoint antiactivist judges, who sought to undo the Court's antidemocratic paternalism. Their purpose was to reverse *Roe v. Wade*, not because of their personal views on abortion but because the Constitution does not require or allow the Court to resolve the abortion controversy.

President Bush and the Reagan Revolution

In the 1988 campaign, Bush seemed to say enough to make clear that he would continue the Reagan revolution. His emphasis was on continuity and loyalty to Reagan. He also pledged unambiguously not to raise taxes, and he showed his contempt for the cultural liberalism or elitism of his opponent, Michael Dukakis. But, as president, Bush did not make it clear enough whether he remained true to Reagan's constitutional principles or his policies. In 1990, for example, he seemed to say he had come to believe that a large deficit was a greater evil than higher taxes. Negotiation and compromise with Congress, guided by this perception, led him to break his antitax pledge. To his credit, he departed from his antirhetorical precedents and attempted to explain to the American people why his promise was broken. His explanation included hardly any opposition to Congress in principle or policy. He was followed on television by Senator George Mitchell, the Democratic leader, who also broke with custom to agree with the president in the name of good government. The budget agreement seemed a perfect example of the bipartisan process Bush hoped to establish.[8]

Bush said a bipartisan agreement could bring the deficit under control, and that its rejection would bring recession. The recession came anyway. The deficit continued to increase rapidly. The president, not Congress, got most of the blame. He quickly repudiated the agreement, refusing to take responsibility for what he had done and confusing the voters even more.

Bush's aim to create a bipartisan or "good government" approach to the deficit problem led to the worst political mistake of his administration. Probably only the indifference to principle that is the precondition for this bipartisanship could have convinced the president that he and the Democratic congressional leaders could really agree to reduce the deficit. He should have known that any such agreement would mainly focus the contempt the people have for government's irresponsibility—even if it is largely a reflection of their own irresponsibility—on the president. He was counted on to follow Reagan's lead in firmly and publicly resisting Congress.

Bush's new position, that the main economic worry is the deficit, and his irresolution about taxes probably combined to reduce Americans' long-term confidence about their economy. This combination certainly made the president look more unprincipled than he really was. Because of it, he was vulnerable to the charge that the deficit was the creation or the responsibility of the Reagan-Bush presidency or of divided government ("gridlock"). This made the deficit seem less the particular responsibility of the Democratic Congress.

The deficit, according to the Bush's critics, was the main cause of America's economic decline or lack of competitiveness. It caused not only the recession, but a broader and more critical economic malaise. The focus on the deficit, always avoided by Reagan but prepared for 1992 by Bush, leads people to doubt what prosperity they do enjoy. They believe that the economy is not performing as well as it seems. Of course, this uneasiness empowers opposition leaders.

Perot masterfully used this uneasiness to wean prosperous conservatives away from the president. He said that the economic crisis could be resolved only by a de facto suspension of the ordinary operation of the separation of powers. For him, gridlock did not mean divided government but constitutional separation. He flattered the American people almost beyond belief. He suggested that a simple majority would willingly accept the combination of severe budget cuts and higher taxes that he said were required to bring the deficit under control.

The demagogue Perot sounded dangerous, but he was not. He naively believed that the president, through rhetorical leadership, could become much more powerful than he is really permitted to be under the Constitution. His impressive vote came partly from those apolitical Americans most easily seduced by simple or demagogic solutions. But it also came from those who really believed that the deficit was the nation's major problem. This belief should not have produced a vote for Perot. Comparative analysis shows that the separation of powers, by distancing government some from the people's inclinations, actually retards deficit growth.[9] Bush missed this and many other rhetorical opportunities for a defense of American constitutionalism.

Clinton had the only plausible proposal for ending gridlock. A Democratic president must be elected to go with the inevitably Democratic Congress. But as a means for deficit reduction, this proposal was plausible only if one does not believe that the Democratic Congress has been the deficit's main cause. To make divided government seem preferable, a Republican president repeatedly and effectively has to make the case against Congress. The budget agreement, based on Bush's nonpartisan constitutionalism, fatally undermined his ability to make that case. He allowed the argument to prevail that divided government is the enemy of progress.

To defend divided government, Bush had to continue the Reagan revolution by employing its sometimes confrontational tactics and aggressive rhetoric. He should have publicly confronted Congress in 1990 and 1992. He should have said clearly and often that tax increases do not have a history of reducing deficits. By stifling economic growth and providing the means for more government spending, they in the long run increase them. Because he seemed to conspire with Democratic leaders to allow a record tax increase in 1990, Bush could not credibly call for a tax cut to get the country moving again in 1992. Nor could he credibly blame the recession on excessive taxing and spending. Because he passed up these opportunities for rhetorical leadership, he was accused effectively by opposition leaders of being insensitive to the suffering and insecurity produced by the recession. He really believed, and with good reason, that there was little he could do to bring the recession to an end. On the level of actual policy, he did not panic. He was served well by his inclination to believe that government intervention usually makes things worse.

But, stung by the charge of insensitivity, Bush was reduced during the campaign to promising Democratic-style programs and gimmicks. This demagoguery was ineffective because it was obviously unprincipled. Clinton and Perot had no trouble calling attention to the mere expediency of these last-minute ideas, as well as to their tacit admission of failure. They certainly did not characterize the Bush's administration as a whole. (The same sort of analysis applies to the leader-aroused perception of a health care crisis.)

Bush's rhetorical leadership on behalf of the continuation of the Reagan revolution would have been less demagogic than his attempt to campaign without relying on that leadership. His ineffective demagoguery seemed to come from his conviction that all rhetorical appeals are equally unworthy. He also seemed to see little connection between campaign rhetoric and the requirements of governing. He might have been reelected, and even had a successful second term, had he made his principles clear, as well as the connection between them and his policies. Unfortunately, where Reagan was strongest, Bush was weakest.

As things were, Clinton learned more about revolutionary leadership under the Constitution from Reagan than did Bush.[10] He spoke generally of change, and followed Reagan in making opportunity and responsibility the principles on which Americans' should rest their hopes for a better tomorrow. He did not speak as a Democratic reactionary, a defender of discredited entitlements. He always sounded more progressive, and often more like a Reaganite, than Bush.

Clinton's shrewd, Democratic addition to Reagan's principles was that Reagan and Bush did not really believe in them. He portrayed them as economic elitists who believe that low taxes and deregulation for the rich would benefit all. Clinton promised to extend the benefits of Reaganism to all.

Bush was easy prey for this leadership because he did not give the democratic argument for the economic liberty favored by Republicans. He did not explain why the free market does not primarily benefit, as Clinton charged, his rich friends. He did not even begin to defend Reagan from the tired charge that his policy was "trickle down." What the part of the world emerging out of the rubble of communism had discovered about the interdependence of democracy and liberty, the American, Republican president seemed not to know.

Culture and Quayle

There were other issues besides economic ones in 1992, and on each of them Bush was less vulnerable. The campaign focused on the economy, as Clinton intended, mostly because Bush was ineffective in raising other issues. I have already considered foreign policy. Much more promising were the "family values" issues, especially when connected to what Vice President Dan Quayle called "cultural elitism."

Bush used these issues to good effect to discredit his opponent in 1988. Differences in style and better campaign management made Clinton a more elusive target than Dukakis, but Clinton's genuine positions on the social or cultural issues were probably no less vulnerable. When Bush was charged early in the campaign with diversion and demagoguery when he raised these issues, he for the most part dropped them. He did so because he seemed not to believe in them. It was not clearly his view that the deterioration of personal and parental responsibility can be traced to bureaucratic regulation and judicial fiat. He also seemed not to see that the decay of the conditions that make possible parental responsibility affects especially the lives of ordinary and disadvantaged Americans. Again, Bush did not follow Reagan in giving the democratic argument for his principles and policy.

Actually, Bush's policies in resisting cultural deterioration had been fairly steadfast. He could have taken some pride, for example, in his antiactivist judicial appointments. But because he did not defend the antiactivist position in a principled, democratic way, he left the rhetorical field to the leadership of his opponents. The media soundly defeated him, as they never did Reagan, only because he did not effectively engage them. He seems to have believed the media elite when they reported that the Republican cultural positions are somehow both unpopular and vulgar. He also seemed to agree that the constitutional arguments on behalf of these positions are outside the respectable mainstream of constitutional discourse.

Yet despite almost everything one reads and hears, the fact is that even a majority of those who voted with the abortion issue in mind—and this was the most contentious and problematic of the cultural issues—voted for Bush. What if he could have actually explained the relationship between his policies and "family values"? What if these explanations had compelled Clinton actually to make clear and defend the Democratic positions on these policies and values? Bush seemed to believe he could win without arousing cultural or moral animosity.

But Clinton's talented advisers, who said "the economy, stupid," believed that only such animosity might reelect the president.

Quayle made a spirited effort to confront the media on the cultural issues. He failed not because his positions were wrong or unpopular,[11] but because he is inarticulate and not very intelligent. He, like the president, experienced exceptional difficulty in presenting coherent explanations, although he seemed to have a greater interest in doing so.

An important presidential power, by party custom, is the selection of his running mate. Bush chose badly in 1988, even though he had plenty of time. The intelligence and rhetorical abilities of his choice seemed to be of no interest to him. Yet the right vice president might have supplied what he himself lacked. The choice of Quayle is evidence of the extent to which Bush believed he could govern effectively without rhetorical leadership. Bush's critics, with good reason, said it confirmed the contempt for *logos* they already discerned in his own speech.

The magnitude of this careless miscalculation was large, if difficult to measure. A respectable running mate, polls show, would have given Bush a clear landslide in 1988. The cumulative effect on the administration's reputation of the innumerable jokes, articles, and even books based on Bush's and Quayle's verbal gaffes must have had a significant effect in 1992. Many of the criticisms, of course, were unfair. But many serious citizens both liberal and conservative were embarrassed and repulsed by the "bully pulpit" having become the "silly pulpit." The comparison of Bush and Quayle with the glib Clinton and Gore was striking. The Democrats were able to give quick, detailed, plausible, and often edifying explanations about every issue under the sun. Because they were so much more articulate, many voters came to believe that they must be more competent.

Conclusion: Bush's Impossible Conservatism

President Bush believed he could resist the tendencies of his rhetorical, anticonstitutional time by winning reelection without resorting much to rhetorical leadership. But his deeds did not overwhelm his opponents' words. They were still able to create a perception of crisis. In dealing with that perception, Bush, because he was inarticulate, seemed incompetent.

Bush seemed to believe that, for him, a successful presidency would not be hard, and most commentators agreed with him for most of his term. But all American experience, not just that in our rhetorical time, pointed to his failure. Walter Dean Burnham has shown that presidents elected as "promising conservators of the 'revolution' carried out by others" seem always to fail. Such "regime conservators" are never good at making policy visions their own, and so they cannot provide "positive, sustained leadership in dealing with the country's problems."[12] Their conservatism is always too constitutional or not revolutionary enough. Even under the Constitution, too extreme an attachment to regime conservation leads to defeat by those who aim at "change," or regime transformation. Presidential leadership is essential for presidents to resist leadership effectively.

Notes

1. See, for example, Jeffrey K. Tulis, *The Rhetorical Presidency* (Princeton: Princeton University Press, 1987) and James Ceaser, *Presidential Selection: Theory and Development* (Princeton: Princeton University Press, 1979).

2. *The Federalist*'s view of leaders is presented in greater detail in my "*The Federalist*'s Hostility to Leadership and the Crisis of the Contemporary Presidency," *Presidential Studies Quarterly* 17 (Fall 1987): 711-24.

3. On Bush's strategy, see Michael Duffy and Dan Goodgame, *Marching in Place: The Status Quo Presidency of George Bush* (New York: Simon and Schuster, 1992). See especially pp. 58–62. All I do is give a more friendly or less muckraking view of the information they present. I also found the chapter, "Making the Process Work: The Procedural Presidency of George Bush," in Aaron Wildavsky's *The Beleaguered Presidency* (New Brunswick, N.J.: Transaction, 1991), pp. 301–52, quite useful in pointing the way to Bush's constitutional conservatism.

4. I am greatly indebted to the analysis and information concerning Bush's understanding and use of presidential power in Terry Eastland, *Energy in the Executive: The Case for the Strong Presidency* (New York: Free Press, 1992).

5. See James Ceaser and Andrew Busch, *Upside Down and Inside Out: The 1992 Election and American Politics* (Lanham, Md.: Littlefield Adams Quality Paperbacks, 1993), pp. 35–6, 53, note 8. Also, Seymour Martin Lipset, "The Significance of the 1992 Election," *PS: Political Science and Politics* 26 (March 1993): 7–16.

6. See William K. Muir, *The Bully Pulpit: The Presidential Leadership of Ronald Reagan* (San Francisco: Institute for Contemporary Studies Press, 1992).

7. See Wildavsky, pp. 213-40. Compare with the analysis of Reagan's strategy in Harvey C. Mansfield Jr., *America's Constitutional Soul* (Baltimore: Johns Hopkins University Press, 1991).

8. See Eastland, pp. 49–63.

9. See James Q. Wilson, "Does the Separation of Powers Still Work?" in Robert E. DiClerico, ed., *Analyzing the Presidency*, 2nd ed. (Guilford, Conn.: Duskin Publishing, 1990), p. 105.

10. On the superiority of Clinton's rhetoric and explanations, see Harvey C. Mansfield Jr., "Change and Bill Clinton," *Times Literary Supplement*, Nov. 13, 1992, pp. 14–15.

11. See Barbara Dafoe Whitehead, "Dan Quayle Was Right," *The Atlantic Monthly* 271 (April 1993): 47–83.

12. Walter Dean Burnham, "The Legacy of George Bush: Travails of an Understudy," Gerald M. Pomper, ed., *The Election of 1992: Reports and Interpretations* (Chatham, N.J.: Chatham House, 1992), p. 2.

6

Living Without Congress

David M. Mason

His January 1992 State of the Union address was declared, in the weeks leading up to it, to be the most important speech of George Bush's career. Although he was still a favorite for reelection, his poll numbers had started to slip, and the American economy had remained distinctly mushy through the Christmas shopping season. In the fall of 1991 he had ignored entreaties from Congressional Republicans to call Congress into a special session to deal with the economy. Through December and early January his advisers rejected increasingly urgent calls for a statement on the economy, responding "wait for the speech."

Many doubted that any speech could live up to the expectations, but Bush's last State of the Union nearly did. While his economic program was tepid, his challenge to Congress was bold: act on his plan by March 20, a mere 52 days. "From the day after that," vowed Bush, "if it must be: the battle is joined." Hard-line Republicans were cheered: George Harry Truman Bush was laying the foundation for a fall campaign against the do-nothing (Democratic) Congress. Congressional Democrats were faced with the choice of giving Bush a victory on his economic plan or taking the heat for failing to act. Not only might this strategy return Bush to the White House, it could produce a working or real majority for Republicans in Congress. Anti-incumbent sentiment was being fed by the House Bank scandal, public disgust at the Clarence Thomas nomination fiasco, and the Keating Five. Adding Democratic obstruction of a forceful Republican economic program could complete the recipe for a GOP electoral sweep.

This was not the first critical juncture at which Bush had issued an economic challenge to the Democratic Congress. His 1988 acceptance speech had been as much a challenge to Congress as a pledge on taxes.

"Congress," said Bush, "will push me to raise taxes." His reply, he promised, to repeated congressional entreaties would be "read my lips." Bush's retreat on taxes with the 1990 budget deal was no less a retreat from his promise to face down Congress. The latter failure was viewed by Bill Clinton's strategist James Carville as no less important than the former in forming the public's negative opinion of Bush.

Unfortunately the pattern of blustery challenge and voiceless retreat was repeated. The day after the State of the Union address a large banner was hung from the Republican National Committee offices, across the street from congressional office buildings, demanding action on Bush's economic plan. But Bush and his team failed to follow up with vigorous lobbying or appeals to the public. As the weeks wore on, with no significant movement by Congress, Bush even offered to extend the deadline, on the pretext that his original target fell on a Friday, a day on which Congress does not usually meet. The RNC banner was quietly removed. Congress took no action. As late as July Bush's former drug czar, William Bennett, and other conservatives were urging Bush to renew his economic challenge to Congress. But Bush allowed his challenge, his program, and his presidency to slide into oblivion. Rather than a fastball down the middle, the former Yale pitcher gave Congress an intentional walk.

In the waning days of the campaign Congress actually passed a tax bill based very loosely on the package Bush had submitted in January. Congress had transformed the bill from a modest but general economic stimulus plan into a loophole-laden lobbyists' delight, however, and Bush threatened to veto it. Unlike Bush, Congress persisted, delaying submission of the bill to the president so that he would not receive it until after election day. Counting on a by-then predictable Bush loss, the tax bill's congressional sponsors hoped that Bush would play true to form and sign their bill in a final feckless act. Though disappointed by Bush's ultimate veto, Congress was so inured to his unpressed challenges that nothing could have dissuaded them from giving it one more try.

While Bush vacillated, Clinton simply ignored Congress. July's Democratic convention was notable for the near-total exclusion from the program of Democratic congressional leaders. While that decision was perhaps understandable given Congress's low approval ratings, the prominent roles played by congressional Republicans at their party's August gathering provided a sharp contrast. In a mild disagreement with congressional leaders, Clinton did campaign in favor of a presidential line-item veto, a position he shared with Bush. But Clinton's intent was to illustrate his own fiscal reserve, rather than to criticize congressional spending habits, much less to make any broader point about the balance of powers between executive and legislature. That Clinton viewed the item veto as principally symbolic is illustrated by his record in Arkansas, where he wielded the item veto only eleven times in a dozen years as governor.

Clinton mentioned Congress in speeches infrequently and usually indirectly. Unwilling to defend Congress, or to embrace congressional Democrats, Clinton criticized Bush for Congress-bashing. Bush's failed leadership, charged Clinton, was the real problem. Clinton promised to end gridlock on an anti-anti-Congress platform: he did not seek or claim congressional support, but argued that his superior program and leadership would lead to progress. By shifting Bush's criticism of Congress back to the incumbent president, Clinton was able to neutralize the Congress card without allying himself with the discredited institution. So wary was Clinton of associating himself with the Democratic Congress that he avoided the argument, advanced by many, that having the presidency and Congress controlled by the same party would end gridlock. Candidate Clinton kept Congress at a nonhostile but politically necessary arm's length.

Seemingly strange, especially in light of subsequent polls showing his supporters' unreserved antipathy for Congress, outsider Ross Perot virtually courted Capitol Hill. His support for a line-item veto was tepid—offered, he said, so that Bush would "stop whining about it."[1] When Bush brought up the item veto during the debates, Clinton seconded the proposal but Perot ignored it. He would just "get under the hood," with Congress, see what the problem was, and fix it. On issue after issue Perot had no position, only a methodology: to gather the experts, somehow induce them to come to a consensus, and implement that agreement. By participating in these exercises, Congress, far from being a barrier to progress, was to be part of the solution.

Strangest of all in the Perot campaign was his failure to support term limits. Clearly Perot's popularity and the enthusiasm for term limits sprang from the same well of anti-elitist populism. One pro-term limits group, THRO (for Throw the Hypocritical Rascals Out), invited Perot to address their national rally, an invitation that was initially accepted but later declined. On the November ballot in fourteen states, term limits propositions outpolled each of the presidential contenders in those locales. Surely identification with this popular cause, and cooperation with term limits organizations, would have boosted Perot's support. Perhaps Perot genuinely expected to be able to recruit Congress to the cause of cleaning up the mess of which it was so obviously a part, but his mysterious reluctance to criticize Congress left the legislature largely out of presidential campaign discourse.

The Compromised Executive

While Bush, Clinton, and Perot all failed on this point, it should have been obvious by 1992 that a serious, political discussion of relations between the presidency and Congress was essential to improve the functioning of the American political system. For at least twenty years Congress has been continually expanding its control over the administrative apparatus of the executive branch. Much of the legislation accomplishing these congressional power grabs is constitutionally suspect. All six presidents serving since passage of the War Powers Resolution of 1974, for instance, have maintained its unconstitutionality. Presidents have also, however, reported to Congress "consistent with" war powers requirements while Congress corporately has withheld from pressing the resolution's restrictions on the length of time U.S. forces can remain in hostile situations without explicit congressional approval. The constitutional standoff has clearly compromised to some degree the president's constitutional authority as commander-in-chief.

The inherent powers of the president in foreign affairs and the urgency of armed conflict have allowed presidents and Congress to arrange a modus vivendi on war powers. Similar restrictions on executive action in domestic affairs have proved more troublesome. The early and mid-1970s saw an explosion of legislative restrictions on the executive.[2] These include the Congressional Budget Act, National Environmental Policy Act, Freedom of Information Act, revisions to the Administrative Procedures Act, the Ethics in Government Act (with its executive branch independent counsels), the creation of numerous independent agencies, and the widespread use of legislative vetoes (a practice which has continued informally despite the Supreme Court's decision invalidating their formal use). These restrictions on the executive did not represent, however, limitations on what or how much the federal government did. In fact, these statutes limiting the powers of the president and his immediate lieutenants were accompanied by a remarkable expansion in the size and scope of the federal government. As Congress increased governmental (i.e., executive) responsibility, it limited executive power. The result is a governmental runaway freight train, in the form of continually expanding regulation and deficit spending, with no engineer to apply the brakes or steer the engine onto another track.

The loss of effective executive control over most operations of the government greatly expanded the degree to which Congress, particularly through subcommittees and even individual members' actions, could influence or control administrative and regulatory activities.[3] In particular, Congress is unaffected by (because it is exempt from) the formal requirements and restrictions limiting executive branch flexibility and even general presidential oversight of executive activities. The measurement and chronicling of congressional micromanagement, as this phenomenon is often but inadequately termed, has progressed from academic books[4] and articles through editorial pages (especially the *Wall Street Journal*) to newsmaking theatrics such as Defense Secretary Richard Cheney's display at a 1990 news briefing of a 10-foot-high stack of the 661 Defense Department reports required by Congress in a single year. If the reports were merely a waste of money ($38.5 million in Cheney's example) and a distraction for bureaucrats (370 man-years),[5] we could be little concerned. But each document represents an effort to give a congressional subcommittee, even a particular staffer, the tools and information needed to control in detail some operation of the Defense Department. The distinction between making the laws and enforcing (or implementing) them has been largely abandoned. Rather than a pilotless runaway train we have a crowded freeway with hundreds of vehicles being steered from the backseat. The result is gridlock.

Gridlock represents a constitutional crisis in the broadest sense: a challenge to the ability of the nation to govern itself. Old programs cannot be terminated, new programs cannot be started, the government cannot take effective action on problems considered critical by its citizens. Contrary to the premise of Perot's town meetings and the advocates of unified partisan control of the executive and legislative branches, political gridlock is not caused by policy disagreements. Policy arguments normally are subject to compromise, if not to political efforts resulting in defeat or victory for one view. Gridlock occurs when the political system blocks rather than facilitates the resolution of policy disputes. Congressional efforts to disperse power while increasing governmental activity, stretching, bending, and violating the Constitution in the process, are at the root of gridlock.

That the 1992 presidential field failed to recognize or address this problem is not to say that the executive-legislative relationship was unaffected by the campaign. The failure to address the immediate and serious controversies over the Constitution's division of governmental powers set the stage for further breaches in the separation of powers, made more worrying for the lack of controversy attendant to the violations. Even if candidates overlooked the need, for the sake of our political system, for a discussion of executive-legislative relations, they should have seen the utility of such a discussion for a president's ability to govern. Without such a discussion, leading to a vigorous political effort to change not only the balance but the very grounds of executive relations with Congress, each of the three candidates was bound to fail. While presidential candidates can't seem to live with Congress, presidents can't live without it. The failure to resolve disputes during the campaign, before the relationship is consummated, leads to trouble on the honeymoon or soon thereafter.

The Campaign and the Compromised Executive

With no congressional constituency (either by running his own candidates or by endorsing selected candidates in both parties), a Perot victory would have almost certainly led to a politically dangerous standoff between Congress and the president. Perot's remedy to structural political (i.e., constitutional) problems was to ignore the structure. It was never evident, for instance, how his proposed electronic town hall would relate to existing political institutions. The desire to sweep away barriers to progress (as Perot defined it) without apparent acknowledgment (much less understanding) of the basis of those barriers was doomed to failure. Unlike chairmen of closely held corporations, American presidents cannot dictate; they must convince. Absent comprehension of the institutional environment, and lacking political backing to change it, Perot's sojourn as president would have been no more successful than his tenure on the board of General Motors. His demagogic efforts to brush aside intermediary political forms certainly would have failed, with possibly catastrophic constitutional consequences.

Bush seemed to have the right principles, but lacked the commitment to press his point. A Bush reelection, absent a Trumanesque campaign explaining *why* Congress needed to be changed, would have meant four more years of divided government, with intractable disagreement about the goals and direction of the nation. Even a "do-nothing" campaign that produced Republican gains short of a congressional majority would have given Bush a moral and politically useful claim that voters wanted Congress to get in line behind him. Bush's failure on this point was a disappointment to more than just Republican partisans. Early in his administration Bush launched an executive powers effort coordinated by Presidential Counsel C. Boyden Gray and high-ranking Justice Department officials. The objectives of the effort were to identify and oppose congressional encroachments on executive powers, to expand as far as possible the scope of independent executive action, particularly in the area of foreign affairs, and to frame conflicts, whether with the legislature directly or in the courts, in the most favorable manner possible. If, as argued here, congressional encroachment on executive authority presents serious constitutional problems, this was just the sort of effort needed to address the issue.

Two theories of inherent presidential powers, either of which would have worked a revolution in relations with Congress, were advanced by the Bush team. Most widely noted was the claim that the president might have an implicit line-item veto authority, based on the constitutional requirement that "every order, resolution, or vote . . . be presented to the President" for his approval or veto.[6] Since the presentment clause had been the basis of the landmark Supreme Court ruling (*INS* v. *Chadha*[7]) invalidating legislative vetoes, the theory that it might be held to further restrict Congress's ability to tie the executive's hands, through take-it-all-or-leave-it omnibus legislation for instance, was arguable if somewhat divergent from common conservative views of judicial interpretation. After several years of flirting with this theory, however, Bush's Justice Department released an opinion disavowing it without a court test.

The second and more plausible claim of Bush's executive powers team was that the president had the authority to ignore and effectively invalidate specific provisions of laws he believed to be unconstitutional. The question in this case was not whether the president had to obey an unconstitutional law, but whether his declaring part of a law void made it so. Despite the popular impression, shared by too many in Congress, that this task is exclusive to the Supreme Court, all three branches of government share responsibility for interpreting and applying the Constitution. The simplest path for the president is to veto legislation he believes to be unconstitutional. But the advent of complex, omnibus bills has complicated the question. Should he veto an entire bill, perhaps shut down major governmental functions, in order to settle a constitutional quibble over one obscure provision? If he overlooks the blemish in approving the bill, is he then bound by a blatantly unconstitutional requirement until released by a court? Bush argued that he could sign legislation while reserving the right to refuse to comply with objectionable provisions of it.

So important was this shield veto, as it later came to be called, that Bush included it among the topics he discussed with Attorney General Richard Thornburgh when asking him to remain in the new administration. Sooner or later, Bush told Thornburgh, a good test case will come along allowing them to secure a court ruling buttressing this claim. In fact, Bush invoked the shield veto scores of times, singling out offensive provisions in signing statements accompanying the legislation and declaring his intention to refuse to comply with the law. He did not argue, however, that his signing statements actually excised the suspect requirements. In fact, each item became, with Bush's signature, the law of the land. The statute books swelled with arguably invalid laws, but only this particular president's judgment stayed their enforcement. In the absence of a Supreme Court declaration on it the shield veto undermined the rule of law while leaving unconstitutional requirements to be enforced by a less scrupulous successor. Still, over the course of four years, the Bush administration could find no claim ripe for adjudication. While it is true that the administration had the upper hand in each individual case—the president was declaring laws invalid and making them so by nonenforcement—and Congress failed to press a challenge, the temporary nature and lack of agreement about the administration's claims made them weak and unsustainable in the long term. (A court's declaration on constitutionality does not lapse merely by virtue of a change in judicial personnel.) Rather than waiting for a challenge on what opponents believed to be its weakest ground, or allowing a successor to reverse its position, the administration should have chosen its strongest case and sought judicial confirmation. Bush governed, however, as he campaigned, with firm principles and flaccid application. Consequently the shield veto, and Bush's entire executive powers effort, may merit only a footnote in the history of executive-legislative relations.

Democratic Monopoly and the Compromised Executive

The accurate predictions of continued gridlock under Perot or Bush should have been as easily made about President Clinton, as he discovered very early in his term. Senate opposition caused the withdrawal of his first nominee for attorney general (Zoe Baird) while subsequently numerous lesser nominations were nixed more or less quietly. Two of Clinton's major social policies, providing federal funding for abortions and ending the ban on homosexuals serving in the military, were rejected by Congress. His economic stimulus plan was stopped cold, and his overall budget plan was diced and dismembered with the remnants passing by the barest of majorities. Only partisan solidarity prevented congressional leaders from declaring Clinton's budget, like those of his Republican predecessors, dead on arrival.

Clinton brought some of these problems on himself: his economic and social policies were not overwhelmingly popular and the views of some of his nominees were, by his own admission, indefensible. But there was more to this roughing up of a freshman president by his own party in Congress than his specific policy failures. As much as congressional Democrats wanted their new president to succeed, they may have become incapable of allowing him to do so.

Two less prominent controversies early in the Clinton administration shed light on this phenomenon. During his presidency, Bush had proposed to elevate the Environmental Protection Agency to cabinet status. Rather than simply redesignating the EPA as a Department of Environmental Protection, as Bush recommended, however, congressional committees with environmental jurisdiction wanted to alter the agency's structure and operations in the process. Among the most controversial proposals was to create an independent office to gather and disseminate environmental statistics. Bush objected, on constitutional grounds, to an agency not responsible to the president within a cabinet department, and the EPA cabinet elevation bill died without a vote.

After campaigning on environmental concerns, Clinton likewise moved to create an Environment Department. Though he was more flexible than Bush on restructuring proposals, Clinton's request also languished in Congress. Some congressmen objected to Clinton's decision to abolish the Council on Environmental Quality, a White House agency, on the grounds that the office had been mandated by Congress in the National Environmental Policy Act (NEPA), and held up the cabinet elevation bill in an effort to win their point. Other members of Congress had other concerns. The Senate committees on Governmental Affairs and Energy and Natural Resources were at loggerheads, as were the House committees on Government Operations, Merchant Marine and Fisheries, Energy and Commerce, and Natural Resources. Disputes within Congress and between Congress and the executive were little affected by the switch in the partisan identification of the president. In fact, yet new grievances were added. The outcome is entirely foreseeable. Sooner or later Clinton will capitulate to a greater or lesser number of congressional demands about the structure and operations of the new department. Each of the changes will decrease the president's ability to control an executive agency and increase the degree to which Congress and its various subcommittees can control operations of the bureaucracy.

While compromising executive branch management authority is old (though not necessarily unimportant) news, another environmental controversy moved Congress into federal law enforcement in an unprecedented way. House Energy and Commerce Committee Chairman John Dingell had been engaged in a years-long dispute with the Justice Department's environmental crimes section. Though anyone familiar with the prosecutorial ethos may find it mind-boggling, Dingell accused federal prosecutors of going too easy on suspected criminals. In an illustration of how congressional interference begets more congressional interference, the charges were reportedly brought to Dingell by EPA bureaucrats who had lost out in interagency discussions about how various cases were to be handled. Dingell demanded to interview individual prosecutors in the environmental section. The Reagan and Bush Justice Departments had steadfastly refused to allow Congress to interfere in this fashion with executive law enforcement responsibilities, and prior to Congress's disputes with those Republican administrations such a request would have been unthinkable. The constitutional separation of powers has an obvious practical purpose: one can imagine the abuses when individual congressmen find themselves able to summon law enforcement officials and demand investigations of political opponents. While abuses are possible within the executive branch, canons of prosecutorial ethics and statutes prohibiting irregular contacts between political appointees and law enforcement officials erect barriers to improper behavior. Congressional bludgeoning of prosecutors in back rooms and without records is subject to no such restraint.

The Bush administration offered senior political appointees to discuss the standards used by the environmental crimes section in investigating and prosecuting cases. Congress could have investigated those standards and challenged them, through public argument or by changes in laws. But Dingell wanted a scalp, specifically that of the career official who headed the section. More than petty venality, Dingell's approach threatens to obliterate the distinction between making laws and enforcing them. Personal vilification of individual prosecutors would make every case subject to congressional micromanagement: prosecutors ignoring the advice of congressional staffers would risk having their careers ruined. Dingell's demands to interview individual prosecutors in secret sessions had nothing to do with law or policy and everything to do with his desire to dictate the application of laws and policies in specific cases. It is difficult to imagine a more obvious violation of the principle of separation of powers.

Centuries of precedent were swept away at the beginning of the Clinton administration by Attorney General Janet Reno's capitulation to Dingell's demand. She, or her White House supervisors, just did not want to fight with Congress about it. In dealing with Congress, Clinton was even weaker than Bush, and that weakness threatens genuine constitutional damage. The first level of Clinton's weakness was political. By failing either to oppose or to join with Congress (even with particular candidates for the most part) in his campaign, Clinton was left without substantial support there. In striking contrast to Ronald Reagan, for instance, there was no Clinton faction in Congress, even among the large Democratic freshman class. While Democrats were willing to support him on various specific policies, no significant group was willing to risk their own political careers, much less to sacrifice their institutional interests, in support of the president or his principles. Structurally as well, Clinton was weaker in dealing with Congress than his Republican predecessors. Even absent strong personal support for Bush, congressional Republicans found it in their interest on political and policy grounds to support the president in disputes with Congress. The combined weight of executive argument with a sizable legislative minority frequently was sufficient to secure a satisfactory compromise, if not outright victory, in interbranch disputes. Several of Bush's vetoes, sustained with unified Republican support, were on institutional points. Bush vetoed a State Department authorization bill in 1989, for instance, objecting to restrictions on his authority to negotiate treaties. Despite overwhelming Congressional support for the bill (the original version passed 338 to 87 in the House), congressional Republicans supported Bush's veto, and a new bill was passed absent the objectionable provisions.

As the majority party in Congress, Democrats have no similar interest in compromising their institutional prerogatives in cooperation with a Democratic president: they can get their way without his vetoes. Neither will Republicans rally to Clinton's cause on institutional questions, since doing so would only abet policies they oppose. Efforts by

Vice Presidents Bush and Dan Quayle to establish a centralized, administration-wide regulatory review apparatus were sustained with some limitations for a dozen years despite opposition by congressional Democrats, including then-Senator Al Gore, who claimed that the regulatory review operations violated the Administrative Procedures Act (APA), Freedom of Information Act (FOIA), and various other congressionally imposed restrictions on executive branch operations. Regulatory review having become a partisan cause, President Clinton with great fanfare dissolved the Competitiveness Council, which Vice President Quayle had employed to oversee such efforts, as one of his first official acts. By June, however, Vice President Gore's staff concluded that someone needed to be watching the federal government's various back, side and rooftop regulatory apertures to lend some semblance of order to the administrative gusher. Gore's staff proposed a presidential order giving the vice president's office authority to review and recommend changes in all federal regulations. Having endured a dozen years of partisan jibes about the inappropriateness of such an arrangement, and fearing the uses to which such authority might be put by Gore's staff, Republican Representative Bill Clinger quickly offered an amendment intended to stop the proposal. Rather than defending their president, key House Democrats registered their opposition with the White House which quickly backed away from the plan.

The new Democratic president was thus deprived by the Democratic Congress of a key tool for managing his regulatory responsibilities. Why? Because limiting the president's role in regulatory affairs proportionally expanded congressional influence, which, by the way, is wielded without regard to the niceties of the APA, FOIA, and other laws requiring public disclosure of the rationale for regulatory decisions. Forbidding effective executive-branch oversight of regulatory policy is also a recipe for even more gridlock. While unifying party control of the White House and Congress produced some policy consensus, given an administration unwilling to defend its institutional prerogatives, the combination lowered barriers to congressional raids on executive authority. Since it agreed with Congress on goals, the administration ignored the importance of form and method. Ambition failed to counteract ambition, and Congress moved to annex yet larger swaths of executive territory. With neither firm friends in Congress nor a political base for institutional opposition, Clinton is left at the mercy of Congress.

Were a failed presidency alone at stake, Americans might not need to be concerned. Some might even rejoice at the partisan opportunities. But unless the next switch in executives is accompanied by a more coherent discussion of the political and institutional challenges facing any president, we will be no better off. Indeed, should Clinton stumble, the failure is likely to be perceived as his alone, setting the stage for another failed campaign, given over to ever shriller calls for leadership. As John Wettergreen suggests,[8] this impasse could persist indefinitely. Should a real crisis ensue, however, congressional hegemony could be replaced by a presidential dictatorship. The authority (scope of activity) of government is more easily limited than its power. Congress has been comfortable expanding executive authority only because it has seized executive power. A war or economic crisis might allow, even force, a president to reclaim his inherent authority and work a revolution.

If ending gridlock is not reason enough, the possibility, even if remote, of renewed executive dominance shows that it is in the interest of Congress, as indeed of all Americans, to undertake a serious reexamination of the practical applications of the Constitution's separation of powers. The usual forum for such a debate, a national campaign, might be had despite the failures of presidential candidates thanks to the nationwide term limits effort. Referendums in fourteen states in 1992 covered much of the country, and serious debate on term limits has now begun in many state legislatures. Advocates on both sides address fundamental constitutional issues: the nature of representation, the means of citizen control of government, the role of the legislature. That the tone of debate is not as elevated as an academic seminar, and the motives of interlocutors not unmixed, is natural to politics. Certainly for the next several years the term limits debate represents the best forum to discuss, and offers an arguable remedy to address, the ills of government. A serious and sustained public debate over term limits might even prepare the way for a more coherent effort to address the nature of the presidency and its relation to Congress in the presidential campaign of 1996.

Notes

1. "Angry Voters See Perot Riding in Like Cavalry," Los Angeles *Times*, March 22, 1992.

2. For a further discussion of this development see John Adams Wettergreen, "Bureaucratizing the American Government" in Gordon S. Jones and

7

The Supreme Court and the 1992 Election:
The Dog That Did Not Bark

Ralph A. Rossum

"Is there any other point to which you would wish to draw my attention?"

"To the curious incident of the dog in the night-time."

"The dog did nothing in the night-time."

"That was the curious incident," remarked Sherlock Holmes.

—Arthur Conan Doyle

In one of Arthur Conan Doyle's short stories, *Silver Blaze*, Sherlock Holmes is able to solve a crime because of the "curious incident" of a dog that does not bark. The question to be addressed here is why the Supreme Court did not "bark" during the 1992 presidential election. Why, despite the high stakes involved, did it not figure more prominently in the campaign strategies and rhetoric of the two major parties?

There were many reasons why the Court and, in fact, the entire federal judiciary, should have been a major campaign issue. In 1991 there was the bitter controversy surrounding the Senate's confirmation of Clarence Thomas as an associate justice of the Supreme Court, which served to focus national attention on the debates over abortion, affirmative action, criminal procedure, and more generally, the role of the Supreme Court in the shaping of public policy. There was the likely prospect of two or three retirements from the Supreme Court (by March 1993, Justice Byron White had already announced his intention to retire at the end of the 1992–93 term of the Court) and the opportunity that would give to George Bush or Bill Clinton to mold the

Court in his own image. There were the 107 court vacancies at the federal district and appellate level that the new president would be able to fill immediately, plus, assuming the usual number of resignations and retirements over the next four years, two hundred additional judges to name. Finally, there was the clear possibility that Congress would create an additional two hundred new judgeships, allowing the new president to make an indelible mark on the future of the federal judiciary.

Despite these compelling reasons, the Supreme Court and the lower federal courts never became an election issue. Although Clinton boldly announced in his acceptance speech at the Democratic National Convention that he would appoint only those justices who would protect the Court's abortion decision of *Roe v. Wade* (1973) and "guarantee a woman's right to choose," this promise to impose a "litmus test" was neither challenged by the Republicans nor scrutinized by the news media. Likewise, Clinton's talk of appointing Mario Cuomo to the Supreme Court and his declaration that Harry Blackmun (author of the majority opinion in *Roe*) was the one current justice he would have appointed to the High Bench failed to attract attention or notoriety. So why did the Supreme Court (and the federal judiciary) not bark? Why did it remain a nonissue? Why was the opportunity to appoint two or three new judicial conservatives to the High Bench (and perhaps more than five hundred lower federal court judges) not exploited by Bush in 1992, as it had been by Ronald Reagan in both 1980 and 1984 and as it had even been by Bush himself in 1988? Why, likewise, did the Democrats not raise the prospect that Bush, if reelected, would appoint justices (and lower federal court judges) opposed to abortion and hostile to civil rights, as they had also done in past elections?

The Court and the 1992 Election

Several explanations present themselves. To begin with, Anita Hill's testimony during Thomas's confirmation hearing put Bush and the Republicans on the defensive. Instead of heralding his appointment of a self-restrained black justice opposed to racial preference and the judicial creation of new rights and entitlements, Bush appeared embarrassed by his choice.[1] Senator Arlen Specter of Pennsylvania found himself in the political race of his life because he had been willing, as a senior Republican member of the Senate Judiciary Committee, to subject Hill's allegations that she had been sexually harassed by

Thomas to vigorous cross-examination.[2] The media and various feminist groups considered any defense of Thomas and his judicial philosophy of self-restraint as an affront to women everywhere and tantamount to defending sexual harassment.[3] Thus, despite his excellent qualities of mind and his industry on the bench (he had the most productive year of any first-year justice in recent memory, writing twenty-two opinions while serving, because of his extended confirmation, slightly less than the full term), Thomas quickly became the most unpopular justice in both academe and the media. For example, in a symposium issue devoted to his hearings, the *Southern California Law Review* published twenty-five essays opposing his confirmation and not a single essay supporting him; eager to heap even more opprobrium on him, the editors promised that they would soon publish an article by one of Hill's lawyers entitled "The People v. Anita Hill."[4] The *University of Pennsylvania Law Review* published an "open letter" by Federal Court of Appeals Judge A. Leon Higgonbotham Jr., assailing Thomas for his views on civil rights and racial preference and urging him to reflect on the impact that civil rights attorneys and groups, the removal of voting barriers, and civil rights gains in housing and privacy had on his own personal achievements.[5] The *New York Times* editorialized against him because of his dissent in an Eighth Amendment case, labeling him "the youngest, cruelest Justice."[6] Still another newspaper published a book review that expressed the hope that "maybe, just maybe, Clarence Thomas will not turn out to be the worst Supreme Court Justice since James McReynolds."

Just as Bush and the Republicans appear to have avoided mentioning the Supreme Court in part to keep Justice Thomas and the Anita Hill episode from unnecessarily resurfacing, Clinton and the Democrats appear to have avoided mentioning the Court because, quite simply, the judiciary has never really been a Democratic issue. Democrats have generally defended rather than attacked the Court, and, thus, even though the Supreme Court has been dominated for the past two decades by justices appointed by Republican presidents, the public has come to identify the Democrats rather than the Republicans with busing, affirmative action, criminal procedural decisions that favor the criminal and handcuff the police, taking prayer out of the public schools, protecting pornography, and embracing unbridled judicial activism.

It is difficult for Democratic presidential nominees to argue that they should be elected so that they can appoint activist judges who will substitute their policy preferences for those of the public at large. It has been much easier for them to argue against voting for Republican presidential nominees for fear that, if elected, they will appoint judges who will overturn landmark precedents (e.g., *Miranda v. Arizona* [1966] or *Roe v. Wade*) and turn a deaf ear to those most in need of the solicitude of the Court, i.e., those who are victims of discrimination because of their race, gender, sexual orientation, or class. This was the strategy that the Democratic party pursued in the three previous presidential elections when they raised the specter of back-alley abortions brought on by Reagan and Bush appointees to the Supreme Court intent on overturning *Roe*.

By 1992, however, this strategy had played itself out. It was clear to both to Clinton and Bush that the appointment of six justices to the Supreme Court by Reagan and Bush (in fact, eight of the nine sitting justices had been appointed by Republicans) had neither advanced the conservative agenda nor reversed past liberal gains. Liberals in the electorate were no longer particularly worried by the prospect of Republican appointments. But even more to the point, conservatives and moderates could no longer perceive additional Republican appointments as doing any good. After twenty-four years of continuous appointments to the Supreme Court by Republican presidents, the country remained, and in all likelihood would continue to remain, "just one more good appointment away from a 'conservative' Court."[7] Bush and his Republican supporters could not make the Court into an effective political issue, because their constituency saw no payoff in keeping judicial appointments out of the hands of the Democrats.

A brief review of the decisions the Court was handing down during the 1992 presidential campaign season dramatically illustrates why Bush could not mobilize political support by pointing to the importance of preserving control of judicial appointments. These decisions reveal the Court to be conservative neither in the positive sense of advancing conservative causes nor even in the negative sense of being unwilling to advance liberal causes.

Turning first to criminal procedure, in *Morgan v. Illinois*, the Court created a new right for defendants in capital cases to ask prospective jurors whether they would "automatically" impose the death penalty on conviction and to remove jurors who respond in the affirmative; this prompted Justice Antonin Scalia to observe in dissent "that the Court strikes a further blow against the People in its campaign against the death penalty." In *Dawson v. Delaware*, it held that the admission of evidence that the defendant was a member of the Aryan Brotherhood, a white racist prison gang, was not relevant to his character and violated his First Amendment right of association and, on that basis, overturned the death penalty the jury had imposed on him for the robbery and brutal murder of a woman during a prison escape. In *Hudson v. McMillian*, it held that use of "excessive physical force" by prison guards subjected a prisoner to "cruel and unusual punishment" even though no serious physical injury resulted. In *Jacobson v. United States*, it expanded the definition of entrapment (holding that the prosecution must prove beyond a reasonable doubt that the defendant was disposed to commit the criminal act not only before the government induces the commission of the crime but even before the government makes initial contact with him) and on that basis reversed the federal conviction of a 56-year-old Iowa farmer for receiving child pornography through the government's use of a "sting" operation. It reversed a conviction for conspiracy to import and distribute cocaine in *Doggett v. United States* on the ground that an eight-and-a-half-year period between indictment and trial denied the defendant his constitutional right to a "speedy" trial; it condemned the "Government's egregious persistence in failing to prosecute" the defendant, even though the defendant was not held in detention during that period and claimed to be unaware he was under indictment, and despite the fact that the government was unaware of his whereabouts.

The Court's free speech and equal protection decisions during the presidential campaign likewise provided no consolation for conservatives or encouragement for Bush to use the Court as a campaign issue. Concerning the former, the Court continued to discover in the First Amendment various impediments to legislative efforts to provide for social order. In *Simon & Schuster, Inc. v. New York Crime Victims Board*, it invalidated New York's "Son of Sam" law, which sought to prevent perpetrators of sensational crimes from profiting by selling their stories for publication, and in *Lee v. International Society for Krishna Consciousness*, it declared unconstitutional a New York Port Authority restriction on the distribution of "literature" at airports. And concerning equal protection, the Court made it clear that it had not abandoned its efforts to compel school racial integration, even in higher education. In *United States v. Fordice*, it found that Mississippi's colleges and universities were being operated in violation of the Fourteenth Amendment because they remained racially imbalanced.

Perhaps most devastating of all to the argument that a Republican needed to be reelected so that conservative justices would continue to be appointed were the Court's decisions concerning abortion and prayer. In *Planned Parenthood v. Casey*, the Court reaffirmed *Roe v.*

Wade, with the plurality opinion written by Sandra Day O'Connor (a
Reagan appointee) and joined by Anthony Kennedy (appointed by
Reagan) and David Souter (appointed by Bush), and in *Lee v. Weisman*, it invalidated invocations and benedictions at public high school
graduation ceremonies in an opinion written by Kennedy.

Two principal factors explain the Court's failure to advance the
conservative agenda of Reagan and Bush or to reverse the liberal
constitutional gains of the past. The first is that deep fissures exist
within judicial conservatism, and the second is that most conservatives
who turn to the Court for relief seek defensive rather than offensive
victories. Each will be examined in turn.

The Meaning of Judicial Conservatism

A debate is raging among the justices appointed to the Court by
Reagan and Bush over what constitutes judicial conservatism. The
debate is among the "textualists," who argue that primacy must be
accorded to the text, structure, and history of the document being
interpreted; "majoritarians," who argue that the Court should defer to
legislative choices; and "incrementalists," who are committed to
gradualist approaches to change in law and who give great weight to
stare decisis and "settled doctrine."[8]

Scalia is most closely identified with the "textualist" position. He
argues that the job of the judge is to apply the clear textual language of
the Constitution or statute, or the critical structural principle necessarily implicit in the text. For Scalia, it is always the original and objective
meaning of the language itself that counts, not the subjective intentions
of those who wrote it. Thus, Scalia searches out the ordinary meaning
of the words used when the provision was adopted. Applying this
textualist approach in *Harmelin v. Michigan* (1991), he held that the
cruel and unusual punishments clause of the Eighth Amendment does
not prohibit the imposition of a mandatory term of life in prison
without possibility of parole for possessing more than 650 grams of
cocaine. Announcing the judgment of the Court, he rejected the
plaintiff's contention that his sentence was unconstitutional because it
was "significantly disproportionate" to the crime he had committed,
noting that "this claim has no support in the text and history of the
Eighth Amendment." Concerning the text, he observed that "to use
the phrase 'cruel and unusual punishment' to describe a requirement
of proportionality would have been an exceedingly vague and oblique

way of saying what Americans were well accustomed to saying more directly." Concerning history, he surveyed English constitutional history since the promulgation of the English Declaration of Rights of 1689 as well as eighteenth- and nineteenth-century American constitutional and legal history to show that the cruel and unusual punishments clause was designed only "to outlaw particular modes of punishment" (e.g., drawing and quartering, breaking on the wheel, flaying alive), not to require that "all punishments be proportioned to the offense." He was led, therefore, to argue that *Solem v. Helms* (1983), in which the Court had held that the Eighth Amendment does contain a proportionality guarantee, was "wrong" and should be overturned.

While his textualist approach led Scalia in *Harmelin* to reject the defendant's claim, it does not always. Thus, in *Coy v. Iowa* (1988), it led him to uphold the right of a criminal defendant (in this case, a man convicted of two counts of engaging in lascivious acts with a child) literally to "be confronted with the witnesses against him" and to overturn his conviction because Iowa law allowed the two thirteen-year-old girls he was charged with sexually assaulting to testify behind a large screen that shielded them from the defendant. For Scalia, the text was unequivocal and governing:

> As Justice [John Marshall] Harlan put it, "[s]imply as a matter of English," it confers at least "a right to meet face to face all those who appear and give evidence at trial." Simply as a matter of Latin as well, since the word "confront" ultimately derives from the prefix "con-" (from "contra" meaning "against" or "opposed") and the noun "frons" (forehead). Shakespeare was thus describing the root meaning of confrontation when he had Richard the Second say: "Then call them to our presence—face to face, and frowning brow to brow, ourselves will hear the accuser and the accused freely speak."[9]

For Scalia, textualism is a means of constraining judicial discretion. Believing that the rule of law is the law of rules,[10] he argues that where the text embodies a rule, judges are simply to apply that rule as the law. Where the text fails to supply a rule, there is no rule and, hence, no law to apply and, therefore, no warrant for judicial intervention. The source of a legal rule must be found elsewhere, i.e., in the actions of the popular branches.

While Scalia is most closely identified with the textualist approach, Thomas seems, during his first years on the High Bench, to have adopted very much the same approach. Thus, in *Hudson v. McMillian* (1992), he dissented from the Court's opinion that held that the use of excessive physical force against an inmate may constitute cruel and unusual punishment, even in the absence of significant injury. Noting that "for generations, judges and commentators regarded the Eighth Amendment as applying only to tortious punishments meted out by statutes or sentencing judges, and not generally to any hardship that might befall a prisoner during incarceration," he dismissed the majority opinion as an unfortunate consequence of the Court having "cut the Eighth Amendment loose from its historical moorings." Likewise, in *White v. Illinois* (1992), he argued in concurrence that both "the text and history" of the confrontation clause make it clear that it was to apply only to a witness who actually testifies at trial or to formalized extrajudicial statements such as depositions, and not to out-of-court statements admitted under the traditional hearsay exception. Given Thomas's emphasis on "text and history," it is perhaps not surprising that he agreed with Scalia in 85 percent of the cases in which he participated during his first term.

Chief Justice William Rehnquist is the Court's leading "majoritarian." He argues that the Constitution "was designed to enable the popular branches of government, not the judicial branch," to govern.[11] Congress and the president were "to furnish the motive power within the federal system, which was in turn to coexist with the state governments." These popular branches, "having a popular constituency were looked to [by the Framers] for the solution of the numerous and varied problems that the future would bring."

Rehnquist is not a simple majoritarian, unmindful of the problems of majority tyranny. As he notes, "limitations were indeed placed upon both federal and state governments in the form of both a division of powers and express protection of individual rights." These limitations, of which the Court is one, "were not themselves designed to solve the problems of the future." Rather, they "were instead designed to make certain that the constituent branches, when *they* attempted to solve those problems, should not transgress these fundamental limitations." Rehnquist's majoritarianism and deference to legislative authority are apparent in his opinion upholding the constitutionality of the independent counsel statute in *Morrison v. Olson* (1988); his opinion in *Payne v. Tennessee* (1991) overturning *Booth v. Maryland* (1987) and upholding the constitutionality of the introduction of victim impact statements in death penalty cases; his dissents in the flag burning cases; his regular votes to sustain state laws against constitutional challenges brought by criminal defendants; his dissents in the commercial speech cases in which the Court has struck down laws limiting advertising on First Amendment grounds; and his dissents in *Roe* and its progeny in which the "right to privacy" has been invoked by the Court to invalidate legislative restrictions on abortions.

Appointed in 1990, Souter has quickly become the leading "incrementalist" on the Court. Souter, the "stealth" nominee, has established himself as a classic, common-law jurist who regards all law, including constitutional law, as "evolving" and who sees the role of the judge as intimately involved in the "making" of law through the ongoing process of refinement of earlier precedents. Souter pays great deference to the work of previous courts. Precedents reveal not only what past courts have done, but why they have done it; they show how past courts have balanced the various interests involved and provide Souter with a rich source of the multifactor balancing tests he is fond of applying.

For Souter, the text of the law itself is less important than the purpose the law is to serve, and that purpose is to be found in what earlier courts have said about it or, in the case of a statute, in its legislative history. When Justice Scalia ridiculed him in *United States v. Thompson/Center Arms Co.* (1992) for resorting "to that last hope of lost interpretive causes, that St. Jude of the hagiography of statutory construction, legislative history," Souter defended his antitextualist approach by quoting Justice Felix Frankfurter:

> A statute, like other living organisms, derives significance and sustenance from its environment, from which it cannot be severed without being mutilated. Especially is this true where the statute, like the one before us, is part of a legislative process having a history and a purpose. The meaning of such a statute cannot be gained by confining inquiry within its four corners. Only the historic process of which such legislation is an incomplete fragment—that to which it gave rise as well as that which gave rise to it—can yield its true meaning.[12]

Souter's penchant for balancing and incrementalism and his attachment to precedent are apparent in such cases as *Doggett v. United States* and *Lee v. Weisman*. In *Doggett*, he ritualistically applied the four criteria of *Barker v. Wingo* (1972) and concluded that the petitioner, who was not brought to trial until eight and a half years after his indictment, had been denied his Sixth Amendment right to a speedy trial, despite the facts that the petitioner did not even know he had been indicted and that the government believed he was in prison in Panama. Thomas was prompted to observe in dissent that "so engrossed is the Court in applying the multifactor balancing test set forth in *Barker* that it loses sight of the nature and purpose of the speedy trial guarantee set forth in the Sixth Amendment.'' In *Lee*, Souter concurred in the Court's opinion that prayers at public school graduation ceremonies indirectly coerce religious observance and therefore violate the First Amendment. He proclaimed that ''we hold true to a line of precedent from which there is no adequate historical case to depart.'' Reviewing the Court's establishment clause cases, he pronounced them ''settled law. Here, as elsewhere, we should stick to it absent some compelling reason to discard it.''

Souter's incrementalism appears to have won as converts both O'Connor and Kennedy, who have failed as yet to articulate a discernible or consistent judicial philosophy of their own. O'Connor voted with Souter 89 percent of the time in the 1990 term and 78 percent in the 1991 term, and Kennedy voted with him 84 percent of the time in the 1990 term and 87 percent in the 1991 term. Their adherence to precedent and acceptance of the propriety of incremental judicial lawmaking were perhaps most apparent in their plurality opinion in *Planned Parenthood v. Casey* (1992). In it, they held that even though *Roe* was wrongly decided, it should not be overturned. They argued that if the Court were to overturn *Roe* merely because newly appointed justices regard it as a bad decision, it would create the impression that the justices yielded to political pressure and more generally that constitutional decisions are determined by politics. That, they insisted, would result in ''both profound and unnecessary damage to the Court's legitimacy, and to the Nation's commitment to the rule of law. It is therefore imperative to adhere to the essence of *Roe*'s original decision, and we do so today.'' Rehnquist objected: ''Our constitutional watch does not cease merely because we have spoken before on an issue; when it becomes clear that a prior constitutional interpretation is unsound we are obliged to reexamine the question.'' Rehnquist's objection, however, was unavailing. As Thomas Hobbes observed in his *Dialogue Between a Philosopher and a Student of the Common Laws of England*, ''precedents prove only what was done, but not what was well done.'' Hobbes's words, however, were unpersuasive to Souter, O'Connor, and Kennedy; for them, proving and approving what was done in *Roe* were essential. Sustaining bad law rather than correcting judicial error was their highest duty, for to overturn the precedent that *Roe* had set would jeopardize the very

character of a Nation of people who aspire to live according to the rule of law. Their belief in themselves as such a people is not readily separable from their understanding of the Court invested with the authority to decide their constitutional cases and speak before all others for their constitutional ideals. The Court's concern with legitimacy is not for the sake of the Court but for the sake of the Nation to which it is responsible.[13]

The debate among the Reagan and Bush justices over what constitutes judicial conservatism explains in part the Court's failure to advance the conservative agenda of the presidents who appointed them. Their disagreement over whether to defer to the words of the text, the popular branches of government, or previous courts means that even when they reach the same conclusion, they often do so for different reasons and are unable to agree in a common opinion. The result is that the Court increasingly does not speak with an authoritative voice to renounce and reverse past liberal constitutional gains and to establish new conservative principles. To cite one example, in *Harmelin*, while all the Reagan and Bush justices agreed that Michigan's law imposing a mandatory term of life in prison without possibility of parole for possessing more than 650 grams of cocaine did not violate the cruel and unusual punishments clause of the Eighth Amendment, they divided on whether *Solem v. Helms* (1983), in which the Court had previously concluded that the Eighth Amendment contains a proportionality principle, should be overturned. Scalia, making a textualist argument, said that it should; the incrementalist Kennedy, wishing to adhere to precedent and therefore arguing implausibly that the Michigan law somehow passed *Solem*'s proportionality test, said it should not. The result was reported in the *U.S. Reports* as follows:

> Scalia, J., announced the judgment of the Court and delivered the opinion of the Court with respect to Part V, in which Rehnquist, C.J., and O'Connor, Kennedy, and Souter, JJ., joined, and an opinion with respect to Parts I, II, III, and IV, in which Rehnquist, C.J., joined. Kennedy, J., filed an opinion concurring in part and concurring in the judgment, in which O'Connor and Souter, JJ., joined. White, J., filed a dissenting opinion, in which Blackmun and Stevens, JJ., joined. Marshall, J., filed a dissenting opinion. Stevens, J., filed a dissenting opinion, in which Blackmun, J., joined.

Because of their failure to agree on whether they should defer to the text of the Eighth Amendment or to the decision of a past Court, the Reagan and Bush justices—even though they upheld the Michigan law—ended up canceling out each other, and a liberal precedent was allowed to stand.

The numerical predominance of the incrementalists in the debate over what constitutes judicial conservatism provides another reason as well for the Court's failure to act as a conservative Court. In *Casey*, three of the six Reagan and Bush justices were so wedded to *stare decisis* that they were unwilling to overturn *Roe* (or at least to admit they were doing so) even though they thought it had been wrongly decided, and even though they discarded the trimester framework that *Roe* had created and sustained a variety of restrictions on abortion contrary to the Court's original holding in *Roe*. To overturn *Roe* would be to "surrender to political pressure" and would unjustly repudiate "the principle on which the Court staked its authority in the first instance." For them, fidelity to precedent was more important than following their own understanding of the Constitution. Since most precedents are liberal, it is hardly surprising that the Reagan and Bush justices (dominated as they are by the incrementalists) have yet to overrule "a single major decision that produced the drastic social changes of the past four decades."[14]

Offensive and Defensive Court Strategies

The second principal factor explaining the Court's failure to advance the conservative agenda of Reagan and Bush or to reverse the liberal constitutional gains of the past is that most conservatives who come before the Court for relief seek defensive rather than offensive victories. While the Reagan and Bush justices may quarrel among themselves concerning what constitutes judicial conservatism, it must be acknowledged that they all are conservative and that they have handed down many more decisions that are pleasing to conservatives than to liberals. Most of these decisions, however, have given conservatives what David Bryden has termed "defensive" as opposed to "offensive" victories.[15] And while liberals have won far fewer cases before the Reagan and Bush justices, most of the victories they have secured have been offensive ones.

An offensive victory is achieved when a litigant obtains a constitutional right; offensive victories are absolute, for they nullify all defeats in the political arena. *Roe*, *Miranda*, *Mapp v. Ohio* (1961), the reapportionment decisions, and the school prayer decisions all exemplify liberal offensive victories; they constitutionalized portions of the liberal political agenda by trumping conservative victories in the political arena. A defensive victory, by contrast, merely thwarts the other side's efforts to obtain an offensive victory, transferring the issue from the judiciary back to the political arena; defensive victories are contingent, for they leave the ultimate resolution of the policy issue in the hands of elected officials. *Bowers v. Hardwick* (1986) is an example of a defensive victory for cultural conservatives. In it, the Court refused to extend constitutional protections to private homosexual acts but left liberals free to lobby for repeal of sodomy statutes, which they have been highly successful in doing.

Table 7-1 below divides into five categories the constitutional decisions of the Supreme Court handed down from the beginning of the 1986 term of the Court, when Rehnquist was elevated to chief justice and Scalia was confirmed as an associate justice, through the end of the 1991 term of the Court in late June 1992. The five categories are conservative offensive victories (CO), conservative defensive victories (CD), liberal offensive victories (LO), liberal defensive victories (LD), and decisions in which the Court did not divide along conservative or

Table 7-1

Major Constitutional Victories in the Rehnquist Court, 1986–1992

	CO	CD	LO	LD	N	Total
1. Criminal Law and Procedure	0	26	6	5	4	41
2. Establishment of Religion	0	2	3	0	0	5
3. Freedom of Speech	0	12	4	4	4	24
4. Search and Seizure	0	9	0	0	0	9
5. Takings	2	1	0	1	0	4
6. Equal Protection	1	4	2	0	2	9
7. Federalism	1	1	2	2	2	8
8. Free Exercise	0	2	0	0	0	2
9. Due Process	0	3	0	2	3	8
10. Eighth Amendment	0	4	50	3	0	7
11. Eleventh Amendment	0	0	0	0	1	1
12. Separation of Powers	0	1	0	0	4	5
13. Right to Privacy	0	2	2	0	0	4
Totals	4	67	19	17	20	127

Note: CO = conservative offensive, CD = conservative defensive, LO = liberal offensive, LD = liberal defensive, N = no division.

Total conservative victories: 71(55.9%)   Total liberal victories: 36 (28.3%)
Conservative offensive victories: 4(5.6%)   Liberal offensive victories: 19 (52.7%)
Conservative defensive victories: 67(94.4%)   Liberal defensive victories: 17 (47.3%)

liberal lines (N).[16] The table shows that during the six-year period under consideration, the Supreme Court handed down 71 decisions favoring the conservative side and only 36 decisions favoring the liberal side. That would seem to give conservatives a strong reason to seek to maintain control of the Court and to mobilize support for Bush's reelection. However, the table also shows that only 4 of the 71 conservative victories were offensive, in contrast to 19 of the 36 liberal victories. In terms of their impact on public policy, offensive victories are, of course, far more potent than defensive victories; moreover, the rights created by offensive victories create expectations, rendering them harder to reverse than defensive victories. *Roe v. Wade* is a case in point. As the O'Connor, Kennedy, and Souter plurality in *Casey* noted,

> for two decades of economic and social developments, people have organized intimate relationships and made choices that define their views of themselves and their places in society, in reliance on the availability of abortion in the event that contraception should fail. . . . The Constitution serves human values, and while the effect of reliance on *Roe* cannot be exactly measured, neither can the certain cost of overruling *Roe* for people who have ordered their thinking and living around that case be dismissed.

Why have almost 95 percent of all conservative victories in the Supreme Court been defensive while over half of all liberal victories have been offensive? The answer would appear to lie in the fact that most conservatives seek defensive victories. Given their commitment to federalism and the principle of self-government and given their principled belief in judicial restraint, most conservatives do not turn to the Court to argue that the Constitution requires doing something that the popular branches have failed to do; quite the contrary, they turn to the Court to argue that the Constitution does not prohibit doing something that the popular branches have done or wish to do. They do not argue, for example, that a fetus is a person and that any state law permitting abortion therefore violates the Fourteenth Amendment; rather they argue that the Constitution should not be understood to prohibit the popular branches of state government from restricting abortions if they so choose. They do not argue that school systems without voucher programs in place violate the First Amendment rights of parents who wish to send their children to parochial schools; rather they argue that a school voucher program is not unconstitutional assistance to religion. They do not argue that "victim's rights" are mandated by the Constitution; rather they argue that they are not precluded by the Sixth Amendment. Moreover, if they win on these matters before the Court, all they have won is the opportunity to try to persuade the popular branches to their point of view. Most liberals, by contrast, seek offensive victories. They wish to create new rights based on freedom of speech, the establishment or free exercise clauses, due process, equal protection, or the concept of privacy in order to trump the political victories of their opponents in the political arena. Since most conservatives go before the Supreme Court seeking defensive victories and most liberals go there seeking offensive victories, it is not surprising that the Court has generally accommodated both sides.

Conclusion

Given the debate among the Reagan and Bush justices over the nature of judicial conservatism and the numerical predominance of the incrementalists in this debate who are inclined to defer to precedent, even liberal precedents, and given the Court's inclination to provide defensive victories to conservatives and offensive victories to liberals, it was impossible for Bush to use the Court as a way of galvanizing political support for his reelection. Likewise, there was little about the Court's performance that Clinton could use to excite fear and alarm in his constituency. Even had the state of the economy not been such an overriding consideration and had Bush been a more effective campaigner, the Court would not have surfaced as a major issue. The Court had no bark, because no bite. Twelve years of Republican occupancy of the White House and twenty-four continuous years of Republican appointments to the High Bench had shown the Court to be neither the means of political salvation some conservatives had fervently desired nor the threat to their most cherished rights and liberties some liberals had feared.

Notes

1. On Bush's behalf, it must be said that he defended his nomination of Clarence Thomas and supported his efforts to secure Senate confirmation much more vigorously and successfully than did Reagan when he nominated Robert Bork for a seat on the Supreme Court in 1987. See Terry Eastland,

Energy in the Executive: The Case for the Strong Presidency (New York: Free Press, 1992), pp. 245–57.

2. See David Brock, *The Real Anita Hill: The Untold Story* (New York: Free Press, 1993).

3. See, for example, Toni Morrison, ed., *Race-ing Justice, En-Gendering Power: Essays on Anita Hill, Clarence Thomas, and the Constitution of Social Reality* (New York: Pantheon Books, 1992).

4. "Symposium—Gender, Race, and the Politics of Supreme Court Appointments: The Import of the Anita Hill/Clarence Thomas Hearings," 65 *Southern California Law Review* 1279 (1992).

5. A. Leon Higgonbotham Jr., "An Open Letter to Justice Clarence Thomas From a Judicial Colleague," 140 *University of Pennsylvania Law Review* 1005–28 (1992).

6. *New York Times*, Feb. 27, 1992, p. A18.

7. Lino Graglia, "A Conservative Court? No," in Terry Eastland, ed., *The Public Interest Law Review, 1993* (Washington, D.C.: National Legal Center for the Public Interest, 1993), p. 164.

8. The following discussion relies heavily on Michael Stokes Paulsen, "The Many Faces of 'Judicial Restraint,' " and John O. McGinnis, "The 1991 Supreme Court Term: Review and Outlook," both in Terry Eastland, ed., *The Public Interest Law Review, 1993*.

9. 487 U.S. 1012, 1016 (1988).

10. Antonin Scalia, "The Rule of Law as the Law of Rules," 56 *University of Chicago Law Review* 1175 (1989).

11. William H. Rehnquist, "The Notion of a Living Constitution," 54 *Texas Law Review* 693–707 (1976).

12. 112 S. Ct. 2102, 2109, n.8.

13. 112 S. Ct. 2791, 2816.

14. Graglia, "A Conservative Court? No," p. 157.

15. See David P. Bryden, "Is the Rehnquist Court Conservative?" *The Public Interest*, No. 109 (Fall 1992), pp. 73–88. The following discussion relies heavily on this article.

16. Table 7-1 updates the work of, and utilizes the methodology employed by, Bryden in his article, "Is the Rehnquist Court Conservative?," pp. 77–78.

8

The Politics of Change and the Public Service: The Bureaucracy, the 1992 Campaign, and the Clinton Presidency

David E. Marion

Considering the dominance of domestic issues in the '92 campaign, voters reasonably might have expected that the federal bureaucracy would come in for considerable attention from the candidates. At a time when foreign policy matters loomed much larger, candidates Jimmy Carter in 1976 and Ronald Reagan in 1980 gave the organization and power of the bureaucracy a central place in their campaign oratory. While federal agencies and their personnel did not go unnoticed by George Bush, Bill Clinton, and Ross Perot, the bureaucracy never became the lightning rod issue that might have been predicted in an election devoted to domestic policy problems. To appreciate why this was the case it is necessary to take note of a change—brought about by Woodrow Wilson and other Progressives—in the way Americans think about electoral politics and the role of the bureaucracy in governance. More specifically, what must be appreciated is the success of the Progressives in making the choice of which political leader's vision will prevail the decisive act of American political life; all else, including the actions of administrative-class officials, is of secondary and derivative significance. The campaigns of all the candidates in 1992, including that of Bush who once deprecated "that vision thing," reflected to one degree or another Wilson's views on electoral politics and administrative governance.

Where James Madison believed that the federal bureaucracy, the party system, and national electoral politics could properly be left in the shadows of the Constitution, nineteenth- and early twentieth-century reformers such as Wilson concluded that these things all needed to be elevated in political importance if we were ever to purify the democratic bona fides of Madison's republic. The Constitution's virtual silence on such subjects as the federal system of administration, political parties, and national electoral politics was for Wilson evidence of the incompleteness, and indeed the defectiveness, of the political thinking and labors of the Founding Fathers. In point of fact, Founders such as Madison, Alexander Hamilton, and George Washington recognized the connection that existed between all these things and the shape of the republic that would finally emerge from their work at the Constitutional Convention. They understood that care would have to be taken to see that matters bearing on administration, the electoral process, and political parties would be handled in a way that complemented rather than conflicted with the requisites of a decent and competent democratic republic. They certainly did not underestimate the difficulty or importance of this task, as they did not underestimate the significance of their work at the Constitutional Convention. While they recognized that questions of administration or electoral politics could not be divorced from the principles and thus the limits of the Constitution itself, they did not believe that it would be either prudent or necessary to draft a comprehensive plan for the republic at the Convention of 1787. They expected that the principle of limited government and the related priority of individual rights that informed the Constitution would also define policy related to administrative or electoral matters. Only by understanding the change in our thinking about the guidance available from the original Constitution on matters of administration and policy that was initiated by progressive reformers such as Wilson can we fully appreciate the full significance and implications of the treatment given the bureaucracy in the 1992 campaign and during the first months of the Clinton administration.

Some Contextual Considerations

There is ample evidence that the 1992 campaign was fought largely within the parameters established by the political reformers of the latter part of the nineteenth century. Thus, for example, while the 1992 campaign was distinguished by the repeated pledges of the candidates to solve problems related to the health care system, the environment, or deficit spending, and to reduce corruption and inefficiency in government, it was the Progressives who gained notoriety as the first major political group whose efforts were visibly informed both by an attack on corrupt and ineffective government and by the view that society is open to perfection through deliberate human action. Connected to this reasoning was the claim that government has an obligation to facilitate full participation by all citizens in the enjoyment of the fruits of a vibrant community of rights. Hence the defense by the Progressives of such devices as the initiative and referendum. While full participation in an open political process was treated as a fixed feature of true democratic government, substantive matters of policy were to be entrusted to the people for disposition at their pleasure. In short, the Constitution was treated as being silent on the substance of, say, economic or education policy, which was held to be separable from the procedures of democratic government.

The practical consequences of the thinking of the Progressives cannot be underestimated. Within the context of this reasoning it is permissible to build a coalition around virtually any set of policy preferences, something that the New Dealers used to full advantage in the 1930s and 1940s. Electoral power could now replace reflection on permanent constitutional principles as the decisive action responsible for shaping the way of life of the people. Thus, for example, whether to regulate production or hours and wages was treated as an electoral matter, not an issue to be decided in terms of what the original Constitution stipulated. A related effect of freeing public policy from the limits of the Constitution was the separation of many administrative concerns from such limits. The key consideration in terms of the bureaucracy was ensuring that the system of administration was equal to implementing the results of electoral politics. A technically neutral bureaucracy became the natural complement to Wilsonian and New Deal electoral politics.

In its most radical form, then, Wilsonian and New Deal-style liberalism involved a shift of attention away from a concern for preserving the way of life originally associated with the Constitution, or even understanding the meaning of the Constitution as the decisive guiding document on policy issues, to finding out how best to mobilize public opinion and interest group support behind a set of preferences. Here was the new approach to legitimizing government action. One obvious consequence is that the satisfaction of public preferences ends up driving governmental action and rhetoric. In addition, this thinking encourages the general good to be defined in terms of the aggregation of satisfied individual or group goods, whether of laborers and Catholics and Jews in the 1930s and 1940s, or of pro-choicers and gay activists in the 1990s. Not surprisingly, the end result is the emergence of the opinion that the attainment of happiness, and not merely provisions for the pursuit of happiness, is the decisive measure of the respectability of government. As will become evident below, this shift away from a fixed view of the American way of life and toward the sanctification of the achievement of happiness through facilitative governmental action was writ large in the rhetoric and politics of change that defined both the 1992 campaign and the early period of the Clinton administration.

Besides a change in thinking regarding what is required to legitimate social or economic or defense policy, the Progressives and New Dealers promoted a new view of the role of the president as the leader of the nation and head of the executive department. This second change is perhaps best captured in a report that received favorable attention from Franklin Roosevelt. The 1937 report of the Brownlow Committee, clearly the critical administrative document of Roosevelt's presidency, provides concrete evidence of the transformation in thinking that had occurred since the founding on the means and ends of American republicanism. One hundred and fifty years after the Philadelphia convention, the executive was cast in the 1937 report principally as a political leader or, to use the language of the document, the "leader of [the] people," whose aim ought to be to raise "the level of the happiness and dignity of human life."[1] Here is the New Deal vision of the means and ends of democratic goverment. This report dramatizes the connection of the executive to the people and legitimizes presidential decision-making that treats the Constitution as a "practical instrument of government" designed to promote the general social welfare.[2] So construed, the Brownlow version of positive government would not only be available to satisfy majority preferences, it would be seen as deserving respect in direct proportion to its success in "raising the level of the happiness of the people."[3] In an observation that anticipates much of the rhetoric of the 1992 campaign and the Clinton White House, the Brownlow report observes that "there is much bitter wrong to set right in neglected ways of human life."[4] There is a distinct presumption on the part of the authors of the report that proper exertions of human will can correct such bitter wrongs. Not surprisingly, the belief in the ability to correct such wrongs feeds a conviction that there is a moral responsibility to correct them. In short, what is possible is treated as being necessary.

In sum, the modern thought that helped shape the 1992 campaign weds moralistic idealism with faith in modern technology and science in a fashion that is in contrast to the cautionary thinking of Founders such as Madison and Washington. Needless to add, the effect of this new thinking on governmental action is magnified by the desire of the people for solutions to economic and social problems to the end of contributing to a heightened form of comfortable preservation. Importantly, neither the emphasis on the satisfaction of popular preferences nor the commitment to technical neutrality in the bureaucracy provides meaningful long-term substantive direction for administrative agencies.

The 1992 Campaign and the Bureaucracy

It has become the rule for candidates to devote their campaigns to the twin tasks of shaking up the public "to want some change" and then "to persuade them to want the particular change" that the candidates want, to paraphrase Wilson's description of what should happen in the electoral process.[5] The 1992 campaign, with the heavy use of talk shows, instructional-style programs, and the introduction of the activist audience model for presidential debates, represents the fullest extension yet seen of Wilsonian electioneering. The change mantra of the 1992 campaign was a logical extension of Wilson's legitimization of the politics of change. Even Bush, the so-called establishment candidate, spoke of the need for change; witness for instance his promise to "reinvent" American education or his pledge to meet with the hundred-plus new members predicted to be entering the House of Representatives after the election in order to change the way the executive and legislative branches interact. Significantly, Bush later explained his defeat as a result of a failure to effectively articulate how he planned to change the country. In keeping with Wilson's advice, the candidates sought not only to energize the people as a force for change but, as importantly, to get them to agree with the need for particular reforms. Indeed, too little attention has been given to the fact that the heavy reliance on the talk-show circuit was not so much intended to allow the candidates to familiarize themselves with the preferences of the people than to permit them to sell health care reform (Clinton) or deficit trimming (Perot) or new initiatives in education and general regulatory practices (Bush) to what was expected to be a receptive audience. The object was to convince the people that they desired the very reforms to which the candidates were committed as a result of their own reading of the prevailing mood of the people. The specifics, however, were almost always obscure, an obvious consequence of the fact that the candidates' commitment to particular ends often turned out to be soft or insufficiently thought out. Bush's call for "reinventing" American education, for example, came with few particulars, while Perot and Clinton often found themselves backtracking when they did make specific suggestions for dealing with the health care system or the deficit. It clearly was more important to be seen as an agent of popular changes or reforms than to have the answers regarding specific measures that should be taken. If the politics of change ushered in by the Progressives had come of age, so had the politics of simplification and generalization. It should not be surprising, then, that out of the rhetoric of the campaign came Clinton's observation in his inaugural address that it is left for each generation of Americans to define for themselves what it means to be an American. What better statement could be offered of the perceived open-endedness not only of electoral politics but of policy-making in general?

Implicit in the rhetoric of change is an instinctive faith in the malleability of the bureaucracy. That the promises of deficit reduction, or improvements in the health care system or regulatory practices, might not match the capacity of administrative agencies to act is not a matter of serious scrutiny. There is the presumption that if the people desire particular results or endorse candidates committed to specific reforms, then a technically neutral bureaucracy's only responsibility is to supply the requisite action. Thus, for example, it is quite clear that Clinton expected the armed services merely to accede to his demand that the ban on homosexuals be lifted. It is equally clear that, if successful in his bid for the presidency, Perot expected to deal with a compliant bureaucracy. While Bush understood better than his competitors the true complexities of the administrative system and the value of a career civil service that participates fully in managing the business of government, he opted to be publicly silent on the contribution that, say, professionals in the defense or state departments are poised to make based on their experience and knowledge of long-term national interests while at the same time following the lead of his competitors in pandering to popular opinion. What the rhetoric of the campaign obscured was not only the intricacies of the federal administrative order and the utility of a professional civil service to the effective implementation of public policies but, and related to this, the limits of bureaucratic action. Insofar as the people are encouraged to demand services or benefits beyond the capacity of the administrative service to supply, whether in terms of quantity or quality, the federal bureaucracy is set up to fail and, by extension, public cynicism regarding the competency of the national government can only be intensified. Ironically, while such a result is at odds with the idealism characteristic of the politics of change, it actually serves the interests of the politics of change by creating the ground for unending appeals for reforms.

The linkage between Wilsonian political thought, with all its internal tensions and ambiguities, and the 1992 campaign was given unmistakable expression in Clinton's inaugural address. Just as Wilson called variously for perfecting the work of the American Founders and for fashioning a democracy that would be open to the unlimited desires of the people, which presumably will not always coincide with the original intentions of the Founders, so Clinton spoke simultaneously of "renewing" America and of "reinventing" America. In short, his language could be seen as pointing both backward and forward, to both preservation and re-creation. Insisting that change must be made "our friend," Clinton observed that as each generation of Americans has the right to define what it means to be an American so they also have a responsibility to do this for themselves. Echoing a theme from Wilson, Clinton called on the American people to do something that he claimed no generation had hitherto done, to invest while cutting national indebtedness. Again in Wilsonian fashion, Clinton spoke of a new and better world that could be ushered in if only we had the courage to make the necessary sacrifices and to act with the requisite boldness. True to the tradition that informed both the campaign and his inaugural address, the fleeting references to "renewal" ended up having almost nothing to do with preserving specific substantive commitments on the part of the Founders and almost everything to do with defending an exaggerated and mistaken view of the Founders' vision of decent democratic government. The Constitution of the Founders is reduced to a political framework for comprehensive democratic (meaning populist) government. What is envisioned is a system that merely serves as a medium for facilitating the enjoyment of any "way of life" desired by the present majority.

Like Wilson, Clinton alluded in his inaugural address to the valuable contribution that might be made by representatives of the people who exercise independent judgment, but his underlying populist political convictions really ended up undercutting any substantive ground for true deliberative decision-making by government officials. What predominates is the view that public policy is to be "the product of officials whose responsibility to public opinion will be direct and inevitable." Public opinion is to rule, not only with respect to the actions of elected officials but, obviously, in the case of the civil service as well. Hence the declaration that public service personnel should be "intimately" connected to popular thought through "constant public counsel." Here is language that could have been lifted directly from the writings and speeches of Progressives or New Dealers. Insofar as the president is visualized as the spokesman for the dominant opinion or "will" of the day, especially on matters having to do with perfecting the democratic order, the implication that a "steady, hearty allegiance" to the policies of the executive is expected from the civil service fits in perfectly with the thrust of the New Deal assumptions of the Brownlow committee. The possibility for true formative leadership by the president, however, ends up being effectively weakened by the repeated pledges, in the name of open, democratic government, to seek the constant counsel of the people on matters of policy, both great and small. With administrative concerns already decoupled in large part from the Constitution, the additional weakening of the institutional presidency threatens the possibility that any part of the executive branch can supply the energy and responsibility that the Framers knew would be needed from this department if the republic was to make good on the great objectives set out in the Preamble of the Constitution.

As noted previously, it was not primarily from explicit baiting and bashing that the bureaucracy suffered in the 1992 campaign. This is not to say that federal agencies and their officials escaped completely unscathed, but harsher treatment might have been expected. Perhaps the most memorable attack came in Perot's critique of the Agriculture Department and specifically of its figurative agent who was said to have been found weeping after he learned that the one active farmer for whom he was responsible had passed away. This sort of imagery, however, was the exception rather than the rule. What was more typical were the Bush administration's announcements of plans for spending more on job training and for new health and education programs or the unveiling of new regulations coming from the Environmental Protection Agency, presumably with the president's blessing, during some of the critical preelection weeks of October. These promises more than offset Bush's complaints about unnecessary federal paperwork requirements and his call for a voucher program in education that would include private, and not just public, schools. What suggestions Bush did make for decentralizing or deregulating some activities were either not believable or just not convincing given his willingness to continue most domestic programs and even enlarge some.

For Clinton's part, the real culprit is not big government, but a government that is not meeting preconceived criteria of a good democracy. From expansions of federal Head Start and jobs programs to passage of a national bottle bill and more demanding federal fuel efficiency standards for automobiles, to the creation of a new economic security council in the White House, there is little evidence of uneasiness with the federal bureaucratic system. The commitments to reform the health care system and stimulate economic growth were not presented as pledges to reduce the size or power of the national government. As with Bush, Clinton's emphasis on new programs and new spending obscured the occasional pledge to reduce the federal work force over several years or to reshape the Arms Control and Disarmament Agency or to ease banking regulations. When it came to cuts that should be made, Clinton's best and almost only example during the campaign of a program that might be ended was the subsidy for honey producers. The overwhelming commitment is to fashion an activist government in keeping with the slogan, "What have I done today to make anyone's life get better?"[6] This "do good" philosophy is consistent with the New Deal view both that bitter wrongs exist which must be corrected and that proper exertions of the human will are sufficient to rectify such wrongs. This is the real core of the "new covenant" that Clinton touted in his acceptance address at the Democratic National Convention.[7]

To repeat, the candidates focused less on big government than on inefficient or ineffective government. They both cultivated and appealed to a public frustration with paying more and getting less from government. Each did his best to persuade the people that an administration under his guidance would best squeeze every possible ounce of blood from each federal dollar spent. Witness in this connection Clinton's unveiling of an 800 number for exposing governmental waste and fraud. For his part, Perot did not seek an end to Head Start-type programs as the way to reduce the deficit, but emphasized the elimination of waste in government, which he calculated to amount to tens of billions of dollars. Perot was fully prepared to lead a government that would give the people what they want, ideally determined by a willingness to pay for federally provided services. Consider his call for national town meetings where elected officials would receive their marching orders directly from the people. Responsiveness of the sort invited by Perot clearly is compatible with a substantial administrative jurisdiction or, more to the point, a substantial national administrative jurisdiction. This is an important point. As a group, the candidates either could not or would not challenge the prevailing preferences of the people or special interest groups for more governmental services, grants, or benefits. The absence of the will and substantive grounding for erecting a challenge to the popular impulse both to demand that government "raise the level of the happiness of the people" and to believe that an infinite variety of bitter wrongs need redressing is a direct legacy of the Wilsonian and New Deal tradition. In keeping with the instrumentalist view of administration that emerged from this tradition, the bureaucracy is reduced in a matter of fact way to being an instrumental device for assisting the president in making good on campaign promises.

Reflecting a common theme from Wilson, all the candidates in 1992 spoke of taking control of the bureaucracy, to the end of achieving a better-managed democratic government. A neutrally competent bureaucracy attuned to the will of a president armed with a popular mandate was never far from the surface in the campaign. And, indeed, the view that the future is ours to create, and that administration is one of the major modern devices by which people can control their destiny, links the campaign, as well as Clinton's presidency, in a special way with the Progressives and New Dealers. Ironically, however, the populist rhetoric that dominated the campaign, building on the historical tendency of the American national spirit to be suspicious of a professional bureaucracy, really ends up endangering the possibility of efficient and professional government since both experience and practical and theoretical knowledge are undercut as independent sources of legitimacy for participants in governance. Hence, below the surface of the opening for national administrative action of significant proportions that characterized the recent campaign, and is a mark of the Clinton administration, are currents that have the potential for substantially limiting the full contribution that might be derived not only from representative government but from a professional class of administrative officials. The absence of firm sources of meaningful guidance for administrative decision-making can only undermine the possibility of deriving the full benefits of a career bureaucracy that is essential to satisfying the very popular preferences that drive the contemporary electoral process. Neither Wilson nor Madison could be pleased with the result: the possibility that we have yet to identify the formula for a perfectly efficient democracy would not sit well with Wilson, while the movement away from true deliberative government toward plebiscitary democracy would not be well received by Madison—what better evidence that the time has come for a general re-examination of electoral politics and the requisites of decent and competent democratic governance?

Bureaucracy and Democratic Republicanism

There is a modern schizophrenia regarding the place and role of administrative-class officials in governance that is strikingly visible in Wilson's political thought. His writings supply a justification for viewing public service personnel merely as servants of the public will on the one side, and as independent contributors to governance on the other. This dual view of administration corresponds to the competing modern desires for government based on consent as well as for competent government capable of protecting rights and advancing the comfortable preservation of its members. In the end, however, it is the commitment to government based on the consent (meaning the desires) of the people that predominates in Wilson's political thought and in contemporary electoral politics. Thus, for example, his writings lend support to the view that at the core of democratic government stands the principle that the laws of the community should give expression to the prevailing will of the people. In the context of such reasoning, a professional bureaucracy would be responsible for selecting the means most adapted to carrying out the specific objectives desired by the citizen body. Such a view of democratic government places administration squarely and solely at the end of the policy process. Here is the thinking that is visible in the 1992 campaign, especially in Perot's explicit, and Clinton's sometimes explicit sometimes implicit, defense of plebiscitary democracy.

There is another view of administration, however, that emerges in Wilson's writings. In his 1887 essay on the science of administration, he bluntly observes that public opinion is often insufficiently enlightened and needs the counsel of students of administrative science who not only know how to make government more efficient, but understand what governments can properly and successfully do. Presuming that many administrative class officials will also be students of the science of administration, this alternative view of the place and role of the bureaucracy provides an opening for justifying formative action of major significance by unelected officials. This second view reflects the traditional reservations, seen in the work of the Founders, regarding the perfectability of pure democratic government or of governance on the basis of raw public opinion. There is nothing in Wilson's historicist faith in democratic government, however, that supplies a dependable substantive principle for a bureaucracy, or an executive department, that isn't limited to carrying out the preferences of the people. In the end, all claims that the popular will might be defective, and thus all checks on the will of the people, are rendered suspect by Wilson. This fact is important to a full appreciation of what followed in the form of New Deal thinking and in the 1992 campaign.

In contrast to Wilson's administrative thought is the thinking of Founders such as Hamilton, called by Wilson a "great man, but . . . not a great American." For Wilson, Hamilton could not qualify as a "great American" because of his reservations about tailoring governmental action to coincide with the opinions and interests of the "common man." In truth, Hamilton and Madison, among other Founders, believed that the opinions and interests of the "common man" ought to be made to coincide with a republican political order that recognized the dangers of allowing uninformed or illiberal opinion to rule. Informing this position is the understanding that not all opinions are salutary or even tolerable. According to this reasoning, interests and opinions should not be permitted to roam at will, but ought to be guided to promote the best national interests. As a result, leadership that is formative in nature receives a secure grounding in the practical requisites of a competent republic of rights. By contrast, the crucial problems for Wilson, and this turns out also to be true for Clinton, Perot, and even Bush, are largely instrumental or functional in nature. That is to say, Wilson and the New Dealers after him are principally identified with seeking to legitimate reforms that will improve the capacity of the political order to respond to the popular will. Here is the litmus test of the true democratic bona fides of the political system.

While Wilson devoted attention to the ministerial side of democratic government, Founders such as Hamilton and Madison, despite their known disagreements, counseled attention to the formative side of republican government, especially the hospitability of the republic to substantive political leadership or, better yet, statesmanship. Their goal was competent as well as consent-driven government. Both understood that direct democratic government could not be counted on to produce quality democratic government. It might be added that Madison and Hamilton understood the tragic side of the human condition that makes government itself necessary; witness the famous lines from *Federalist* 51: ". . . what is government itself but the greatest of all reflections on human nature? If men were angels, no government would be necessary. If angels were to govern men, neither external nor internal controls on government would be necessary." Among other things, this knowledge led the Founders to recognize that republican government, to be competent and decent, must be able to rise above the lowest common denominator of public opinion. Modern liberal thought, however, no longer admits to a tragic side to political life, in part because the principle of equality leads to a rejection of the idea that there are deep-seated differences that warrant disparate treatment of persons and also because of the conviction that modern science finally can rid society of intractable difficulties. We may have tough problems to address, according to the prevailing thinking, but there is nothing in nature that makes the human condition inherently tragic.

Madison's and Hamilton's appeal for competent republican government would have been heartily endorsed by Wilson and Roosevelt, but they could not have readily accepted the Founders' understanding of the existence of limits to what even good governments can accomplish. The difference of opinion regarding the limits of governmental action is reflected in a difference of opinion regarding both political rhetoric and action. The consequences for the bureaucracy are not insignificant. The thinking of Founders such as Madison and Hamilton ends up cultivating less cynicism because it restrains expectations while also providing more protection and legitimacy for a professional bureaucracy whose institutional knowledge and experience can have a beneficial influence on governance. They would caution us both to avoid inflaming public passions in a way that might enervate government and to educate the public to understand the importance of drawing on the full contribution that might be made to our well-being by persons whose participation in governance is based on the possession of a specific body of knowledge and experience, certainly to include administrative-class officials. Unlike Hamilton and Madison, the tradition arising out of the thinking of the Progressives and New Dealers provides no effective substantive basis for challenging petitions raised on behalf of unrefined public opinion. Such a result not only diminishes the contribution that might be acquired from nonelected officials but carries the potential for weakening the presidency since candidates no longer defend the principle that the executive's authority is constitutionally defined and legitimated as compared to being a function of public opinion. Evidence that this danger is real is not difficult to find, witness the fact that presidents are forced to fight harder to maintain their traditional authority against congressional encroachment. As for the bureaucracy, with the institutional presidency weakened and most domestic public policy and administrative matters decoupled from the Constitution, federal agencies and their officials are virtually set up to fail in practice, in part because too much is promised, at the same time that their actions are rendered suspect in theory. Against this back-drop, the existence of some measure of what has been called bureau-cratic free enterprise, or independent and self-serving actions by government agencies, should not be surprising. Indeed, there is no principled basis left for resisting efforts not only by the citizen body, but by elected and career officials as well, to expand governmental programs and power.

It can be hoped that the full unfolding of Wilsonian thinking in the 1992 campaign and the policies of the Clinton administration may well trigger serious scrutiny of the comparative merits and weaknesses of the electoral and governmental practices that seemingly follow from Madisonian political thought on the one side, and the political thought of the Progressives and New Dealers on the other. By returning to the political thought of Wilson and the New Dealers, as well as of Madison and Hamilton, we can deepen our understanding of the competing arguments on behalf of rule based on popular opinion in a system fashioned to promote the efficient implementation of the majority will, and rule based on the deliberate will of the community in a political order intended to moderate and even check illiberal, unreasonable, and uninformed popular inclinations. A proper understanding of the principle of official responsibility that should govern the conduct of all public officials, including administrative-class personnel, will be decisively affected by the selection that is made between these alterna-tive views of the nature and purposes of a defensible modern republic, including its system of administration. Here is an exercise befitting the true friends of American democracy.

Notes

1. *Report of the President's Committee on Administrative Management*, pp. 1, 2 (1937), chaired by Louis Brownlow. Hereafter referred to as the Brownlow report.

2. John Rohr, *To Run a Constitution* 129, 145 (Lawrence, Kans.: University of Kansas Press, 1986).

3. See President Franklin D. Roosevelt's letter to both the House of Repes-entatives and the U. S. Senate of January 12, 1937, accompanying the report of the Brownlow Committee. 81 *Congressional Record*, Pt. 1, 188. For his part, Roosevelt specifically noted that there was nothing "revolutionary" in the recommendations of the committee.

4. Brownlow report, p. 2.

5. Woodrow Wilson, "The Study of Administration," *Political Science Quarterly* 2 (June 1887), 208.

6. "First, We Have To Roll Up Our Sleeves," *Time*, Jan. 4, 1993, p. 36.

7. *Richmond Times-Dispatch*, July 19, 1992, p. F2.

9

Forgotten Federalism

H. E. Scruggs

The key difference between Democrats and Republicans, former U.S. Attorney General Edward Levi once observed, is that Democrats want to run America and Republicans don't want them to. This glib distinction is helpful in understanding the stakes at play in the 1992 presidential race. The campaign, just as Bill Clinton claimed, was not about ideology—it was not clear whether any of the candidates had one. It was about who would run America.

One of the most troubling facets of the contest was the unchallenged assumption that this country's domestic affairs needed to be run by the national government. The only question was which candidate would have the opportunity to sit at the financial and regulatory controls. The notion that states might have a role to play in areas traditionally reserved to them—education, health, and law enforcement—was unrepresented. The absence of any significant discussion of federalism during the 1992 campaign is an indication that the safeguard of "a territorial allocation of authority secured by constitutional guarantees"[1] lies dying somewhere in the political cellar of the republic. Search the newspapers, the commercials, the speeches, and the debates; federalism was never seriously discussed as an issue or an option in crafting solutions to society's problems.

Meaning in Nothingness: The Absence of Rhetorical Federalism

In virtually all previous presidential campaigns, candidates have felt an obligation to at least pay lip service to the role of the states in governing. But in a year when much attention was paid to the reading of lips, the words "states," "governors," or "federalism" were rarely even mouthed. It is hard to imagine that federalism has ever received less attention in a presidential campaign than it did in the 1992 contest. This neglect is especially telling in a year when all three candidates—a Republican incumbent, a sitting Southern Democratic governor, and a Texas populist—should have been naturally predisposed towards a restoration of federalism or, at very least, in favor of stopping the states' free fall from political prominence.

Perhaps none of them felt the need to address the role of the states, assuming it was well known that they were guided by an understanding of and a respect for federalism. A more likely explanation, however, is that George Bush, Bill Clinton, and Ross Perot felt compelled by difficult economic times to offer national programs that would solve everyone's problems with minimal individual or local inconvenience. Any talk of shared sacrifice was saved for postelection speeches. There was a general or shared perception that *change* in 1992 had to be promised in terms of sweeping national reforms rather than by encouraging the diversity and experimentation which characterize the truly federal.

Bush was so harried in his efforts to reclaim his position as the *national* leader that any focus on his role as a *federal* officer was avoided as distractive. How could he afford to acknowledge that not only did he lack a secret plan to end the recession but that most of America's other domestic problems were the responsibility of the states? Instead, Bush's campaign, like his administration, appeared to pride itself on coming up with programs that were almost as extravagant, almost as burdensome, and almost as intrusive as those proposed by Clinton or the Democratic Congress.

How was it possible that a Republican president—the heir to Reagan's New Federalism—with some ambition to be known as a conservative allowed himself to be drawn into a campaign competition to outbid the opposition with promises of bigger, more nationalized government? Perhaps Bush's preoccupation with the New World Order afforded little time, energy, or inclination to contemplate the subnational.

Bush's failure to federalize the issues of the race might be dismissed as just one more casualty of a reelection campaign that appeared dazed and disorganized from the outset. (Bush and his top aides may still be wondering how they could have slipped from Desert Storm war heroes to recessionary goats at such supersonic speed.) By comparison, Clinton's focus-group-distilled themes and messages were purely market driven. If Bill Clinton didn't talk about federalism in any way, shape or form, it was because his pollsters as well as his own finely honed political instincts told him that the voters didn't care which level of government promised to solve their problems.

There are essentially no references in the Clinton and Gore campaign tract, *Putting People First*, to federalism or related topics. The word "governor," for example, occurs only as a title for Clinton. The Clinton-Gore attitude could be adequately described as unquestioning commitment to the national government, regardless of the issue. Crime will be dealt with by a new "National Police Corps" and education improved through "a national examination system." If America's legislatures and governors like money and mandates, they will love Clinton's "federalism."[2]

In his announcement speech, in what may have been the only federalist rhetoric by any major candidate in the entire 1992 campaign, Clinton expressed pride in what Arkansas had "done to become a laboratory of democracy and innovation," but then moved on quickly to attack the Bush administration for turning over responsibility for "education and health care and social policy . . . to [the] fifty states."[3] Times have changed when a Democratic challenger thinks, apparently with good reason, he can wound a Republican president with such a charge. At the Democratic National Convention, Clinton made it clear that his Little Rock training would not inhibit his Washington agenda as he described his "New Covenant" in terms which totally bypassed the states—a "solemn agreement between the people and their [national] government."[4]

Perot's enigmatic campaign was nearly indistinguishable from Clinton's in its approach to the subject of federalism. Except for one reference to giving "the elected leadership in our cities and states the tools to do the job," while using the national government to "instigate, prod, and encourage good results,"[5] there was no mention of it. When Perot looked under America's hood, the last thing he wanted to see was fifty different engines in need of fifty diagnoses. Imagine his infomercials with a pie chart and homespun slogan for every state. One wonders whether President-cum-CEO Perot would have simply eliminated states as redundant departments and laid off governors as excess middle managers in the government corporate structure.

Such a scheme would fit well with Perot's expanded populism, which envisioned a much less mediated relationship between the people and the national government to be accomplished by devices such as the electronic town meeting and through the abolition of the electoral college. In his book, *United We Stand*, proposal after proposal calls for a national program. The only political subdivisions singled out for more autonomy are local school districts[6]; all other units of state and local government are promised money and mandates, differing from Clinton's proposals only in magnitude.

The Rise and Fall of American Federalism

Today's widespread tendency for Americans and their political leaders to see the various states as little more than administrative units of the national government is a relatively recent development that both obscures our view of history and disorients us politically.

The Founders did not invent federalism; they remodeled it. They were driven by the desire to design an arrangement by which the states would be more effectively unified for reasons of convenience and, more importantly, in their resistance to enemies of freedom both foreign and domestic. The resulting division of power—James Madison called it a "compound republic"[7]—was then understood as an important device in thwarting despotism: first, by keeping most governmental functions at the level closest to the people; and second, by limiting the power of both the state and national governments. In much the same way that the separation of powers between the three branches of the national government protects against tyranny by dividing authority and responsibility between the Congress, the president, and the courts, federalism divides power between the states and the national government. "[T]he power surrendered by the people," according to James Madison, "is first divided between two distinct governments, and then the portion allotted to each subdivided among distinct and separate departments. Hence a double security arises to the rights of the people."[8]

It would be a mistake, however, to characterize the Founders' view of federalism exclusively as a device to curb abuses by the central government. David Broyles has observed that under the Articles of Confederation, liberty was threatened by the actions of various state governments as well as by foreign enemies.

[F]ollowing the Revolution the states had done much to deserve . . . criticism, . . . and not just from headstrong nationalizers. . . . [I]rresponsible states were blocking national measures for which there was widespread support. . . . But, more importantly, . . . states were being untrue to republican principles by passing biased legislation to the advantage of favored classes of society.[9]

A federal division of power was intended to protect citizens from tyranny at the state as well as the national level. A national guarantee of a republican form of government for every state was understood as a necessary precaution against factional tyranny in the states. Nevertheless, the Founders clearly reserved a positive role in the constitutional order for state and local officials who, because of their proximity to the people, would be more responsive than national representatives. The wording of the Tenth Amendment reserving all nondelegated and nonprohibited powers to the states "or to the people" was no doubt crafted with this in mind.

The Founders hoped to create a political environment that would not only establish limited government but would also facilitate good government. Most of the affairs of Americans would be dealt with at the local level, because that is the level at which they would be best administered. The Founders were not antigovernment; they were against bad government—government that was either abusive or ineffectual. To Alexander Hamilton, "[t]he true test of a good government is its aptitude and tendency to produce a good administration."[10]

If most governmental functions would be handled at the state and local levels, with what would the national government concern itself? Madison noted that "great and national objects"[11] would not only be the focus of those sent to the nation's capital but that such issues would attract a moral and intellectual aristocracy[12] that would transcend the petty and partisan preoccupations that tended to prevail at the state level. Since the states would be left to manage most of America's regulation, taxation, and division of the spoils, those with the best minds and morals involved at the national level would struggle with the great issues of the day—"war, peace, negotiation, and foreign commerce."[13] State and local governments were crucial to the success of the central government because they served both to restrict and to liberate the range of national power to truly national interests.

The newly constituted form of government was understood and presented as "neither wholly federal nor wholly national."[14] Great deference was paid to the ongoing importance of the various states. This was done to assure citizens that the level of government with which they were most familiar and that they were most able to control would continue to be the most active in the regulation of domestic and economic affairs. Significantly, one of Madison's arguments that the proposed Constitution was indeed federal was that the states were the political units by which the people would approve it:

> [R]atification is to be given by the people, not as individuals composing one entire nation, but as composing the distinct and independent States to which they respectively belong . . . The act, therefore, establishing the Constitution will not be a *national* but a *federal* act."[15]

The Evolution of Federalism

The words *federal* and *national* have become synonyms. The confusion, if it can still be called such, is not new and it may be deserved. Even casual students of the Founding are aware that those working in favor of the initial ratification of the U.S. Constitution purloined the title *Federalists* in order to mask the strong national component of the document. Prior to the Constitutional Convention the thirteen former British colonies were "federal" in the traditional sense, since they interacted according to the Articles of Confederation under which there was in reality no national government. At that time "federalism meant . . . exactly what we mean now by confederalism: 'a sort of association or league of sovereign states.' "[16]

Neither the new Constitution nor its adherents were clear on the theoretical definition or practical operation of federalism. Alexis de Tocqueville observed:

> The first difficulty which the Americans had to face was how to divide sovereignty so that the various states of the Union continued to govern themselves in everything to do with internal prosperity but so that the whole nation, represented by the Union, should still be a unit and should provide for all general needs. That was a complicated question and hard to resolve.
>
> It was impossible to define in advance, completely and exactly, the share of authority which should go to each of these governments dividing the sovereignty.[17]

Two hundred years of experience have not clarified this division of power in name or practice. Whatever *federal* might have meant in the late eighteenth century has little in common with its contemporary usage.

How did the political environment change in America to cause the word *federal* to evolve in practical meaning from confederal to national? By 1788, Madison was already challenging some of his own earlier representations as to the federal nature of the Constitution.[18] Always the pioneer, Madison was one of the first to enter the debate on original intent. It is doubtful that the Founders ever reached an explicit consensus as to the operational boundaries of a federal system. If they did, any such understanding evaporated during their lifetimes.

The nationalizing policies of the Federalist party and early Supreme Court decisions affirming the supremacy of the national government,[19] as well as the Court's own power to review and strike down state laws,[20] launched the trend toward modern federalism before the new nation was half a century old.

The reformation of the founding which took place during the Civil War severely qualified the notion of state sovereignty. President Abraham Lincoln declared:

> Our States have neither more nor less power than that reserved to them in the Union by the Constitution—no one of them ever having been a State out of the Union. . . . Much is said about the "sovereignty" of the States; but the word even is not in the National Constitution, nor, as is believed, in any of the State constitutions. . . . [N]o one of our States except Texas ever was a sovereignty. . . . The States have their status in the Union, and they have no other legal status . . . This relative matter of national power and State rights, as a principle, is no other than the principle of generality and locality. Whatever concerns the whole should be confided to the whole—to the General Government; while whatever concerns only the State should be left exclusively to the State.[21]

Clearly, Lincoln did not believe the states were sovereign in the sense that they had the option to secede, but he gave nearly total deference to the states in terms of governing activities within their borders. The short-term effect of the Civil War was a "new and invigorated federalism in which both the states and the [central] government gained power" and in which there remained a "strong respect for states' rights."[22] The longer term implications of the Civil War amendments, which nationalized the meaning of citizenship, were not to unfold for decades.

The progressive era with its social and economic reforms ushered in the next major erosion in the remaining areas of state primacy. Misconduct by industries with the resources to control or evade state regulatory efforts prompted unprecedented national intervention in economic affairs and ushered in a new willingness by the American people to look to Washington rather than to their state capitols for protection from domestic threats to health and safety. Part of the legacy of Wilsonian progressivism was an increasingly large role for the national government. Reacting to the "gridlock" of his day, Woodrow Wilson advocated a shift away from traditional checks and balances in favor of a process that would serve as a "guiding and adjusting force—[a] single organ of intelligent communication between the whole Nation and the Government which determines the policy of that Nation."[23] The national government, through vigorous personal leadership in the presidency, would lead the nation in the cause of progress.[24]

Any residual popular resistance to an expanding national role was overwhelmed by President Franklin Roosevelt's vast programmatic responses to the Great Depression and World War II. As national dollars pumped life into the economy, states began surrendering autonomy in exchange for assistance and millions of Americans developed a new, personal relationship with their central government. V. O. Key described the changes and the times:

> The federal government underwent a radical transformation after . . . 1932. It had been a remote authority with a limited range of activity . . . and performed . . . functions of which the average citizen was hardly aware. Within a brief time, it became an institution that affected intimately the lives and fortunes of most, if not all, citizens.[25]

Harry Truman added stability and permanence to the expanded government and, by professionalizing the civil service, guaranteed a bureaucratic inertia that would long outlive him and other disciples of the New Deal.

Dwight Eisenhower attempted to delegate responsibility and authority back to states by establishing "the Commission on Intergovernmental Relations with the explicit charge to identify areas of federal involvement that could feasibly be 'returned' to the states."[26] He was unsuccessful not only because of resistance by Congress and the bureaucracy but also because of the governors' reluctance to accept control of politically challenging programs.[27]

Lyndon Johnson's Great Society constituted another giant leap in the growth of the national government. The states did not resist. Governors and mayors were more than happy to receive the flood of federal dollars even if they were accompanied by burdensome paperwork and regulation. Many found the programs so loosely supervised that it afforded them a flexibility never intended by Congress. The age of fiscal federalism had begun.

The New Federalism heralded by Richard Nixon was far more managerial than philosophic. It was not at all evident that Nixon disagreed with the expanded and expensive range of government services; he just wanted them delivered efficiently. The push toward flexible grants to state and local governments was not so much motivated by a desire to restore states to their rightful place in governance as it was an admission that the programs had grown so complex and comprehensive that they were no longer effectively managed out of Washington. By sending dollars with fewer strings to state capitols and city halls, more and more communities and organizations became dependent on funding from the national government.[28]

Jimmy Carter's main contribution to the evolution of federalism was massive infusions of federal dollars directly to the cities. This development, on the heels of the Nixon administration's scattering federal dollars, was to change the meaning of federalism to connote aid to cities that did not pass through the states.[29]

While paying homage to the role and rights of the states had long been standard fare for nearly all presidential candidates, Ronald Reagan made "the role of the states in the federal system a major campaign issue" in 1980.[30] Throughout his campaign and in his first inaugural address he employed the term New Federalism as a rallying cry for cutting the national government rather than in the Nixonian sense of spreading around more dollars through different channels. Reagan's efforts to send programs back to the states without dollars was greeted skeptically by state and local leaders. Nevertheless, Reagan's anti-big-government election mandate, combined with growing fiscal pressures, enabled him to substantially reduce the level of aid to subnational units of government. What governors and mayors pejoratively referred to as "Fend-for-Yourself Federalism"[31] temporarily replaced fiscal federalism.

After decades of free spending, most big-city mayors claimed that the financial crises faced by cities during the 1980s were exacerbated, if not caused, by Reagan's New Federalism. Such claims were not totally unfounded. Between 1980 and 1987 federal aid to urban areas declined by 47 percent. At the same time, all other federal grant programs, most of which were administered by the states, experienced a 47 percent increase.[32] However, most governors and legislatures, because of fiscal challenges of their own, lacked the capacity and/or willingness to come to the rescue of the large urban areas.[33] And they were hardly willing to offend their political subdivisions by defending the New Federalism, especially since many believed that Reagan's approach was less interested in balancing the federal system than in balancing the federal budget at their expense.[34] In short, by the end of Reagan's first term, New Federalism had come to represent little more than painful cuts in national programs and burden shifting to states and especially cities. Politically speaking, the issue was losing its appeal.

Bush attempted both to soften and to sophisticate Reagan's approach by pitching what might be called a New and Improved Federalism. In 1989 he met with governors at an Education Summit that produced a set of national education goals (e.g., national standards for English, history, math, science, and geography) and established targets for funding increases in areas determined by the governors to be the highest priorities. Even so, many governors facing financial difficulties at home were disappointed that more national dollars for education were not made available. Bush came away from the summit convinced that while the national government could play a role in promoting goals and standards, education had to be dealt with at the state level.

The Bush administration also crafted a major welfare reform package in response to requests by governors for greater flexibility to experiment with programs. The effort bogged down in Congress and was replaced by a waiver program allowing states to petition for exemption from certain national regulations. Only a few states opted to participate.

Bush's final attempt to implement his kinder and gentler federalism was the "turnback" proposal included in his 1991 State of the Union address. Governors had complained that their states would rather receive fewer national dollars in exchange for a reduction in the number of restrictions accompanying those dollars. Bush offered to consolidate large numbers of programs—many of which dealt directly with the cities—and turn them back to the states. Congress did not appear to be interested in reducing the number of programs under its direction. Cities and counties howled that they would rather deal directly with Congress than risk having their funds diverted by state governments with their own financial problems. Governors appeared no more willing than in Eisenhower's time to expend any political capital in order to ask for more responsibility. The "turnback" proposal died for want of a second.

Partisan politics also hampered Bush's attempts to develop a federal partnership with governors. As the 1992 election approached and his political vulnerability became more apparent, fewer and fewer

Democrats were interested in working closely with the president. This was especially true in the aftermath of the Los Angeles riots.

The Los Angeles riots briefly refreshed Bush's interest in federalism, but without much in the way of results. Several of his domestic policy team lobbied forcefully in favor of an aggressive urban renewal package including enterprize zones, reform in education and welfare, stimulus for capital formation, and anticrime measures. Congressional Democrats appeared disinterested in doing anything which might help Bush politically while House Republicans calculated that such programs were unlikely to help their reelection hopes since most GOP voters live in the suburbs, not the inner city.

Bush ended up backing a relatively modest emergency aid package for cities which passed Congress with little Republican support.[35] Perhaps convinced of the need to focus his own political efforts on the suburbs (i.e., middle class), Bush thereafter avoided big-city issues as well as big-city mayors.

Federal Cities

As campaign issues or areas of thematic focus, states and governors played a negligible role in 1992, but cities and mayors were prominent. Weary from years of decaying economic conditions exacerbated by reduced federal funding, the mayors organized early to extract pledges of support from presidential candidates. Their position was strengthened as a result of two developments. First, the dynamics of the three-way race elevated the impact that big-city voters would play in deciding the winner; and second, the Los Angeles riots dramatically highlighted the plight of large urban areas.[36]

Bush got off to a rough start in his reelection campaign effort to court urban voters. In his 1992 State of the Union address he attempted to imply support for and from mayors by announcing he had met with representatives from the League of Cities, which represents smaller municipalities, and that at their request he was going to appoint a commission on America's urban families. Boston Mayor Raymond Flynn, president of the U.S. Conference of Mayors (the organization which represents most of the larger urban centers), immediately blasted Bush, citing the President's refusal to meet with big-city mayors.[37] The following day, Baltimore Mayor Kurt Schmoke attacked Bush for "ignoring the mayors' pleas to include funding for urban economic initiatives in his 1993 budget . . . [and for failing] to address urban problems."[38]

The mayors were also unhappy with the Democratic contenders. Claiming they were dissatisfied with the level of commitment to funding the needs of the cities, the U.S. Conference of Mayors held off on endorsing a candidate in the Democratic primaries. They apparently never considered supporting Bush.[39] In an effort to "push urban needs higher on the presidential agenda" the organization hosted a debate between the Democratic hopefuls early in 1992 but came away frustrated "at their inability to get . . . candidates to devote much time to urban issues."[40] Flynn explained that "none of the major contenders performed strongly enough to merit" the organization's support.[41]

The obvious Democratic leanings of most big-city mayors did not restrain them from playing the Perot card in an effort to leverage more support for their issues. "We're loyal to the people of our cities," declared Mayor Flynn. "We're not loyal to any person or party."[42] Flynn had earlier vowed "to make candidates understand that if they don't address our needs, they're not going to have our support."[43]

In June 1992, several mayors—including Flynn—accepted Perot's invitation to give him "an honest evaluation of how . . . the federal government could be helpful meeting needs of American cities."[44] Perot promised to study their proposal for a $34 billion urban revitalization proposal, but declined to commit. Perot's book *United We Stand* was similarly short on specifics. He expressed a desire to make the "cities gleam" and a willingness to give inner-city residents a "lift to the first rung" of the ladder of opportunity. He promised to provide federal support for law enforcement and to fund a beefed-up program of enterprize zones. He was, however, critical of the "billions [spent] on urban renewal and model cities programs."[45]

Notwithstanding their brief flirtation with Perot, by late June the U.S. Conference of Mayors was ready to give Clinton some help. Even though he was running third behind Bush and Perot in the opinion polls at the time, Clinton had the Democratic nomination wrapped up and had come out in support of $200 billion in new domestic spending.[46] It was to this group's annual meeting that Clinton personally unveiled his long-awaited revised economic blueprint. The mayors' positive reaction to Clinton's plan was considered an important boost for his campaign at a critical time.[47]

Promising money to the cities was as close to federalism as any of the major candidates got in 1992. It is revealing of the state of the states that no effort was made to include governors in discussions of what ought to be done to assist cities. And the governors did not seem to mind. As the mayors hammered and hammered at the candidates for promises of more dollars, there is no record of any expression of the slightest concern about the onerous regulations which always seem to accompany such funding. Mayors appeared ready and willing to swap local governance for national money. The Founders' federalism had given way to the funder's federalism—which is no federalism at all.

The Procedural Federalism of Presidential Elections

The electing of a president, which is routinely referred to as a celebration of democracy, might also be recognized as a vestigial tribute to federalism. The principles of federalism can be credited for inspiring both the creation and the retention of the electoral system. The principles of federalism are also responsible for the degree to which states continue to control the time, place, and manner of presidential primaries and caucuses. Modern American presidential elections, even when they ignore federalism rhetorically, are still very federal experiences.

The source of the procedural autonomy of states in determining the allocation of presidential electors is found in Article II, Section 1 of the U.S. Constitution: "Each state shall appoint, in such manner as the legislature thereof may direct, a number of electors, equal to the whole number of senators and representatives to which the state may be entitled in the Congress."

The Supreme Court has long recognized the authority of each state to determine its own method of choosing and apportioning electors.[48] Convinced that it maximizes their political clout, most states allocate their electoral votes on a winner-take-all basis. But with all the complaints that the electoral system is too complicated and too detached from the vox populi for contemporary tastes, why has there been so little movement toward a state by state abandonment of the tradition of awarding all electors to the candidate receiving the most votes? Just as the Constitution suggests, any state legislature can opt for a more proportionate method of casting its electoral votes. Maine and Nebraska have exercised this right and use a modified winner-take-all approach by allocating only two of their electors on a statewide basis and awarding the others according to the preferences expressed by the majority of voters in each congressional district.[49]

The dearth of discussion about states altering their method of distributing electoral votes—a possible improvement short of discarding the entire electoral vote system—suggests that if elections are indeed tributes to federalism, they are tributes made in ignorance. With so little of a truly federal nature left in America, we ought not be too surprised if a constitutional device rooted in federalism goes unrecognized. Yet, however unappreciated, the Court has resisted efforts by several states to have the electoral system judicially dismantled.[50]

It was federalism that, in 1992, allowed Iowans to meet in January caucuses while Californians waited until June to vote in a primary. This very federal process requires presidential candidates and their strategists to do what most presidents and their bureaucrats avoid: treat states as states. Our current system of presidential primaries is a stark acknowledgment that in a day and age when states have retained very little authority over anything remotely affecting things national, state legislatures still decide whether to have a presidential primary, when it will be held, and what procedures will be followed. Considering the impact of primaries and caucuses on the choices available to voters in November, it is no small matter that states still exercise power over the timing and type of procedure used for selecting delegates to the national nominating conventions.

It is, however, important to note that the states' authority in this area is not absolute. The Supreme Court has ruled that in exercising discretion over time, place, and manner, state legislatures must conform to the rules established by the national committees of the political parties involved.[51] Interestingly, the practical impact of this ruling is that all states—if they want to hold the Democratic and Republican primaries or caucuses on the same day—must abide by the stricter and more numerous rules promulgated by the Democratic National Committee.[52]

Elections are the strongest remaining evidence of the federalism which once served as a defining attribute of American constitutional government. Whether they continue to be a useful instrument for limiting government or are now merely a well-preserved artifact of a bygone era is not clear. What is clear is that the U.S. Constitution provided that the various states would control elections. The structure of American presidential elections ought to refresh our awareness of and commitment to the principles of federalism, but the campaigns of 1992 had little corrective effect on our course toward minimizing the role of the states as meaningful governing units.

Should We Care About the Demise of Federalism?

In *Marbury v. Madison* (1803), Chief Justice John Marshall declared that one of the central purposes of the Constitution was to "define and limit" the power of the national government.[53] How prominently does federalism figure into these purposes? Can it be demonstrated "that the preservation of federalism . . . [is] as important to the preservation of liberty as is the safeguarding of individual rights"?[54] If a large, powerful central government without formal external checks is understood to be a threat to liberty, then federalism is an indispensable safeguard.[55] The continued erosion of the status of states, however, should alarm those committed to republican principles for reasons beyond the immediate prevention of tyranny.

Federalism is also important because it encourages good government. For example, state and local elected officials are far more accessible and accountable to the citizenry than those at the national level. Furthermore, each state is different and each community is different. Each has varying needs in terms of government regulation and services. National laws, programs, and policies are much less likely to take such differences into account. Federalism is vital in any area of governance where one size is unlikely to fit all.

The value of accountability is especially obvious when it comes to government spending. Forty-nine states have some form of balanced budget requirement which imposes the kind of fiscal discipline no member of Congress can imagine, much less emulate. For governors and state legislators the nexus between taxes and governmental services is a reality with which they and their constituents are well acquainted. Moreover, the fact that all but eight legislatures are part-time means that most state lawmakers spend more time paying taxes than spending them. Contact with other taxpayers is far more regular and meaningful than that experienced by their congressional counterparts.

The national government has proved itself to be incapable of limiting its appetite for spending. Programs bloat, deficits soar, and waste prevails. Even advocates of expanded national involvement in subnational affairs acknowledge that as a result of fiscal discipline, most states weathered recent recessionary stresses surprisingly well.[56] States make hard choices and balance budgets while the fiscal irresponsibility at the national level encumbers not only current citizens but future generations as well.

Perhaps one of the reasons that state governments have fared relatively well in recent decades is that the intense competition for power and resources which the Founders believed would be the burden of state legislatures has largely been absorbed by the national government. The national role and passion of interest groups has greatly intensified because Congress has become the primary focus of efforts to manipulate the distribution of public goods and services, the regulation of moral and economic interests, the collection of revenue, and the ratification of life-styles. The rank and file citizenry have become increasingly isolated, alienated, and poorly represented. Suspicion is growing that patriots possessing the best minds and morals are no longer interested in seeking a seat in a Congress which now busies itself with "lesser interests." Should we be surprised if those most inclined to concern themselves with "the great and national objects" presently find themselves disinclined to spend their lives trading pork-barrel projects, determining the availability of vitamins and the content of food coloring, setting rates for cable television, chasing misplaced Social Security checks, and running other reelection abetting errands under the rubric of "constituent services"?

The Founders' high-minded vision of a national government directed toward great and national objects seems remote from the contemporary political scene. The states, which were anticipated to be the locus of passion and pandering, now play only a supporting role in the national government's preoccupation with legitimizing and underwriting every imaginable individual desire. The level of government best situated by constitutional design to control public passions now services them recklessly.

If both the state and national governments have suffered from fading federalism, so too have the people. The more remote a government is from the citizens it governs, the less capable it is of teaching respect for laws and imparting the benefits of participation.[57] If what we think doesn't matter to the lawmakers, then the laws they make are less legitimate and less likely to be obeyed. The resultant decline in virtue endangers the republic, for the morality of the people was and is the primary precaution against the loss of liberty.[58] It also signals a corresponding reduction in human happiness. The Founders viewed morality as more than a "device employed by the statesman's prudence for political purposes"; for them virtue was understood to be an essential "ingredient in human happiness."[59]

But Who's Running America?

Does any of this matter if skeptics are right in their claim that what people really care about "is not which government proposes to act, but what action some government proposes to take''; and, that ''[i]nsofar as federalism blocks a national approach to a national problem, it makes policy less coherent and effective than it might otherwise be''?[60] In other words, if solecisms such as ''It's the economy, stupid'' are the soul of the new politics, are the ideas of limited government and division of power simply anachronistic inefficiencies preventing the trains from running on time? The campaigns conducted by all three candidates in 1992 suggest this may be the case.

Twentieth-century presidential rhetoric has evolved from New Deal to New Federalism to New Covenant. What is this new covenant that some claim we have entered into by virtue of the 1992 election results? And what constitutes the old or existing covenant that should now be discarded as obsolete? Are we being asked to abandon the covenant which serves as the very foundation of federalism—the covenant described by Daniel Elazar as the means by which free people ''form political communities without sacrificing their essential freedom and without making energetic government impossible''?[61] If so, it is no wonder that talk of sacrifice was postponed until after the election.

If the elections of 1992 did indeed signal the last gasps of federalism, we may want to consider the consequences of its approaching demise in terms of reduced personal freedom and happiness. Such remorse is hardly new. After Madison witnessed the excesses of the Alien and Sedition Acts, he modified his nationalistic views and longed for the safety provided by more vital states.[62] Is some similarly shocking development on the horizon that will persuade candidates in the 1996 campaign to at least discuss the need to revive the states? Time will tell. There would appear to be a surplus of potential crises and a scarcity of credible national solutions. How desperate must conditions become before those who would run America are willing to consider a truly federal approach? When and if these conditions occur, any renaissance of American federalism will need to be preceded by a recovery of its meaning. For neither voters nor candidates can be expected to value what they do not understand.

Acknowledgment

I am grateful to my colleague Ralph C. Hancock for his thoughtful comments, suggestions and support. Special thanks to Brant Bishop for his very valuable assistance. Research assistance was also provided by Matt Fairholm and L. J. Godfrey.

Notes

1. Samuel H. Beer, "Introduction," in Timothy Conlan, *New Federalism: Intergovernmental Reform from Nixon to Reagan* (Washington, D.C.: Brookings Institution, 1988), p. xii.

2. Bill Clinton and Al Gore, *Putting People First: How We Can All Change America* (New York: Times Books, 1992), pp. 56, 85–86.

3. Clinton and Gore, *Putting People First*, pp. 188, 190.

4. Clinton and Gore, *Putting People First*, p. 226.

5. Ross Perot, *United We Stand: How We Can Take Back Our Country* (New York: Hyperion, 1992), p. 83.

6. Perot, *United We Stand*, p. 79.

7. Clinton Rossiter, ed., *The Federalist* 51 (New York: New American Library, 1961), p. 323. All references are to this edition and will hereafter be cited as *Federalist*.

8. *Federalist* 51, p. 323.

9. David Broyles, "Federalism and Political Life," in Charles R. Kessler, ed., *Saving the Revolution: The Federalist Papers and the American Founding* (New York: Free Press, 1987), p. 71.

10. *Federalist* 68, p. 414.

11. *Federalist* 10, p. 83.

12. Thomas G. West, "The Rule of Law in *The Federalist*," in Kessler, ed., *Saving the Revolution*, pp. 159–62.

13. *Federalist* 45, p. 292.

14. *Federalist* 39, p. 246.

15. *Federalist* 39, p. 243.

16. Martin Diamond, "What the Framers Meant by Federalism," in Laurence J. O'Toole, ed., *American Intergovernmental Relations* (Washington, D.C.: Congressional Quarterly Press, 1985), p. 29.

17. Alexis de Tocqueville, *Democracy in America*, ed. J. P. Mayer, trans. George Lawrence (New York: Harper & Row, 1988), 114.

18. Jean Yarbrough, "Madison and Modern Federalism," in Robert A. Goldwin and William A. Schambra, eds., *How Federal is the Constitution?* (Washington, D.C.: American Enterprise Institute, 1982), pp. 84-96.

19. *McCulloch v. Maryland*, 4 Wheaton 316 (1819).

20. *Ware v. Hylton*, 3 Dall. 199 (1796).

21. Abraham Lincoln, *The Life and Writings of Abraham Lincoln*, ed. Philip Van Doren Stern (New York: Random House, 1942), pp. 670-671.

22. Alfred H. Kelly, Winfred A. Harbison, and Herman Belz, *The American Constitution Its Origins and Development* (New York: Norton, 1983), p. 327.

23. Arthur S. Link, ed., *The Papers of Woodrow Wilson*, Vol. 24, 1912 (Princeton: Princeton University Press, 1977), p. 418.

24. James Ceaser, Glen E. Thurow, Jeffrey Tulis, and Joseph M. Bessette, "The Rise of the Rhetorical Presidency," in Thomas E. Cronin, ed., *Rethinking the Presidency* (Boston: Little, Brown, 1982), p. 239.

25. V. O. Key, quoted in Conlan, *New Federalism*, p. 5.

26. Laurence J. O'Toole Jr., ed. "Overview," in *American Intergovernmental Relations*, 9.

27. Jeffrey R. Henig, *Public Policy and Federalism* (New York: St. Martin's Press, 1985), p. 23.

28. Conlan, *New Federalism*, p. 96.

29. Roy W. Bahl Jr., "Changing Federalism: Trends and Interstate Variations," in *The Changing Face of Fiscal Federalism*, p. 56.

30. Scott M. Matheson and James Edwin Kee, *Out of Balance* (Salt Lake City: Peregrine Smith Books, 1986), p. 22.

31. John Shannon, "The Deregulation of the American Federal System: 1789-1989," in *The Changing Face of Fiscal Federalism*, p. 28.

32. Helen F. Ladd, "Big City Finances in the New Era of Fiscal Federalism," in *The Changing Face of Fiscal Federalism*, p. 130.

33. Ladd, "Big City Finances," p. 148.

34. Matheson and Kee, *Out of Balance*, p. 30.

35. Ann Devroy, "The Reluctant Activist," *Washington Post*, August 17, 1992, p. A1.

36. David S. Broder, "Flynn, Jackson Seek Clinton's Urban Commitment," *Washington Post*, June 13, 1992, p. A12. Steven A. Holmes, "Undeclared Candidate; Mayors See Attention for Cities with Perot in Race," *New York Times*, June 9, 1992, p. A24.

37. Michael Rezendes, "Flynn and His 35 Guests Didn't Like What They Saw; STATE OF THE UNION ADDRESS," *Boston Globe*, Jan. 29, 1992, p. M17.

38. "Hill Briefs," *National Journal's CongressDaily*, Jan. 30, 1992.

39. Richard L. Berke, "Mayors Appear Unmoved by the Major Candidates," *New York Times*, Jan. 24, 1992, A14.

40. David S. Broder, "Democratic Hopefuls Vow to Aid Cities; Mayors Are Promised an End to 'Decade of Neglect' at GOP Hands," *Washington Post*, Jan. 23, 1992, p. A14.

41. Berke, "Mayors Appear Unmoved," p. A14.

42. Maralee Schwartz, "Perot to Discuss Aid to Cities with Non-Republican Mayors," *Washington Post*, June 8, 1992, p. A10.

43. Broder, "Democratic Hopefuls Vow to Aid Cities," p. A14.

44. Schwartz, "Perot to Discuss Aid to Cities," p. A10.

45. Perot, *United We Stand*, pp. 74–75.

46. David E. Rosenbaum, "Clinton and Tsongas Agree to Keep Brown's Issues Out of Play," *New York Times*, June 28, 1992, p. A16.

47. Jack W. Germond and Jules Witcover, "Clinton Finally Takes The Offensive," *National Journal*, June 27, 1992, p. 1539.

48. *McPherson v. Blacker*, 146 U.S. 1 (1892).

49. Thomas M. Durbin, "The Anachronistic Electoral College: The Time For Reform," *Federal Bar News and Journal* 39 (October 1992): 510.

50. *Delaware v. New York*, 385 U.S. 895 (1966).

51. *Democratic Party of the United States v. Wisconsin ex rel. Lafollette*, 450 U.S. 107 (1981).

52. Robert D. Loevy, "Colorado's First Ever Presidential Primary" (Pasadena, Calif.: Western Political Science Association, 1993), p. 9, photocopied.

53. Pete du Pont, "Federalism in the Twenty-First Century: Will States Exist?" *Harvard Journal of Law & Public Policy* 16 (Winter 1993): 139.

54. Daniel J. Elazar, "Contradictory Trends in Contemporary American Federalism: Courts, Congress and Centralization," *Journal of State Government* 16 (February 1989), p. 49.

55. Yarbrough, "Madison and Modern Federalism," pp. 88–89.

56. Shannon, "The Deregulation of the American Federal System," p. 31.

57. Gary L. McDowell, "Federalism and Civic Virtue: The Antifederalists and the Constitution," in Goldwin and Schambra, eds., *How Federal is the Constitution*, pp. 125–40.

58. *Federalist* 51, p. 322.

59. West, "The Rule of Law in *The Federalist*," p. 166.

60. Beer, in Conlan, *New Federalism*, pp. xi–xii. Beer uses this language to summarize the sentiments of skeptics of federalism's importance.

61. Daniel J. Elazar, "Our Thoroughly Federal Constitution," in Goldwin and Schambra, eds., *How Federal is the Constitution?* p. 61. See pages 58–62 for a more complete explanation of the relationship of federalism to the covenant principle.

62. Yarbrough, "Madison and Modern Federalism," p. 93.

Part Three

Political Issues

10

Pension Fund Democracy: The Economy in the Presidential Election Of 1992

Daniel Casse and Peter McNamara

There is widespread satisfaction with the way the 1992 presidential campaign was conducted, especially when compared to 1988. In 1992, it is said, the election was about "the issues" or rather *the* issue, the economy, whereas in 1988 the issues were lost in an empty debate about "ideology."[1] Economic plans, charts, graphs, and numbers were the unlikely stars of the 1992 campaign. One might even say that facts, rather than values, prevailed. Looked at from the point of view of the Constitution, however, there is reason to question the conventional wisdom. It is one thing to say that the economy is the main issue in a presidential election; it is another to reduce a presidential election to a referendum on economic performance. The latter implies that a political question is really a technical one and politicians need only be technocrats.

Each of the candidates in his own way contributed to turning the debate in this direction. Before taking up the individual campaigns, we need to consider more closely the relationship between the Constitution and the economy.

The Constitution and the Economy

The debate during 1992 presupposed that the Constitution exists to serve the economy by providing government the powers necessary for promoting prosperity. Furthermore, it presumed that the president is responsible for economic prosperity. Two developments of long standing gave shape to the debate.[2] The twentieth-century progressive understanding of the Constitution provided the general framework for the debate. The Progressives viewed the Constitution as a flexible document—a "living constitution"—that provides for activist government and popular presidential leadership of the nation. The second factor shaping the debate was social science. In the postwar era, the progressive view was leavened by the arrival of Keynesian economics which created the hope and, eventually, the expectation that the business cycle could be tamed. Moreover, modern economics produced a wide array of indicators to measure economic change, thereby adding to the appearance that matching policies against results was a simple technical matter. Keynesians now tend to be among the "graybeards," but the notion that the economy can be "fine-tuned" was a lasting legacy, even among the opponents of economic management. A dip in "the numbers" is almost always interpreted as a sign of failure. "Are you better off?" was a winning question for such advocates of the free market as Ronald Reagan in 1980 and, portentously, George Bush in 1988. If the Constitution serves the economy and there are unambiguous measures of economic performance, then the side with the economic theory that promises to keep the indicators moving upward ought to win. Conversely, a politician "caught in the grip of a failed economic theory," as Bill Clinton said of Bush, deserves to lose.[3]

Is this the correct view? The text of the Constitution itself provides no simple answer to the question of its relationship to the economy. It does not even speak of the "economy," but rather of things, at least to our ears, much less concrete, such as "commerce" and the "general welfare." Moreover, it gives to government certain powers over matters connected with the economy such as taxes, spending, borrowing, and so on, without, for the most part, specifying to what precise ends these powers be used. There is no suggestion that the government is directly responsible for economic performance, let alone quarterly economic performance. The reasons for the Constitution's silences are clear. It embodies the classical liberal presupposition that the responsibility of government extends only to providing the conditions, notably "liberty," "justice," and "tranquillity," under which individuals can, as Adam Smith put it, "provide a revenue or subsistence *for themselves*."[4] The performance of the economy is, ultimately, the people's responsibility. Government activism is not ruled out, but to the extent that the government does "regulate" commerce, it ought to respect the basic presupposition of individual responsibility as that most compatible with liberty and, in the long term, best for prosperity.

Furthermore, it seems a matter of simple political prudence to recognize that "liberal or enlarged plans for the public good" often involve temporary setbacks.[5] Thus any short-term responsibility for economic performance would defeat one of the purposes of the Constitution.

Yet it is not simply the case that the Constitution exists to serve the economy. In the first place, to the extent that national wealth is translatable into national power, the economy serves the Constitution by providing the means for its defense. The economy serves the Constitution in a further, less obvious, but perhaps more important way. The Constitution establishes a limited government for the sake of preserving liberty. Limited government requires a certain sort of people: one that does not ask for or require unlimited government. Individuals must believe they can "make it" on their own. If the economy encourages habits and virtues that support limited government, then the economy supports the Constitution. Today, Republicans tend to believe that a free economy promotes individual responsibility, especially when it is supported by strong private institutions like the family and religion. Democrats, by contrast, share in the deep skepticism of earlier Progressives as to the moral implications of a free economy. They see it as tending to promote a culture of irresponsibility which eventually spreads to all aspects of society, including politics. To counter the effects of the market, the progressive movement has tried to blend Alexander Hamilton and Thomas Jefferson, so to speak, by using government activism directly to promote a kind of individual independence and self-reliance. In line with their democratized and historicized understanding of the Constitution, progressive statesmen have been concerned less with maintaining limited government than with guaranteeing the level of equality and security they believe necessary for democratic citizenship and self-realization. In the 1970s, Lyndon Johnson's Great Society incarnation of the progressive movement began to falter as it became more and more clear that its principles set no intrinsic limits to the expansion of government. When Reagan took office in 1981, he could pronounce, with wide public support, that "government is not the solution to our problem," therewith inaugurating an attempt to return to the older view of the relationship between the government and the economy.[6]

Finally, we must ask who is constitutionally responsible for economic management? Again looking to the Constitution itself, we observe that responsibility for the economy seems to be divided, and divided unequally. The president's powers are clear-cut only in the areas of war and foreign policy, whereas his economic powers appear supplemental to those of the Congress. As a result of the dominance of the progressive movement, it is understood today, however, that the president must have a national vision, including an economic plan, for which he seeks the endorsement of the American people, even if this means going over the heads of Congress. Notwithstanding this development, the constitutional ability of Congress simply to ignore the president remains unchanged. Thus candidates are encouraged, beyond the normal incitements of a campaign, to promise more than they can reasonably hope to deliver and, once in office, seem doomed to fall short of expectations.

What ought we expect from a presidential election campaign that is shaped by the Constitution itself and where the economy is the main issue? First, a candidate should recommend those measures he thinks will, in the long run, most promote the general welfare and about which Congress ought to deliberate. Formulating an economic plan is as good a way as any of doing this. For reasons of self-defense once in office, he should make clear the part of his program for which he wishes to be held responsible, perhaps by foreshadowing the kinds of measures he will veto. Second, he must make clear how he will deal with economic issues that are not simply reducible to economics, such as foreign trade negotiations. This is the realm of the unpredictable and the exceptional and, as such, the true constitutional preserve of the president. Finally, he must not be blind to the ways in which the economy serves the Constitution. That is to say, he must make clear that the economic question is not simply a technical question.

The narrow focus on economic performance in 1992 obscured the richness of the choice confronting the people. It presented a particular difficulty for Bush. With the economic indicators either bad or equivocal, he needed to change the terms of the economic debate in order to win. Given the circumstances, this would have been a difficult task for any president. Bush's greatest failing was, however, his reluctance to try.

Caught With His Numbers Down

The failure of the Bush campaign has frequently been ascribed to a "communications" problem—it could not get a clear message to the voters. Yet the difficulties Bush suffered both as president and as candidate in dealing with economic issues are in fact rooted in the deep tensions within his own party regarding fundamental theories of government and economics. Bush, a politician with no appreciable tie to any ideology, found himself trying to please more than one constituency within his own party and several constituencies within the public at large. His economic policy while he was president was characterized by its apparent disinterest in any particular view of the relationship between government and the economy; in this, his presidency finds the greatest contrast with Reagan's, which championed the causes of deregulation and tax cutting. This lack of passion for a particular economic vision turned out to be a fatal weakness during 1992 when the country and media were consumed by economic issues, and both the president's rivals proposed ambitious and far-reaching plans to fix the economy.

Muddling the Message or Muddling Through?

Bush's political insensitivity to economic matters first surfaced in June 1990, less than eighteen months after he took office. Under pressure from Democratic congressional leaders, the Bush administration agreed in writing to discuss tax increases (euphemistically referred to as revenue enhancements) as part of a broader negotiation with Congress over the budget for the following fiscal year. What followed was a long set of closed-door negotiations between congressional leaders and the White House, the final rounds conducted at nearby Andrews Air Force Base to avoid distractions and press leaks. When the summiteers emerged, they announced a "budget deal" that essentially accepted tax increases in exchange for caps on new spending.

After a failed first attempt, the budget package passed the Congress, but not without many Republican defections. Ed Rollins, then the chairman of the Republican Congressional Committee, urged candidates to disavow the budget deal in the November mid-term elections; the Republicans ended up losing eight House seats.

The budget deal of 1990 turned out to be something of a watershed in the Bush administration. Conservative Republicans have tended to mark it as not only a broken promise, but the moment at which the party gave away the tax issue. While the deal continued to have its defenders (most notably Bush's budget director, Richard Darman), at the party's national convention in 1992 the president finally conceded that the deal was a mistake. Politically, however, the party's division over the budget deal characterized Republican schizophrenia on economic issues for the remainder of the administration.

Coincident with the budget deal was the end of more than five years of quarterly economic growth and the formal beginning of the recession. Although the economy showed negative growth for only three quarters, the anemic expansion of the economy throughout 1991 made this economic slowdown broader and longer lasting than the Reagan recession of the early 1980s. Yet the stagnant economy did not become a major issue for the administration until late in 1991, almost on the eve of the presidential primaries. Instead, through late 1990 and the first three months of 1991, the country, as with much of the world, was absorbed by the confrontation in the Persian Gulf with Iraq. The war gave Bush his greatest political strength; one poll showed him with a 91 percent approval rating, the highest in history. It was widely assumed that his success against Saddam Hussein would give him the political capital to take on a more ambitious domestic agenda with the Democratic Congress. Yet when he addressed a joint session of Congress at the conclusion of the war, his domestic agenda seemed focused only on the passage of a crime bill and a transportation bill. Moreover, his advisors were telling him that an economic recovery was just around the bend. As a result, the Bush White House seemed to stumble into the issue early in 1992, when a failed trip to Japan coincided with the media's discovery of voter resentment in economically depressed New Hampshire, and the emergence of Patrick Buchanan as a Republican challenger to the sitting president. Suddenly, the nation's economy was the primary challenge of the nascent Bush campaign.

Bush's Crazy Quilt of Economic Policy

Bush's 1992 State of the Union address struck the economic themes that would be sounded throughout the campaign year: lower taxes, free trade, tax incentives for investment, regulatory restraint, tax credits for education, and health care. His speech included a number of legislative proposals to enact this economic plan, virtually all of which were ignored by a Congress intent on denying a president legislative victories during an election year. Bush's repeated confrontations with Congress were soon overtaken by the emergence of Clinton as the Democratic front-runner and the arrival of Perot on the national stage. These candidates (along with Democratic candidate Paul Tsongas) forced the debate toward economic issues.

Incredibly, throughout the summer and even at his party's convention, Bush had never produced a formal, written description of his economic plan—particularly surprising in a year in which everyone else seemed to be touting a booklet or plan. It was not until September, at a campaign speech to the Detroit Economic Club, that Bush unveiled his "Agenda for American Renewal," a 29-page document that outlined the principal objectives of his proposals to improve the U.S. economy.

While the publication brought together under one roof, as it were, the many economic ideas Bush had promoted over the past three years, the document is most revealing in the way it demonstrated the complexity and confusion of the Republican argument. Although only a brief plan, the "Agenda for American Renewal" was a jumble of rhetoric, budget analysis, guiding principles, six-point action plans, themes, and subthemes, concluding with a thirteen-point strategy. But its basic economic thrust was as familiar as it was compelling: lower tax rates, limits on government spending, less economic regulation, free trade, and incentives for private, entrepreneurial investment. The plan also included—as had much of Bush's previous economic proposals—a far-reaching agenda for reform of the legal system, health care, public education, and job training.

Nevertheless, the agenda failed to capture the public's imagination and two months later Bush was defeated by a politician whose prevailing campaign theme was that the country needed a new economic plan. The reasons for Bush's ultimate defeat at the polls are manifold, but the reasons his economic arguments faltered are linked to the unresolved tensions inherent in the competing economic views that find their home in the Republican party. These tensions made defense of generally conservative, free-market principles (as opposed to the liberal interventionism and industrial policy advocated by Clinton) a difficult if not impossible task.

Growth versus Deficit Reduction. Throughout the Bush presidency, the administration and the Republican party in Congress remained deeply, if not clearly divided on the basic goal of economic policy. The Republican party has traditionally been associated with ideas often described as fiscal conservatism: balanced budgets and limited government spending. Today those ideas mostly take the form of a call for reducing the federal deficit, an idea very much at home inside Bush's administration. His 1990 budget deal was an (unsuccessful) attempt to bring federal spending under control. His speeches throughout the campaign year were full of rhetoric about reducing government waste, and he proposed eliminating dozens of government programs. During the summer of 1992, the White House became engaged in an unsuccessful attempt to pass a balanced budget amendment through Congress.

All these actions had the endorsement of his senior economic advisers and his Treasury Department. But they had only lukewarm support from a group of younger Republicans, led by Housing Secretary Jack Kemp, who advocated a more radical "growth" agenda, focused on reducing marginal tax rates and refocusing government spending to "empower" poor Americans to economic independence. While the debate between these two factions rarely emerged on the campaign trail, the need to appease both sides robbed Bush's arguments of boldness and intensity. The deficit hawks argued primarily from the perspective of restraint: the need to control annual increases in mandatory spending coupled with the gradual reform of current programs. The growth advocates, on the other hand, called for a focus on job creation through tax cuts, privatization, and increased government spending to support entrepreneurial activity in the inner city, regardless of the short-term budget consequences. The former group spoke of regulatory restraint; the latter preferred Reagan-era "deregulation." The tension between the two economic theories resulted in an underwhelming Republican argument for both restraint and renewal, prudence and boldness; it attempted to praise the risk taking of entrepreneurial capitalism while promising economic security.

Government Programs versus Shrinking Government. Bush came to power promising a "kinder, gentler" government. He tried to keep that promise by embarking on government programs, particularly environmental and social programs, that marked a departure from Reagan-era spending cuts and deregulation. In his first two years in office, Bush signed both the Clean Air Act, an ambitious environmental package to control industrial and automobile emissions, and the Americans with Disabilities Act, which provided new protections and mandated services for the physically disabled. These two pieces of legislation were often cited as key accomplishments of the administration.

What he would discover in 1992 was that these laws, along with other programs he had advocated or expanded, were at odds with the type of economy he was espousing. The implementation of the Clean Air Act and the Americans with Disabilities Act created a period of reregulation not seen since the late 1970s. Yet his economic proposals of 1992 argued that burdensome regulation was precisely what had slowed down the economy. Similarly, while Bush chastised the Democratic

Congress for unrestrained spending, it was in fact his administration that had proposed enormous budget increases in social programs that the Reagan Administration had cut or leveled off. Programs long associated with liberal largesse such as Head Start, federally funded drug and alcohol treatment, and literacy grants saw their budgets vastly expanded during the Bush years. Virtually all of Bush's campaign material pointed to budget increases in programs as evidence of the administration's accomplishments in those areas. Hence, the incoherence of the Republican position lay in the confounding argument of promising to cut government, while boasting about having enlarged it. The price of a kinder, gentler America turned out to be exorbitant.

Government Concern versus Laissez-Faire. What the Bush campaign confronted in 1992 was that the slogan it used to sell its economic vision—"government is too big and it spends too much"—required a complete break with the kind of constituent-pleasing spending the administration had encouraged for more than three years. The problem with less spending is that it earns a politician a reputation of cold-hearted callousness; that at any rate was the reputation Reagan cheerfully lived with while he advocated cuts in federal programs. Yet in the winter of 1992, when Bush's pollsters reported to him that the majority of Americans did not believe he cared about how the recession had hurt them, his response was to travel to New Hampshire, the critical primary state, and announce: "Message: I care."

This sentiment, however welcome in New Hampshire, begged the essential question of whether a more caring government was better for the economy and the nation. Much of Bush's economic program implied that the country would do best when government intervened least in the private sector. Lower taxes, less regulation, fewer trade restrictions, and less spending were all indirect methods of showing compassion by stimulating the economy. But in the midst of economic hard times, this argument is difficult for any politician to make. It essentially requires a policy of doing less to demonstrate that you are doing more. This apparent paradox is at the heart of the dilemma that most conservative Republican politicians face when they wish to advance a modified version of laissez-faire economics while courting voters who hold their government responsible for domestic problems.

The solution to the dilemma that Reagan understood but Bush and his advisors never did is that free market economics must, at some point, concede that government itself is the problem; the market controls the economy while the government only interferes with it. For Bush, this argument was out of reach. His campaign depended on too many proposals, agendas, and programs. Economic health would return, he repeatedly argued, if Congress would pass his economic plan. Through these statements, Bush implicitly accepted the role of the nation's chief economic administrator, never appreciating that the components of his economic plan did not depend on who implemented them. Free market policies are government programs that don't require a lot of government. But because Bush wanted to demonstrate how much his administration cared about the economy, he unwittingly weakened his broader argument about the need to diminish government's role in commercial matters.

Putting People First

Coming out of the Democratic National Convention in July, Clinton was in the driver's seat. He held more than a twenty-point lead in the polls, and voters rated him better able to manage the economy than Bush by a two-to-one margin.[7] His task from then on was to avoid the fate of Michael Dukakis in 1988 who had let a large lead slip away between the convention and election day. Good luck and shrewd politics both played a role in Clinton's success.

Clinton's Challenge

The Clinton campaign recognized that the lingering recession was their trump card. "It's the economy, stupid!" read the sign on the wall of campaign headquarters. Given the terms of the debate, which, as we have pointed out, Bush was largely responsible for, only unmistakable signs of a boom might have saved the president. Pinning the blame for the recession on Bush was the thin end of a very large wedge Clinton used to drive between the Republicans and the Reagan-Bush Democrats who had been so critical to past Republican successes. Bush, Clinton argued, had compiled the "worst economic record in fifty years" through mismanagement and neglect. He was portrayed as both incompetent and as unconcerned with the things that concern ordinary Americans. But the real villain was Bush's mentor Reagan, the architect of "trickle-down economics," the economic theory that went along with the "corrupt do-nothing values of the 1980s." As a result of the "something for nothing decade," most Americans—the poor and the "forgotten middle class," those who "played by the rules"—were working harder for less and living in "fear" because of poor health care, or so, at least, went the story line of this economic morality play.[8]

Clinton linked the recession to the sins of the 1980s and, ultimately, to a long-term deterioration of the American economy. Just as he glossed over anything good in the current economic indicators, he also glossed over any of the accomplishments of the Reagan era. The concession that Reagan had not created, but had only greatly exacerbated, the inherent problems of the American economy was really to Clinton's advantage. He was adamant that he was not proposing a simple return to the pre-Reagan era. So as to avoid the "L-word," which Bush had used with such devastating effect against Dukakis, Clinton crafted a timely and accessible message designed to recapture the political center. It offered a "vision" and a "plan." The vision was of a united American people competing successfully in the global economy. The plan—"Putting People First"—was, in essence, an economic plan. Clinton formulated a plan early in his campaign believing, correctly, that it would be an important part of any victory strategy.[9] The plan served as a kind of psychological anchor for the Clinton team, reassuring them that they had something to say and a right to say it.[10] "Putting People First" was a revised version of the original plan. It was presented to the public on June 20 and it constitutes one of the landmarks of the beginning of the resurgence of the Clinton campaign after a period of disarray following the entry of Ross Perot. Careful attention was paid to the form as well as the substance of the plan. While clearly in the progressive tradition, Clinton ran as a "new kind of Democrat" with new ideas and a new vocabulary. Recalling Franklin Roosevelt's Commonwealth Club Address, he promised a "new covenant" between the government and the people: the government would provide "opportunity" and, in return, it would demand "responsibility." While hardly political poetry, the message was both clear and nuanced. The objective was to emphasize Clinton's break with Great Society liberalism's politics of compassion and economics of redistribution.[11]

Rather than respond in detail to Clinton's economic plan or defend the 1980s, the Bush camp tended to be dismissive. Clinton really was "a liberal," they said, but without any sustained attempt to explain why. Clinton responded forcefully to any suggestion that he was a liberal by saying that his new ideas transcended the liberal-conservative gridlock of recent decades and were simply better means for promoting "middle-class values of work, faith, family, individual responsibility, and community." "Ideas, not slogans" was Clinton's challenge to the Republicans.[12] When coupled with Republican ineptitude, this tactic had the effect of shutting off debate on the substance of Clinton's liberalism. Clinton met with considerable success in convincing voters that he was a new kind of Democrat who could successfully manage the economy. In order to determine the character of Clinton's break with earlier Progressive liberals, we must take a closer look at his plan.

The Clinton Plan as Economic Strategy

While "Putting People First" has a populist ring, Clinton is not at all a populist. He means to put "people," not "the people" first. He promised to make the notion of "putting people first" the "fundamental idea that guides our administration," describing it as "the heart and soul of our national economic strategy—and the key to the American future." "Investing in ourselves," he argues, is both the key to economic growth and the key to reversing the "unravelling of the American community."[13]

The plan shows very clearly the mark of Clinton's close friend and campaign adviser, now Secretary of Labor, Robert Reich. It was Clinton's acceptance of Reich's neo-Dickensian worldview that led him to regard a moderate, if somewhat idiosyncratic, recession as a sign of a coming social and economic apocalypse.[14] Reich believes that the internationalization of the American economy has created a crisis for American democracy. He warns that Americans are becoming more independent of each other, at the same time as a privileged few are being integrated into the world economy. As a result, the face of the American community is being reshaped. Those who can make it in the new global economy are "seceding" from the rest of the United States. Because the rich are abdicating their responsibility for the poor, the American community is disintegrating. Crime, poverty, and indifference are the result. During the 1980s, Reich argues, these trends were exacerbated by policies that favored the wealthy and underinvested in people.

The strategy of putting people first has two main elements: the new covenant and investment and growth.

Opportunity and Responsibility. The idea of reciprocal obligations on the part of citizens and government constitutes Clinton's alternative to the boundlessness of the politics of compassion. On close inspection, however, the new covenant proves to be both less than it seems, and not at all what it seems.

Under the "new covenant," the government will provide expanded opportunity, for example job training and education, and in return, it will demand responsibility by requiring that once the training program is completed the beneficiary seek a private sector job. Failing this, he will be required to take a community service job. The stern justice of the bargain is more apparent than real because it is stipulated that the community service job must be "dignified and meaningful."[15] Why then prefer a *real* job? Furthermore, is there enough dignity and meaning to go around and at a price the government can afford? For those with high-paying jobs, the new responsibility simply means higher taxes. Clinton believes that those who disproportionately benefited during the 1980s need reminding that they are part of the American community. The implication is that the American community can be reintegrated through the tax code.

Looked at from a slightly different perspective, the Clinton plan represents not so much a retreat from the progressive agenda, but a radical intensification of the central paradox of the Progressives: the promotion of independence by means of government activism. Clinton's use of the term opportunity involves something of a sleight of hand. The economy itself provides the real opportunities. What he intends to provide is not so much opportunity as the skills one needs to take advantage of an opportunity. The presumption is that one can be held accountable for one's situation only after one has been provided with the skills necessary to take advantage of an opportunity. What is distinctive about Clinton is his understanding of what is necessary to raise individuals to a level where they can be held responsible. Earlier Progressives took for granted social institutions like the family and mores such as responsibility. As a result, they failed to see the unanticipated consequences of their policies. Clinton recognizes the interdependence of the economy, social institutions, particularly those with responsibility for the education and rearing of children, and government. "Putting People First" tries to correct for past failures by recommending that government take these social institutions more completely under its wing. Despite Clinton's disclaimer that "governments don't raise children," the document is replete with remarkable assertions to the effect that through programs and incentives government can inspire parents to be responsible (with "innovative parenting programs") and inspire students with "an ethic of learning."[16] Instead of fewer programs, then, Clinton promises more. Whether this can be done cheaply by "reinventing government" misses the point. The Clinton promise is really one of pervasive government.[17]

He sees this as compatible with "responsibility" because he believes that, ultimately, we are not truly responsible for who we are. The old idea, that one can make it on one's own, forgot the extent to which we are shaped by forces outside of us. The Clinton plan makes no clear division between what is an individual responsibility and what is a governmental responsibility. In fact, it presumes that no such division really exists. The radicalness of Clinton's project, as well its sense of urgency, is deepened by his acceptance of the social revolution of the 1960s which questioned the legitimacy of social institutions earlier Progressives had taken for granted. One can no longer be sure that the traditional family, for example, is a satisfactory way to raise children, hence a need for increased supervision. Furthermore, government policy must respect and cater to other life-style choices. "Putting People First" is, in effect, a program for a postmodern version of the Great Society.

Investment and Growth. Clinton's promise to "grow the economy"—a formulation whose sheer awkwardness ensured that it would stick in voters' minds—represents a reaffirmation of the idea of a progressive economy and a break with the economics of redistribution. Here again the departure from Great Society liberalism is more apparent than real.

The key to growth, according to Clinton, is investment, public and private. The Clinton plan contains provision for a variety of incentives for private investment such as an investment tax credit, tax incentives for research and development, and measures to encourage small businesses. This goal is, however, dwarfed by the emphasis on public investment. The meaning of public investment in the new Clinton vocabulary is expansive. All government expenditures that produce a social return are classed as investments. There is nothing problematic in itself about this definition. What is problematic, however, is the low standard of proof required for establishing the fact of a social return. The Clinton definition of investment is at its widest when it comes to "human" capital. Everything from prenatal and infant health care to vocational training falls under the umbrella of human capital investment. Clinton's theory reverses the Reagan-Bush presumption that the private sector is the engine of economic growth. Instead, he sees the public sector as driving the private sector. This amounts to an inverted supply-side theory of the economy: whereas supply-siders favor continual tax cuts, Clinton favors continual public investment, both in the hope of a future payoff, and regardless of immediate consequences. For Clinton, public investment in human capital is really the equivalent of providing opportunity. As we have seen, the provision of opportunity allows for government involvement in all aspects of life. What the Clinton theory of public investment does is provide an economic rationalization for providing opportunity. In the thrift-conscious 1990s, as opposed to the spendthrift 1960s, this is the kind of argument required to sell activist government. Just as the new language of opportunity and responsibility did not close the door to unlimited government, neither does the language of investment and growth.

A Plan to Govern?

Whatever the intrinsic merits of Clinton's brand of liberalism, the plan was defective in that it did not prepare the way for governing. To begin with, it did not take into account the constitutional limitations on the power of the president. Clinton ran as though he would be all powerful, rather than as an officer in a constitutional government of divided powers. Indeed, he implied that making the economy grow was a power squarely within the grasp of a strong president. In office, he has had to adapt to the realities of governing in a world where inspirational rhetoric gets you only so far. This adjustment has been all the more difficult because the plan did not make clear the choices confronting the nation. Despite its vaunted specificity, the plan was unrealistic and evasive in crucial respects, particularly on the question of the deficit. During the campaign, Clinton used a heavy dose of class warfare rhetoric to unite the poor and the middle class against the rich and the Republicans. In power, he will likely be faced with the choice of either expanding the deficit or reminding the middle class that he has not forgotten them by increasing their taxes and, thereby, putting his coalition at risk. This choice would be difficult at any time, but it will be particularly so after the advent of Perot.

Putting *The People* First

The first installment of the Perot campaign was very successful, but lacked organization and focus. He dropped out just as things were beginning to fall apart. When Perot reentered the race in October, his campaign focused almost exclusively on the deficit. In August, he had issued an economic plan, *United We Stand: How We Can Take Back Our Country*,[18] which contained a program to cut the deficit and promote economic growth.

Perot made the deficit issue his own. As far as he was concerned, it was the "first priority." With the aid of his infomercials, his bar charts, and his homey metaphors, he was able to invest an economic abstraction with moral and practical meaning. The deficit was the "crazy aunt" no one wanted to talk about. It was a "bleeding artery" that had to be stopped. Above all, he drew the analogy between the federal budget and the budgets of individuals and corporations. As a result of the deficit, he argued, the national debt was piling up so fast that future generations would be robbed of their legitimate inheritance. To make his point, he would cite numbers so large they defied human comprehension. Surely there was a crisis! Much could be said of Perot's use of figures, especially his failure to put anything into a relevant perspective. Moreover, he was generally vague as to precisely how the deficit affected economic growth. His chief and, perhaps, only argument was that at some point in the future the United States, like any individual or corporation, would go broke from too much borrowing. Perot's candidacy indirectly helped Clinton because it heightened the sense of crisis. He helped directly by refraining from confronting Clinton on the question of the deficit.

In addition to highlighting the deficit problem, Perot presented a diagnosis and cure. The problem had its source in politicians, bureaucrats, and special interests who had turned the political process into a vehicle for self-enrichment. The cure was a dose of austerity strictly administered by Perot himself. Perot called for a wide variety of spending cuts and tax increases. The plan ventured into areas where most politicians had feared to tread: entitlement reform, especially for more wealthy recipients, cuts in agricultural and mortgage interest subsidies, as well as a hefty increase in the gasoline tax.

The other side of Perot's program was uncannily like Clinton's. He promised incentives for business, greater cooperation between business and government, and more programs (including expanded health care coverage). Only Perot's more forthright rejection of free trade distinguished him clearly from Clinton. The plan earned Perot widespread praise for confronting the unpleasant subject of deficit reduction. Less attention was paid, however, to the question of the plan's implications for economic growth and to the cost of some of his promises, especially on health care. On this score, Perot might be accused of wanting to have his cake and eat it too.

If Clinton was able to give "new class" values a common touch, it might be said that Perot was able to do the same for idiosyncracy. His campaign does, however, have a wider significance. During the campaign he criticized the Constitution as unsuitable for the management of a modern economy. Instead, he spoke approvingly of the "new" constitutions as well as the economic policies of Japan and Germany.[19] He criticized "ideology" as another obstacle to getting on with the job of righting the country's wrongs.[20] Perot brought to the campaign not so much a plan of action as a promise of decisiveness. His special promise was not to let "politics," meaning the political process, get in the way of the will of the people. Perot liberated himself from all but the first three words of the Constitution. With his 19 percent of the vote and his unrestrained populism, he is surely capable of being a political force in the future. Even if his star fades, the Perot strategy is available to anyone who is able to make a similar promise at a time of real or imagined crisis.

The President as Pension Fund Manager

As was pointed out earlier, the election of 1992 was not the first to use past economic performance as a basis for passing judgment on incumbent presidential candidates. Bush used the economic record of his predecessor to help gain the presidency in the first place. But in Bush's case, what seemed a political virtue in 1988 became a vice four years later when his own economic record was scrutinized. He was a prisoner of the arguments that brought him to office.

The 1992 campaign emphasized recent economic performance as the ultimate criterion for presidential selection more than any other past election. The data from monthly and quarterly economic indicators were used throughout the year by all candidates to make their case. Only days before the election, the Bush campaign trumpeted the news that third-quarter GDP figures showed 2.7 percent growth. In this regard, presidential candidates have become something akin to pension fund managers, desperate to hold onto their jobs by pointing to their last quarter profits.

This development cannot be welcome news for either the economy or the Constitution. The undue emphasis on recent swings in the U.S. economy discourages medium to long-term policies that are the only genuine options available to a president who typically must wait the better part of a year for Congress to enact or reject his proposals. More important, the tendency to hold a president responsible for national economic performance is to imply that presidential management and administration have the most direct effect on economic welfare. The Constitution, on the other hand, implies that a president cannot ensure prosperity, but he must be held responsible for ensuring the means to prosperity. This argument has been lost in the current debate over which economic platforms will better reduce unemployment or enhance exports. The tendency to watch the numbers exacerbates the populism inherent in the polity, transferring something of the mood of the investment markets into the political world. On Wall Street, a rumor or an anomalous figure can sometimes scuttle the prospects for an otherwise sound investment or it can become the basis for tales of a new Eldorado.

Clinton's electoral victory is due, in part, to a rejection of the Constitution's view of government and the economy by promising that his administration will make Americans better off. Furthermore, he has promised both to restore the progressive tradition of activist government, while at the same time reining in its tendency toward unlimited government. An examination of his economic plan suggests that its underlying principles do not check this tendency. If there is to be a check on the scope of government, it will have to come from outside through either budget constraints or public opinion. Clinton's principles do put him in a better position to deal with election year questions about the economy. He can always promise to do more. But it was just this kind of activism that precipitated the Reagan revolution. Moreover, the techniques of campaigning he helped pioneer might just as easily be turned against him, magnifying short-term economic problems into crises and preventing his administration from taking a long-term view.

The failure of Bush was a result of conceding the premise of Clinton's argument; although he advocated a limited role for government in the economy, he did so because he believed it would produce better fiscal results. Having seen the fiscal results of four years in office, the public, looking to the future, could still have judged him by his political and economic principles rather than by the nation's economic performance. But because Bush chose the promise of better economic performance rather than principle as the basis for his reelection bid, the American people, taking him at his word, held him responsible for the lackluster economic performance on his watch.

Notes

1. See, e.g., the arguments and data in the essays by F. Christopher Arterton and Kathleen A. Frankovic in Gerald M. Pomper, ed., *The Election of 1992: Reports and Interpretations* (Chatham, N. J.: Chatham House, 1993). See also Joe Klein, "The Year of the Voter," *Newsweek: Special Election Issue,* November/December 1992, pp. 14–15. Self-satisfaction among liberals has led to a certain amount of triumphalism. See, for example, Gary Wills, "The End of Reaganism: How the Feelgood Era that dawned in 1980 foundered on recession, mean-spiritedness and missed opportunities," *Time,* Nov. 16, 1992, pp. 73–76.

2. Jeffrey Tulis brings out the distinctiveness of the Progressive view in *The Rhetorical Presidency* (Princeton: Princeton University Press, 1987). The question of the Constitution and the economy is explored with great insight by Harvey C. Mansfield in Chapter 3 of *America's Constitutional Soul* (Baltimore: Johns Hopkins University Press, 1991). Our argument draws on both these discussions.

3. "A New Covenant," speech to the Democratic National Convention, New York City, July 16, 1992 in Bill Clinton and Al Gore, *Putting People First: How We Can All Change America* (New York: Times Books, 1992), p. 222. This book brought together the Clinton-Gore positions on a wide variety of issues. It incorporated Clinton's economic plan, "Putting People First: A National Economic Strategy for America." All references to Clinton's economic plan are to the version that appears in this volume.

4. *An Inquiry into the Nature and Causes of the Wealth of Nations* (Indianapolis: Liberty Classics, 1981), p. 428 (emphasis added).

5. The words quoted are Publius's, *The Federalist Papers* (New York: Mentor, 1961), 30, p. 191.

6. "First Inaugural Address," *Inaugural Addresses of the Presidents of the United States* (Washington D.C.: Government Printing Office, 1989), p. 332.

7. For a synopsis of the polling data, see Peter V. Miller, "The 1992 Horse Race in the Polls," in William Crotty, ed., *America's Choice: The Election of 1992* (Guilford, Conn.: Dushkin, 1993), p. 142. Data on economic management is presented in Kathleen A. Frankovic, "Public Opinion in the 1992 Campaign," in Pomper, ed., *The Election of 1992,* p. 125.

8. Clinton and Gore, *Putting People First,* pp. 3, 5, 8, 14, 20, 67.

9. Clinton presented the first version of his plan as one of a series of three policy speeches given at Georgetown University in November 1991. A considerable amount of thought went into the speech on the economy. See the account of James A. Barnes, "The Hard Charger," *National Journal,* Jan. 18, 1992, pp. 126–31.

10. "Specificity," said Clinton Communications Director George Stephanopoulos, "is a character issue this year." Quoted in Klein, "The Year of the Voter," *Newsweek,* November/December 1992, p. 15.

11. For example, Clinton's advisers urged him to mention "work" as often as possible in order to emphasize his break with the public philosophy of handouts. See *Newsweek*, November/December 1992, p. 42.

12. "Announcement Speech," Little Rock, Arkansas, Oct. 3, 1991, in Clinton and Gore, pp. 188, 192.

13. Clinton and Gore, pp. 4, 7, 53, 143.

14. Reich's (latest) views are spelled out in his ambitious book *The Work of Nations: Preparing Ourselves for 21st Century Capitalism* (New York: Vintage Books, 1992).

15. Clinton and Gore, p. 165.

16. Clinton and Gore, pp. 17, 60, 85, 221.

17. Note the extraordinary scope of the set of programs Reich would seem to regard as ideal, *The Work of Nations*, p. 247.

18. (New York: Hyperion, 1992).

19. Remarks made on *Good Morning America*, Oct. 22, 1991, reprinted in *Ross Perot Speaks* (Rocklin, Calif.: Prima, 1992), pp. 15–16.

20. Perot, *United We Stand*, p. 35.

11

Religion and Family Values

Gary D. Glenn

In 1992, the family values issue largely took the place occupied by the religion issue in the two Reagan campaigns. Religion, or what people believe about God, and the place of that belief in public life, had been a great issue in 1980 and 1984. Ronald Reagan had then galvanized the hitherto largely apolitical religious right in order to challenge the prevailing secular liberal domination of American public life, especially of public schools. George Bush did not choose to appeal to the religious conservatives in 1992 by a Reaganesque challenge to public secularism as such. Instead of defending Reagan's conviction that religious faith and prayer should be an integral part of our public life, Bush defended the traditional morality shared by many of the religious faithful, regarding abortion, sexual behavior, and especially the family as hitherto understood. Still, religion and family values belong together in analyzing the campaign because family values are dependent on and derived from religion. Hence, an attack on or defense of one involves an attack on or defense of the other.

Religion

Understanding the religion issue in the 1992 campaign requires comparing it with that of the 1984 election. At that time, President Reagan and the Democratic presidential nominee, Senator Walter Mondale, joined by Senator Edward Kennedy and Governor Mario Cuomo, conducted perhaps the most thorough debate concerning the place of religion in American public life ever seen in our electoral politics.[1] This judgment may seem to damn with faint praise, except that important issues are hardly ever debated in modern election campaigns in a serious and thoughtful way.

The 1984 debate began with President Reagan's speech of August 23,[2] immediately following the Republican convention. His concern was to defend a place in public gatherings and public life for public expressions of faith in, acknowledgment of, and reliance on God; and the right of citizens who believed in God to seek to form public policy in light of the moral teachings derived from their faith. Reagan argued that, since 1962 (when prayer was banned from public schools), the Supreme Court had gradually but consistently banned such public expressions of religious faith, on the grounds that this was required by the First Amendment establishment clause. The Court interpreted this clause as requiring a "secular" public life, that is, one conducted without public reference to God, or to morality based on divine revelation, or to a future life of rewards and punishments.

Reagan argued that until the 1960s "the state was tolerant of religious belief and practice" but that since then the courts in particular had become increasingly "intolerant of religion." Beyond public prayer he argued that "those who believe must be free to speak of and act on their belief and to apply [religiously based] moral teaching to public questions." This had been our tradition from the Mayflower Compact down to the beginning of the courts' replacement of religion with secularism in the 1960s. Reagan's attack focused on, but was not limited to, the Supreme Court's removal of prayer and religiously grounded moral standards and instruction from public schools and on the Court's hostility to public financial support for religious schools.[3]

Mondale was reportedly incensed at the "intolerant of religion" charge. Within a few days,[4] he responded with an impassioned speech restating the secular liberal view that suppression of prayer in public schools was true toleration. It was only an "extreme [religious] fringe" of the Republican party that was intolerant, guilty of "moral McCarthyism," and "sought to impose their beliefs on others." And he condemned Reagan for seeking an alliance between that religious intolerance and politics.

Kennedy joined in a few days later. His principal contribution to the debate was to make explicit that it is not only symbolic issues such as prayer in schools that are at issue but moral issues like abortion, prohibition, and sexual identity. Morality, of course, is not religion, although the two are closely connected. To some extent, then, the debate about the relation of religion and politics seemed to be a way of discreetly debating what should be the relation of public policy to the moral behavior of citizens.

Kennedy argued for the widest possible separation of public policy from personal moral behavior. Accordingly, he regarded Reagan's religious supporters' opinions as a disease "infecting" the presidency, and claimed that they had no constitutional right to advocate adoption of their policy positions on abortion, prayer, and sexual identity. They were not only wrong; they were beyond the constitutional pale.

Cuomo shortly thereafter gave a long-scheduled speech at Notre Dame University reflecting on the relation of his Catholic morality and his public duties.[5] He developed the view first articulated by John Kennedy in the 1960 presidential campaign, that a Catholic politician's public policy views had no necessary relation to his personal religiously grounded morality. Cuomo developed this argument more deeply than Kennedy in keeping with the greater importance of the issue Cuomo faced. That issue was abortion. Abortion, he affirmed, was morally wrong for himself and his wife, but it was impracticable to attempt to transform this essentially private morality into public policy. Going further, he advocated the use of public funds to pay for abortions. In defending his policy position, he stressed the great importance of prudence in applying moral principles to politics and to that extent he followed traditional Catholic moral teaching. However, he appeared to depart from that teaching by refraining from saying he thought abortion was morally wrong for others, thus silently accepting the relativist view that what is moral for me may not be for you.

The 1992 campaign saw no similar debate about the relation of religion to politics despite the fact that, during Bush's presidency, judicially imposed secularism proceeded apace, most visibly in public schools. In 1992 the Court had declared officially sponsored commencement prayers unconstitutional.[6] This continued the direction of the earlier prohibition of officially sponsored classroom prayers (1962),[7] Bible reading (1963),[8] the posting of the Ten Commandments (1980),[9] "moments of silence" (1985),[10] and the requirement that creation science be taught along with evolution (1987).[11]

More ominously, during Bush's term the Court ended its twenty-year willingness to compensate religious citizens for requiring them to live, without their consent,[12] in the secular state the Court has created. That compensation had been in the form of court-ordered exemptions (based on the free exercise clause) from otherwise valid secular laws, when the Court judged that their constitutionally protected religious freedom was unnecessarily restricted. However, in 1990 the Court decided that such judicially created free exercise exemptions would no longer be given.[13] Hence, not only was expression of collective religious faith in public gatherings increasingly forbidden, but now previous judicial constitutional protections against legal violations of individual conscience were removed.

Thus, by 1992, judicially mandated public secularism was more thoroughgoing and less accommodating to religious believers than in 1984. Accordingly, what is most revealing about the religion issue in 1992 is how little Bush did to raise it. He did not protest against the removal of religion from public life and public protection during his watch. And it was not Bill Clinton's issue inasmuch as the judicial secularizing of public life since World War II has been led by Democratic justices, mostly appointed by Democratic presidents, and supported by Democratic elected representatives.[14] Public secularism is a liberal Democratic goal. Conservative Republicans like Reagan fight it publicly. Bush's silence reflected his moderate Republican policy convictions, which concern capital gains tax cuts and free trade, not religion. During the campaign, his publicly combative conservative Republican critics like Patrick Buchanan and William Bennett fought that battle.

However, Bush once raised the religion issue in a way similar to Reagan in 1984. In Dallas, again just after the Republican convention, Bush spoke of "the breakdown of the American family" and the "erosion of traditional moral and religious values on which our very Nation was founded."[15] Restoration of what he here, perhaps for the first time, called "family values" requires "increasing our faith in God."

Bush expressed concern primarily about the morality to which religious faith was a means of restoration. In contrast, Reagan also defended the symbolic and ceremonial place of religion—recognition of and thanksgiving and prayer to God—in our public life as a good apart from religion's utility as a foundation for morality. Bush was not inclined to discuss or defend religion publicly or to relate his religious convictions to policy. This difference, like Bush's silence on public secularism, roughly tracks the difference between Reagan's conservative and Bush's moderate Republicanism. Both men, and both sorts of Republicanism, advocate traditional moral values. Bush and moderate Republicanism are uncomfortable with public professions of faith and share with secular liberalism the belief that religion should be a private matter.

Bush did not discuss what government could do about increasing religious faith. "[G]overnment policy" could "make a difference," however, in supporting sound family values. He indicated the policy differences for which he had fought: "welfare law changes to encourage families to stay together, fathers to stick around, children to be able to save a little money when their mother's on welfare, so they can get educated." And he tied these policies to religion by saying that he had successfully fought to make federal child care assistance available in religious settings and supported giving "Federal money to working parents so that they can choose the best school for their children," including religious schools.

Clinton, unlike Mondale in 1984, did not rise to the bait. So there was no serious discussion of religion in public life. Bush's Dallas speech was ignored also by the media except for one statement in which he chided the Democratic party for omitting the word God from its platform. This remark touched off a brief brouhaha, though Clinton seems to have ignored even that. Press commentators generally thought it both in bad taste and mere posturing. The *New York Times* editorially blasted Bush for "questioning the religious convictions of his opponents"; for threatening to "divert attention from Topic A, the economy"; for "an unhealthy revival of the holier-than-thou religiosity America tried to put behind it in 1960"; and for attempting to "exploit" the "explosive division" of "the nation along religious lines." Bush remained silent about this dismissal of religion as merely irrelevant, divisive, and dangerous. Nor did he again try to smoke Clinton out on the platform's failure to pay even the customary lip service to Divinity.

That was the end of the religion issue. Bush did not really try to make an issue of the judicial removal of religion from public life. He said and did just enough to show the flag to his conservative religious supporters, without Reagan's sort of root and branch challenge to liberal secularism.

Family Values

"The heart wants, what the heart wants."[16]

In contrast to religion as such, "family values" was a hot issue in 1992, perhaps the most effective in terms of popular appeal that Bush had going for him. It began with Vice President Dan Quayle's May 19 speech which, along with Patrick Buchanan's address to the Republican National Convention, became one of the two most discussed speeches of the campaign. Originally titled "The Family Comes First," it immediately came to be known as the "Murphy Brown" speech.[17]

Reflecting on the Los Angeles riots three weeks earlier, Quayle argued that "unless we change the basic rules of society in our inner cities, we cannot expect anything else to change." The rules in question were "the baby boom generation's" embrace of "casual sex and drug use, evasion of responsibility and trashing of authority." These had created a "poverty of values" disastrous for all of society but especially for those in the inner cities. The rules breakdown was a generational—rather than racial, ethnic, or class—phenomenon. Those in the inner cities, in particular black and Hispanic minorities, only suffered the consequences of the generational rules breakdown more intensely.

Quayle noted some factual differences between black poverty in the 1960s and the 1990s. In 1967, 68 percent of black families were headed by married couples, whereas in 1991, 48 percent were. And in 1965, 28 percent of black children were born to unmarried mothers, while in 1989, 65 percent were. "Marriage is probably the best anti-poverty program of all," he argued. "Among families headed by married couples today, there is a poverty rate of 5.7 percent. But 33.4 percent of families headed by a single mother are in poverty today."

The speech became famous for its criticism of an event from the popular sitcom *Murphy Brown*. Here is the widely quoted passage:

> Bearing babies irresponsibly is, simply, wrong. Failing to support children one has fathered is wrong. We must be unequivocal about this. It doesn't help matters when prime-time TV has Murphy Brown—a character who supposedly epitomizes today's intelligent, highly paid, professional woman—mocking the importance of fathers by bearing a child alone, and calling it just another "lifestyle choice."

He concluded with a call to talk publicly about the "traditional values" denigrated by "cultural leaders in Hollywood, network TV, and national newspapers" especially the value of "family" which he defined as "two parents, married to each other." It was necessary to define family since, as became explicitly clear in the ensuing uproar, the word no longer had a commonly agreed meaning.

The *Chicago Tribune* would later say that this remark "set off a national debate over family values, single parent households and alternative lifestyles . . . and in September, 70 million viewers tuned in the season premier of 'Murphy Brown' in which she offered her prime-time responses to Quayle's remarks."[18] To characterize what transpired as a "debate" is generous. Syndicated columnist David Broder more accurately noted that Quayle's speech was "serious and sensible" but that "the press went crazy" over the criticism of the television show "and thereafter any real discussion was buried in hoo-haws over Quayle and Murphy Brown."[19]

The press dramatically affected the controversy by the rhetoric in which it reported the speech. The term "family values" did not appear in the text of Quayle's speech. The *New York Times* invented that tag in the headline of its front-page story on May 20. This gave an important spin to the subsequent discussion. "Family values" is substantively empty. Hence, instead of conveying Quayle's support of traditional values and traditional families and as he had described them, it set up Quayle's liberal critics to retort that there are many kinds of families and many kinds of family values. The family values tag also made it seem that instead of properly criticizing morally irresponsible fathers who impregnated women and then failed to stay around to support them and their children, Quayle was heartlessly criticizing only single mothers who were trying to do the best they could in difficult circumstances.[20] Quayle complained about this misrepresentation, but did not connect it to the media's slanting of the terms of debate.

Since Quayle had spoken about what he twice called "traditional values," the more accurate media tag would have been "traditional family values." The *Times'* continuation of the May 20 story headlined the more accurate quote "poverty of values." Mainstream media commentators mostly ridiculed Quayle's "family values" speech. One of the more clever parodies of Quayle was syndicated columnist William Neikirk's satire of Republican "values vouchers," containing the motto "Be Good, Be Rich" and "which conferred good-behavior status, lower insurance rates, cheaper health insurance, first access to job interviews, and a preferred status in hiring," all "without spending a dime."[21] The *Chicago Tribune* editorially objected to the ridicule, noting that Clinton did not share in it but promised to do a better job than Bush at supporting traditional values.[22] Clinton himself apparently said almost nothing else about family values during the campaign. The debate, or rather the manipulation of symbols, was among the media (including "Murphy Brown" herself), Quayle, and media commentators.

There was a small strand of genuine debate about Quayle's speech, represented by syndicated columnists William Raspberry and Joan

Beck. They agreed with Quayle that traditional family values needed to be restored. Raspberry, however, argued that the speech revealed "the absence of common-sense connection between the problems Quayle diagnoses and the treatment he prescribes." Raspberry contended that a common cause of all the problems Quayle cites is lack of jobs. "[W]ith the exception of enterprise zones," however, there was "nothing on it [Quayle's list of proposed reforms] that even pretends to deal with the problems Quayle raised in his speech."[23] Raspberry was silent about whether restoring jobs will be enough to restore the "family structure, personal responsibility and social order." But he seemed to suggest that good economics is primary and good personal moral behavior follows.

On the other hand, Beck suggested that bad personal moral behavior, not bad economics, is the primary cause of broken families. "Unless the number of fatherless children and families headed by a single woman can be sharply reduced," she argued, "current and future remedies for poverty and other social problems will not be maximally effective." Two particular behaviors that needed changing are the sexual revolution—which "removed some of the social constraints on sex outside of marriage"—and that part of feminism which discounts "the importance of men in the lives of women" and which makes "having children without a legal husband a sort of celebrity chic—a lifestyle choice that can be devastating if copied by an inner-city teenage girl."[24]

Angry hostility was the common media reaction to Buchanan's family values speech at the Republican convention. Buchanan declared that American society was being torn apart by a "culture war." Columnist Ellen Goodman saw it as a strategy to "divide and conquer" which "pitted traditional against non-traditional families, working against non-working mothers." R. W. Apple Jr. referred to it as "demonization."[25] After the election, reactions blended into an undifferentiated remembrance of the "family values" theme. Albert Shanker, president of the American Federation of Teachers, praised the Republican defense of "traditional family values."[26] Richard Weissbourd still thought—what was not said about Quayle's version—that the family values issue "seem[ed] intolerant, less an appeal to an ideal than a cudgel"; it "reek[ed] of sanctimoniousness" and "phoniness."[27] David Gergen, then editor of *U.S. News and World Report,* said that many people heard the marching of feet behind the rhetoric.[28]

That some moderates who agreed with the substance of the family values appeal were discomfited by the manner it was presented suggests "how difficult it is to talk about the problem of single-parent families."[29] One reason for the difficulty is that while decent people should admire and encourage single parents who "have managed to raise strong, decent children with solid values," single parenthood is, generally speaking, not as good for children as having two parents. Hence, leaders and policy should publicly support "the overriding importance of two parent families that make child care their central responsibility." To that end, they should encourage marriage as a permanent commitment, not a mere temporary convenience. In particular, leaders should say that it is wrong to bear children out of wedlock.[30] And it is wrong for fathers to be missing from families. The difficulty is that saying these decent truths appears to cast aspersions on, hence demoralize, single mothers struggling to do their best for their children. Moderates are thus uncomfortable criticizing single parenthood and hence uncomfortable with public statements that defend the superiority of traditional two-parent families. In 1992, Republicans seemed unable to find a rhetoric which simultaneously encouraged the person so circumstanced yet also disapproved of the circumstance and of those behaviors which commonly lead to the circumstance.

Immediately after the election, media commentators made an effort to discredit the political efficacy of the family values issue. The *New York Times* asserted that Bush "was widely thought to be hurt by the backlash to the 'family values' appeal." This backlash was said to have been due to the suggestion "that those who failed to follow the prescriptions of Pat Robertson and Patrick J. Buchanan, a pair of right wing orators given prominent time slots [at the Republican convention] were somehow not fully American." The *Times* even suggested that "there were indications that Republican denunciations of non-traditional families may have alienated more voters than they attracted."[31] The *Times'* evidence supporting the alleged "indications" of "backlash" was that "half of single people, half of single parents and more than half of working women voted for Mr. Clinton, while a third of each group voted for Mr. Bush. Seven in 10 homosexual and bisexual votes backed Clinton."

The *Times* did not report the proportion of married people, married people with children, nonworking women, and heterosexuals who voted for Bush although, since Clinton won the election, most of some groups obviously supported him. Contrary to the *Times'* claim that the Republicans "may have alienated more voters than they attracted" with "family values," the following evidence (from the same *Times* articles) might perhaps show that "family values" attracted more voters than they alienated. Clinton won "just over a third of the homemaker vote, with close to half going to Mr. Bush." And "[m]ore than half of those who said abortion should be always illegal or mostly illegal cast their votes for the President." The "backlash" thesis might be true but its truth is established neither by the evidence offered in the *Times* nor by the *Times*' silent omission of contrary evidence.

Abortion and the Family Values Issue

Abortion intruded into the 1992 presidential campaign in a way that shed light on what was really at stake in the family values issue. This was when both Bush and Quayle said, in response to reporters' questions, that they would counsel their own granddaughter or daughter against having an abortion but support her if she decided to have one.[32]

Prominent newspapers gave front-page coverage, as well as editorial support, to abortion rights advocates who said that in this response Bush and Quayle hypocritically embraced *personally* what they reject *politically*; that they had inconsistently but calculatedly adopted the pro-choice position; that they wanted to make an exception for *their* (grand)daughter. Television comments were more venomous, suggesting not only that these Republican males were hoist on their own petard but that they were hardhearted and judgmental toward the everyday woman who wants an abortion but compassionate and forgiving toward their own (grand)daughter who might want one.[33]

Neither Bush nor Quayle intelligently defended their position against these charges. That position rests on the simple thought that decent parents love and stand by their children even when they do something which, by the parents' lights, is a serious wrong. They try to dissuade their children, informing them of their disapproval should they choose to do wrong. If the children do wrong anyway, decent parents do not approve what they *did* but still approve of *them*; support *them*; comfort *them*; are there for *them*. Why? Because they love them and will help them go on, help them learn to live with their past as all of us must learn to live with what we have done. That is one thing it means to "be a family."

This simple thought arises from the more complicated thought that decent parents love *both* their children *and* the right, as it is given to them to understand the right. These loves sometimes conflict. They would have conflicted, for the president and vice president, if the child they loved decided to wrongly kill the innocent human life (as it seemed to her father and grandfather) which she carried. Even those who disagreed about the wrongness of abortion should still have understood that when two loves conflict, there will be a breaking, if only of the heart. Decent parents wish to love their children both because they are theirs and because they live according to the right the parents have tried to teach them. They might have to love their children without that harmony, however, though it should break their hearts to do so. In doing that, parents do not love their own children better than the right. Rather they love their children because they are their own. They are *family*.

Bush and Quayle were accused of hypocrisy but a broken heart does not indicate hypocrisy. Hypocrisy is choosing contrary to what one has declared to be choiceworthy; it is making an exception, for personal advantage, to some rule of right that one has defended. In this case, the alleged hypocrisy is the preferring of one's own flesh and blood, but not the flesh and blood of others, to one's stated principles. But the stated principle in this case was that abortion is a moral evil, not that we should hate or despise those who chose to have one. Where is the hypocrisy in doing what we can to dissuade our children from doing what we think is serious harm, and if we fail, then to do as Bush said, very much from the heart, he would do: "put my arm around her . . . love her, and help her, lift her up, wipe the tears away and . . . get [her] back in the game"?

In truth, the Bush-Quayle political position supported, rather than contradicted, their stated personal commitment to the loving support of their child who might choose to have an abortion. Here is why. Our political system legally permits abortion virtually on demand. This "almost anything goes" public policy puts an enormous moral burden on parents who would counsel their pregnant daughters that deliberate abortion is almost always the unjustified killing of an innocent human life. Present law undermines these parents by teaching their children that abortion is neither right nor wrong, but only a morally neutral choice. Thus, present law undermines the moral influence of pro-life parents over *their* children and supports the moral influence of pro-choice parents over theirs. Bush and Quayle's political position sought to put the moral influence of law on the side of pro-life parents in counseling their children.

Honest pro-choice advocates naturally opposed Bush and Quayle's pro-life political position because they disagreed with it. This is fair political disagreement. Thoughtful and fair pro-choice people could understand that Bush and Quayle were consistent in their political and personal positions. Some, however, saw hypocrisy and a "winking" toward a covert pro-choice position. This revealed how little such people understood about decent parents who stand by their children even when they break their hearts by doing what seems to them seriously wrong, about the love and protectiveness decent fathers have for their daughters, and about the enormous personal moral burden present law places on parents who think abortion morally wrong.

This "hypocrisy" charge sheds light on the family values debate by suggesting that contemporary advanced liberalism fosters a learned incapacity to comprehend primary human attachments, such as family. It is certainly at moral and legal war with families as hitherto understood. Evidence of this, and one of contemporary liberalism's major legal victories in that war, has been to give minor children the legal right to abortion without their parents' knowledge and against their wishes. By this victory, liberalism took away the legal right of pro-life parents to protect their children against abortion. It thereby rejected such parents' morality that abortion is an evil against which their daughters, and their daughters' unborn children, needed to be protected. And it by law imposed on those parents a new morality, according to which deliberate abortion is morally neutral but the right to choose abortion is of the essence of being a free woman. Government thereby erected a moral wall of separation between minor children and their parents.

Contemporary liberalism does not admit that imposing its principles on others by law is imposing a morality. When it imposes on others, by law, its view of how those others ought to live—in this case how parents should raise their daughters respecting abortion—it understands what it is doing as protecting rights—in this case what it now calls "reproductive rights"—not as imposing a particular morality. Thus by definition, only conservatives are capable of imposing their morality on others, which they do by restricting abortions. This semantic sleight of hand conceals the artful repressiveness of contemporary liberal politics which, when adequately understood, both makes defensible and explains its active proscription of even those who are otherwise liberals. *The* campaign example of this was Democratic party leaders' refusal to allow Governor Robert Casey of Pennsylvania to present his pro-life views to the national convention. Speaker after speaker made much of the convention's "diversity" and "inclusiveness." Public recognition, even honor, was given to numerous interests, including sexual life-style interests claiming the name "family," which were not families as hitherto understood. The "diversity" and "inclusiveness" of the convention did not extend, however, to the recognition of pro-life views and interests.

This points to the artfulness of that advanced form of liberalism which controls the present Democratic party. Some more traditional liberals thought the exclusion hypocritical because of the convention's public commitment to inclusiveness. However, it is not hypocritical once one understands that the dominant liberalism's "inclusiveness" excludes some views. Exclusion is injected into, and justified within, inclusiveness by the assumption that *only contemporary liberalism's policies* respecting abortion can legitimately be made into law; *only its view of right* is within permissible policy consideration; and *only its understanding of rights* is within the meaning of the Constitution. On this assumption, opposing views on abortion are not merely wrong but beyond the pale, and hence rightly excluded from the diversity and inclusiveness which informed the convention scheduling.

In other words, the inclusive assumption *prohibits* what the inclusive principle *appears* to require. And since the principle, but not the assumption, was frequently and loudly proclaimed, some who heard the principle were deceived as to its meaning. The artfulness is that "inclusive" used without qualification means something to the ordinary listener that it does not mean to those who understand the assumption. This is deception, not hypocrisy. Does not this explain why, for contemporary liberalism, anti-abortion laws impose one's morality on others, hence are not permitted; whereas pro-choice laws protect rights, hence are compulsory? Because choice is compulsory, it not only justifies but requires government to repress parents' rights until abortion becomes the framework within which family is understood, in order to prevent them from raising their minor daughters according to pro-life moral values.

One might say Bush missed an opportunity to reveal this liberal repressiveness for what it is to traditional liberals and moderates who might not support his pro-life position but might have been more appalled at repressiveness if they saw it as such. However, that expects a great deal of Bush since the repressiveness of such liberal rights is rhetorically well camouflaged. The rhetoric is simple: abolish restraints on what a pregnant child wants to do. How doing that is repressive is more complicated. Can any rhetoric make it intelligible to the generality of Americans? It takes more than a thirty-second sound bite to show the repressiveness behind the talk of inclusiveness, diversity, and choice.

The rhetoric of choice obscures the astonishing boldness of contemporary advanced liberalism's war on the family. That rhetoric claims not to know whether anyone should have an abortion. However, defending minor children's legal right to an abortion against their parents' will implies that liberalism knows what is best for those children better than do their parents. The rhetorical denial of knowledge masks an actual (though implicit) claim to superior knowledge. The war on the family goes deeper. It is a war of ideas before it is a war over power and policy. Its spearhead idea is that minor children are more fundamentally individuals than they are members of families. This idea justifies the state intervening on behalf of a minor individual against her parents not, as hitherto, to prevent manifest harm (such as child abuse) but in a disputed matter of choice. Contemporary liberalism, however, thinks that being unable to choose to have an abortion is a harm that justifies state intervention in a formerly private family relationship so as to legally transfer the right to decide what is harmful from the parents to the child.

The liberal attack on Bush and Quayle's "hypocrisy" was not merely an opportunity to attack them for electoral advantage. It was a further stage in the development of a generation-long liberal legal and moral attack on the traditional legal and moral restraints which support (traditional) families. The spearhead of that attack was *Roe v. Wade* (1973). There liberalism captured the authority of the Constitution and the Supreme Court to teach the American people to be morally indifferent to abortion and thus to permit it legally. Soon thereafter, the same authority took away from parents the right to protect their unwed pregnant child from a predictable consequence of that publicly sponsored teaching, namely, the child's desire to have an abortion.[34]

The attack's plausibility depends on the relativist theory that whether to have an abortion is merely a consumer choice, like preferring Marlboro cigarettes over Camels. Abortion's choiceworthiness is subjective, idiosyncratic, personal, and hence the business of individuals. It is not a matter of moral right and wrong valid for human beings as such and hence not the business of government, law, or society. Law teaches, however, and theories have practical consequences. Relativist theory's practical effect has undermined self-restraint in male/female relations and especially the responsible procreation of children.[35]

The accusation of hypocrisy against Bush and Quayle manifests the latest practical consequence of relativist liberal theory as it progressively transvalues traditional Judeo-Christian morality and the family law derived from that morality. That consequence is that pro-life parents must choose either to denounce and abandon their pregnant child who chooses abortion or else give up their political opposition to abortion. This whipsaw nicely fits pro-choice stereotypes about pro-life parents, namely, that they are rigid, simplistic authoritarian moralists devoid of love and caring about women, who therefore must be hypocrites if they support and love a child who has an abortion. In other words, if you wish to be a loving and supportive parent, you must be a liberal.

By embracing *Roe* twenty years ago, liberalism "reinvented" itself so as to lose its ability to appreciate the sanctity of what it traditionally had regarded as innocent human life. Should we be surprised that it now cannot comprehend a decent man's unconditional love for his (grand)daughter? Bush and Quayle could give no good reasons why they would love and support their errant (grand)daughters. This defect would seem to have arisen out of the ordinariness of their decency rather than out of hypocrisy. They surely never dreamed it necessary to have such reasons because, among ordinary decent people who are neither intellectuals nor philosophers, loving support of erring children is natural and needs no defense. (This is not to say it is easy.) Nature supplies such affection spontaneously if not corrupted by problematic theories about privacy and individualism. That such loving parental support must now be defended with reasons shows the corruption of opinion produced by those theories.

Postcript

The family values campaign quarrel had a remarkable postscript. The April 1993 issue of the *Atlantic Monthly* printed a long article by Barbara Dafoe Whitehead entitled "Dan Quayle Was Right." The thesis was that dissolution of two-parent families is generally harmful to children and that the increasing number of single-parent and stepparent families dramatically weakens and undermines society.[36]

What is this—a mainstream popular magazine printing an article supporting *by name* Dan Quayle and the Republican family values position? And that was not all. A virtually unanimous chorus of media commentators took public notice of the article and agreed with it.[37] No ridicule. No hoo-haws about Murphy Brown. How could Dan Quayle, the fumbling, bumbling, object of media mockery, have been right? And if right, why was he so held up to derision and scoffing? It seems there were media commentators who agreed with Quayle during the campaign, but not only would they not say so, they even ridiculed him. What's going on here?

James Q. Wilson's explanation about the same phenomenon among scholars might apply here. "Many scholars feel, I believe, that to support the claim of family decline is to give aid and comfort to conservative politicians and religious leaders who bemoan that decline and call for the reassertion of 'traditional values.' "[38] That is to say, in the spring of 1993 journalists could say what Quayle and Buchanan said in the summer of 1992 without supporting a conservative or a Republican president against a liberal Democratic challenger.

Moreover, with liberal Democrats controlling both ends of Pennsylvania Avenue, family decline has new liberal political possibilities. Instead of supporting the conservative moral message that parents should sacrifice higher living standards by someone staying home and raising their children, it supports further taxing working fathers and homemaker mothers to subsidize child care for those who won't or can't. Instead of implying moral self-restraint in having children, and self-sacrifice in rearing them, it implies expanding the welfare state to try to cope with the consequences of the lack of these virtues.

The family values postscript shows how hard it is, and how high the price, for honest people in a campaign to speak the truth, as it seems to them, given the prostitute and daring venality, not to speak of the disingenuousness, of contemporary political (especially journalistic) commentary.[39]

Notes

1. I present an interpretation of this debate in "Rhetoric and Religion in the 1984 Campaign," *Political Communication and Persuasion* (1988), Vol. 5, pp. 1–13.

2. There had been some preliminary skirmishes principally in June 1984 when Archbishop John O'Connor of New York had publicly criticized Democratic (and Catholic) vice-presidential candidate Geraldine Ferraro for what he said was her false representation of Catholic teaching on abortion. Ferraro was pro-choice and had circulated a letter to Catholic members of Congress arguing that the Catholic position on abortion was not "monolithic." Therefore, she argued, they could in good conscience also be pro-choice. The Archbishop responded that the Catholic position on abortion *is* monolithic. Going beyond

that, he opined that he could not see "how a Catholic in good conscience can vote for a candidate who explicitly supports abortion." Governor Cuomo defended Ferraro. This incident created considerable public controversy and was the direct inspiration for Cuomo's Notre Dame speech discussed below. See Glenn, 1988, p. 3.

3. See *Weekly Compilation of Presidential Documents*, Monday, Sept. 3, 1984, Vol. 20, No. 35, pp. 1159–61.

4. Mondale's speech is excerpted in the *New York Times*, Sept. 7, 1984, pp. A1-5 and A14.

5. Cuomo's speech was excerpted in the *New York Times*, Sept. 14, 1984, p. A22 and reprinted in full in the *Notre Dame Magazine*, Autumn 1984, pp. 21–30.

6. *Lee v. Weisman* 504 U.S. (to come). 112 S.Ct. 2649 (1992).

7. *Engel v. Vitale*, 370 U.S. 421, 82 S.Ct. 1261 (1962).

8. *Abington v. Schempp*, 374 U.S. 203, 83 S.Ct. 1560 (1963).

9. *Stone v. Graham*, 449 U.S. 39, 101 S.Ct. 192 (1980).

10. *Wallace v. Jaffree*, 472 U.S. 38, 105 S.Ct. 2479 (1985).

11. *Edwards v. Aguillard*, 482 U.S. 578, 107 S.Ct. 2573 (1987).

12. "Without their consent" in the sense that there is no way for citizens to give or withhold consent to Court decisions. They can do so for decisions of their executive and legislative representatives who are elected and removable. The Courts have imposed secularism on religious citizens by declaring unconstitutional laws reflecting that religiosity which have been passed by these representatives. To my knowledge, no acts of elected and removable representatives of the people have required public secularism except those done under judicial constraint or compulsion.

13. *Employment Division, Department of Human Resources of Oregon, et al., v. Smith*, 494 U.S. 872; 110 S.Ct. 1595 (1990).

14. Presidents Roosevelt and Johnson appointed Justices Douglas, Black, Stone, and Marshall. Eisenhower, however, appointed Chief Justice Warren and Justice Brennan. I said *mostly*.

15. "Remarks at the National Affairs Briefing in Dallas, Texas," Aug. 22, 1992, in *Weekly Compilation of Presidential Documents*, Monday, Aug. 31, 1992, Vol. 28, No. 35, p. 1485.

16. Woody Allen justifying his affair with the then minor daughter of his live-in girlfriend Mia Farrow during a custody hearing, spring 1993.

17. This was the title as the speech was printed in *Vital Speeches*, Vol. LVIII, No. 23, Sept. 15, 1992, pp. 711–12.

18. *Chicago Tribune*, Sunday, Nov. 1, 1992, Sec. 4, p. 4.

19. *Chicago Tribune*, Mar. 25, 1993, Sec. 1, p. 29.

20. This was the *New York Times* editorial reaction, May 22, 1992, p. A28. Jesse Jackson called Quayle's criticism "a national demonstration of divisiveness and mean-spiritedness," *Times*, May 23, p. L8.

21. "Finally, the answer to all our problems," in *Chicago Tribune*, May 24, 1993, Sec. 4, p. 3.

22. May 28, 1992, Sec. 1, p. 24.

23. "Dr. Dan's diagnosis is much better than his prescription," *Chicago Tribune*, May 25, 1992, Sec. 1, p. 9.

24. "Don't dwell on the messenger, listen to Quayle's message," *Chicago Tribune*, May 25, 1992, Sec. 1, p. 9.

25. "G.O.P. is flirting with the dangers of negativism," *New York Times*, Aug. 19, 1992, p. A13.

26. *The New Republic*, inside front cover, Nov. 30, 1992.

27. *The New Republic*, Nov. 9, 1992, p. 25.

28. *New York Times*, Aug. 19, 1992, p. A13.

29. William Raspberry, *Chicago Tribune*, Monday, Apr. 12, 1993, Sec. 1, p. 15.

30. James Q. Wilson, "The Family-Values Debate," *Commentary*, April 1993, pp. 29–30.

31. *New York Times*, Nov. 4, 1991, pp. B1 and B3.

32. Quayle was asked first on the television show *Larry King Live,* July 22, 1993. Bush was asked on the NBC-TV News program *Dateline*, Aug. 11, 1992.

33. See *New York Times*, July 24, p. A12. See also *Chicago Tribune*, Aug. 12, Sec. 1, p. 4.

34. 46. *Planned Parenthood of Central Missouri v. Danforth*, 428 U.S. 52, 96 S.Ct. 2831 (1976). Hillary Clinton's idea that children should be able to sue their parents is part of liberalism's long attempt to create the rational family. The rational liberal family denies parents' rights to form their child's character, when those attempts contradict the child's desires and the state's view of the child's liberty. In the summer of 1992 a Florida court upheld a minor child's right to sue for separation from her parents, contrary to established legal doctrine that minors generally cannot sue or be sued in courts of law.

35. See the comments of Eugene Kennedy: "Virtue, as exemplified by fidelity, self-control and other evidences of a functioning conscience, must be committed as privately as possible so as not to offend anybody or to seem to impose one's values on others" (*Chicago Tribune*, Apr. 12, 1993, Sec. 1, p. 15).

36. 35. Vol. 271, No. 4, pp. 47–83.

37. For example, "Was Dan Quayle Right?", editorial *Chicago Tribune*, Mar. 21, 1993, Sec. 4, p. 2. Clarence Page, "Dads who do more can help society do right by children," *Chicago Tribune*, Mar. 24, 1993, Sec. 1, p. 21.

38. Wilson, "The Family-Values Debate," p. 28.

39. It is beginning to look as if this "it's okay if I say it; it has no legitimacy if they say it" approach is becoming the way liberals can now acknowledge as true, the cultural value positions (on political correctness, family, sexual morality, pop culture, educational standards) which they hitherto attacked as false when spoken by conservatives and Republicans. The rhetorical strategy is to ridicule the conservatives and then appropriate their criticisms as their own. See Hilton Kramer, "Stop Thief," review of *Culture of Complaint: The Fraying of America* by Robert Hughes, *National Review*, June 21, 1993, pp. 69–70. This phenomenon attests to the power of ideology, and the personal animosities derived therefrom.

12

Abortion and Health Care

Richard Sherlock

Throughout the West liberal societies are in a period of extended crisis. This crisis is the result of the conjunction of both the inherent character of liberalism and the policies of the welfare state which have in practice come to dominate in the West in the twentieth century. Given the character of liberalism itself, the typical policies of the welfare state seem almost as if they were designed to exploit the fundamental weaknesses of the liberal regime.

The two issues that concern us here, abortion and health care, illuminate this crisis as do few other issues of our time. Health care was, on most polls of 1992, second only to "the economy" as a matter of public concern. Abortion, while not the first or second issue on most lists, is still widely regarded as the most bitterly contested and divisive contemporary political issue. The political response to these two issues is a microcosm of what, properly understood, are the most profound problems confronting American society.

In this chapter we examine briefly one central characteristic of liberalism which underlies the current debates over abortion and health care. We then examine the problems of abortion and health care policy respectively, especially as they presented themselves in the 1992 election cycle. What we shall see is that the character of liberalism itself leads fairly directly to the presentation of these issues as nearly insoluble public problems in the American regime of the 1990s.

The Character of Liberalism

The dream of liberalism's founders was that a political order of security and liberty could be constructed by limiting the reach of politics to the

205

needs of the human body while deliberately minimizing the demands of the human soul. Bodily survival and its logical extension, material prosperity, were minimum goods of nearly universal appeal. A politics that was limited to this universal desire would tame the strife of earlier ages, a strife rooted in conflict over incompatible religious, moral, and philosophic commitments and communal traditions. Political reason and civil law would no longer aspire to the philosophic or religious goal of teaching citizens truths about the ends of human existence, nourishing these commitments in civic life and rendering political decisions in their light. Political reason was now a *techne*, a means or instrument in the service of bodily survival. Politics is now about means, not ends. The ends or purposes of human life are those religious or philosophic intangibles over which people will fight to the death and on the basis of which the civil peace, so desired by liberals, is difficult to fashion.

With its vision firmly limited to this world and not the next, liberalism sought to unleash the inquisitive and acquisitive powers of humankind in the service of more wealth to fulfill the needs and desires of the body and more technology to secure the body against the assaults of nature. The desires for material acquisition and earthly domination that Christianity had regarded with suspicion, liberalism unleashed with delight. Civil peace became the anchor of politics. A politics based on material well-being is always a politics in which compromises can be made between competing interests, or even one interest bought off. Such was the dream of James Madison: the large commercial republic in which politics can be reduced to economic ends, which are ultimately commensurable one with another. A person will almost always be willing to sell his property in the hopes of getting more. Sincere believers, however, will not so sacrifice their salvation for gain. If humankind can be taught to ignore the question of the ultimate ends or purposes of human life, or to treat such beliefs as merely private opinion, politics will certainly go easier and be less dangerous.

The profound religious and philosophic skepticism which lies at the core of liberalism is fully reflected in Thomas Jefferson's powerfully symbolic twist on John Locke's formulation of natural rights. The opportunity to engage in the "pursuit of happiness" is all that Jefferson commits nature and liberal society to provide for human beings and citizens. Neither nature nor nature's god offers any guidance about the meaning of happiness, or the proper limits to its pursuit. Happiness is in the eye of the pursuer, defined by his desires and given voice within the conventions of his culture.

Since liberalism is incapable of articulating the ends or purposes of human existence, it likewise finds itself incapable of setting forth the proper limits to the pursuit of those ends. The citizens of liberal societies, however, intuitively recognize the necessity of limits. Hence liberal politics appears to hover between the absence of any limits on the pursuit of happiness and the imposition of harsh and improper limits. The liberal public seems to have accepted a speciously coherent blend of Thomas Hobbes and John Stuart Mill. From Mill is heard the repeated cry of liberty to "do whatever I want" so long as what I do does not interfere with the rights of others.

For those who do violate this most minimal of standards, however, there are reserved the severe punishments meted out by the Hobbesian sovereign. Hence we have the curious phenomenon in which prosecution of so-called victimless crimes such as adultery, sodomy, or prostitution is vigorously condemned, while the public clamors for ever harsher sentences for murderers, rapists, and pedophiles. We make it easier for parents to shirk their responsibility to nurture their children physically and emotionally by placing almost no limits on divorce. Then when we find that financial desertion follows quite naturally, we try to call a halt with increasingly draconian enforcement measures. Refusing to provide money to one's children is a harm that we can recognize, but failure to fulfill the more intangible but crucial responsibilities of parenthood is not.

As long as the informal limits of the religious and moral traditions of the West were publicly acknowledged, the effect of this fundamental problem of liberalism was muted. But as what Friedrich Nietszche called the "embers of Christian civilization" have grown publicly cold and dim, the crisis at the heart of a "liberalism without limits" is increasingly visible.

Abortion and Liberal Happiness

These observations about the crisis of liberalism are essential for comprehending the public debate about abortion and health care in the 1992 election cycle. Despite what they call themselves—"pro-life" and "pro-choice"—the two most prominent factions in the abortion debate may for our purposes be more accurately termed "none" and "any." The pro-choice position of the left and now the Democratic party is so skeptical that any limits to abortion can be kept within reasonable bounds and so enamored of its social libertarianism that it simply cannot conceive of moderate limits to reproductive choice. The pro-life activists who have controlled the Republican platform writing on this issue in the past three cycles are so fearful that any legal right to abortion will be abused that they demand that it be completely abolished. In their view a limited right will slide inevitably into an unlimited practice.

As hostages to liberal skepticism, both sides have rejected the moral middle where most Americans stand on abortion. To speak for the middle is to reject the polarized all or none dichotomy of the extremes. It is a more conservative middle than some think desirable but it is a position that the public intuitively accepts even if the activists who control their respective parties do not. Perhaps the easiest way to see this middle is to look at the results of numerous polls over the past four years asking in which cases abortion should be legal. The results of these polls by *Newsweek*, Gallup, the Wirthlin Group, and the *New York Times* are strikingly similar and can be represented as shown in Figure 12-1.[1]

Using arguments of the "slippery slope" variety, pro-choice Democrats, who control their party, have in large measure dominated the verbal battle over abortion in the national media. This is the result of two persuasive ploys. First, they have successfully portrayed the opposition as wishing to prohibit virtually all abortions. Second, they have pointed to a series of compelling cases where abortion is, at least arguably, a morally acceptable and accepted option. The unwed teenager living in squalor, the thirty-year-old welfare mother with seven children, the abused housewife—these are the sorts of anecdotes that repeatedly dot the landscape of pro-choice rhetoric. If we start down the road of restriction, it is asserted, we will end up prohibiting legal abortions in all of these compelling cases.[2]

By winning the "battle of the anecdotes," the left has been able to portray itself as "pro-choice, not pro-abortion" (in Bill Clinton's phrase from his nomination acceptance speech). Clearly, however, the reason why the abortion "choice" is so powerfully demanded is precisely because it is seen as the "right" or "best" option in these very compelling circumstances, not because most people support abortion as means of preserving a fast-track career or of selecting the sex of one's child. It is because abortion is seen as right in these extreme cases that the left has been able to so successfully demand from moderates the right to abortion in any case. In contrast, there is

Figure 1

Americans and abortion

Should abortion be legal or not legal in each of the following circumstances?

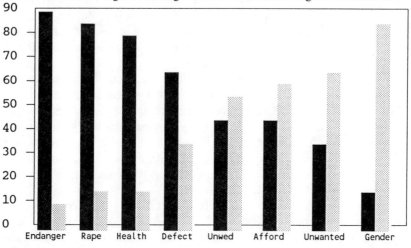

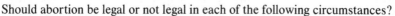

Legal   Illegal

Key

Endanger: Endangerment of the woman's life because of pregnancy
Rape: Pregnancy because of rape or incest
Health: Duration of pregnancy may impair woman's health
Defect: Possibility of baby being born deformed
Unwed: Baby's mother being unmarried
Afford: Baby's mother can't afford to raise child
Unwanted: Pregnancy is inconvenient or unwanted by parents
Gender: Parents want baby of different gender

Adapted from *Newsweek* (Newsweek Poll), April 24, 1989, p. 39.

little clamor to repeal state laws that severely restrict smoking. Prohibiting smoking altogether would be a futile public policy, but it would take quite an imagination to conceive of cases where the best thing to do is "light up."

By focusing their support for abortion on the "hard cases," Democrats have co-opted the language of choice, leaving unsaid their support for abortion per se because most of the public agrees with them on the cases they emphasize. As Republicans have allowed themselves to be viewed as the party of "none" on abortion, Democrats have defended their support for abortion in "any" case by portraying it as support for abortion in "some" cases. A hardly noticed but extraordinary example of this maneuver came during one of the very few extended interviews given to the media by Mrs. Ross Perot. ABC News commentator Barbara Walters questioned Mrs. Perot about abortion, since her husband had a reputation for conservative moral zealotry, in both his personal and professional life, but he was pro-choice on abortion. Mrs. Perot also took a pro-choice stand but justified it with immediate reference to hard cases such as unwed teenagers and women living in squalor.

The dominance of pro-choice politics at the national level has not come about only because the Democratic left has better anecdotes. The compelling anecdote hits home only if the opposition provides a ready target. In this regard few issues have been as badly mishandled over the past fifteen years by the Republican party as its opposition to the abortion practices unleashed by the Supreme Court. Republicans have virtually invited the opposition to call them extremists, because that is how they have styled themselves.

Since 1976, the Republican party platform has called for a constitutional amendment to reverse *Roe v. Wade* (1973) and end the legal regime of virtual abortion on demand that it ushered in. The platform statement has remained almost unchanged for several election cycles and all attempts to modify it have been soundly rebuffed. Republican presidents have spoken by phone hookup to the annual pro-life rally in Washington on the anniversary of *Roe*, and have made certain pro-life policy decisions such as bans on abortion counseling at federally funded clinics. Beyond these relatively meaningless victories, however, Republican conservatives have never thought very carefully about the means of achieving the far distant pro-life goal.

When a constitutional amendment was only a dream and a Supreme Court reversal no more likely than a return to the gold standard, strong pro-life rhetoric was cheap and apparently painless. Unfortunately, this rhetoric, in practice, linked the party's call for a reversal of *Roe* to the position of the National Right to Life Committee, i.e., a constitutional amendment to ban almost all abortions or a reversal of *Roe* in the courts and state legislation that would achieve the same end. By being unwilling to articulate the grounds and details of a policy of some restrictions (and therefore some abortions), pro-life conservatives became the rhetorical captives of the position taken by their most extreme partisans, i.e., no legal abortion. Since they would not discuss what a proper policy might be, it was assumed that they desired what many Americans perceived to be an improper one.

When in practice nothing much could be done, this rhetorical overkill could be conveniently ignored. But as the Supreme Court moved away from *Roe* after 1989 it came to have potentially disastrous political consequences. Not having thought very clearly about what was morally acceptable and politically salable, Republicans were tagged with the position of the pro-life zealots. However morally pure, this position was neither morally nuanced enough for many Americans nor politically salable to a national majority.[3]

The extreme pro-life position is essentially an extension of the premises of liberalism itself, just as is the extreme pro-choice position. Once one grants that the unborn are human beings—and given the liberal view of the state as primarily existing to protect the physical security of human beings from the predatory designs of others—shouldn't abortion be stopped forthwith? If abortion is the equivalent of the gravest crime, murder, shouldn't the law treat it as such?

Furthermore, just like the left, pro-life activists have been extremely skeptical of any middle ground on abortion. If you start compromising on the principle, you will end up with a practice that doesn't protect any of the unborn. Broadly worded "health of the mother" clauses (a position with great public appeal), for example, are considered an invitation to abortion on demand because a doctor can be found to render a "health" judgment anytime anyone desires an abortion for virtually any reason. Since human beings are as selfish and morally obtuse as liberalism's founders held them to be, only strongly restrictive laws can compensate for their individual weaknesses.

A profound skepticism thus informs both of the zealous camps of abortion activists. For many politicians pro-choice became the default position because they either could not find or would not articulate a principled alternative themselves. That abortion seems morally proper in some cases (and is therefore right in such cases) and that it seems only a self-serving reflex in other cases (and is therefore wrong) points to the inadequacies of each of the rigid extremes which are locked in a sort of perverse Hobbesian struggle. Seen as the rigid clash of absolutes, life and liberty, the problem is insoluble. In the Hobbesian world of natural rights each has the absolute right to demand from the other that which cannot properly be given in all circumstances.

In a deep way the conflict over abortion in contemporary America is the struggle of Hobbesian absolutes writ large in civil society. Knowing only survival or liberty, the Hobbesian state asks us to pick either path and it will be enforced to the maximum. Not officially recognizing any higher purpose for liberty or survival beyond brute existence, liberal society finds it difficult to think through what the proper limits to abortion rights might be. An abortion debate centered on virtue instead of individual rights, for example, might ask what kinds of public policies and restrictions encourage individual responsibility, selflessness, and compassion and what extremes of abortion rights pander to only the basest impulses for immediate gratification. That conservatives, who talk so much about public virtue and responsibility, have so thoroughly ignored their tradition and so wholly adopted the Hobbesian language of individual rights, which they have spent a generation condemning, on this issue is surprising.

Compelling evidence from thirty years of polling shows that substantial majorities of Americans have always supported a "conservative middle ground" on abortion. Between 60 and 70 percent of Americans have always supported laws that limit abortion to cases of compelling need: rape, incest, fetal deformity, and health (including mental health) of the mother. They want abortion available in a reasonable number of compelling circumstances, but they reject the concept of an absolute private right that could be exercised at the merest whim.

Abortion in the 1992 Election

The 1992 election cycle was supposed to herald the awakening of a pro-choice giant. Such an event never materialized, largely because no such giant awaits to be aroused. Moreover, the Supreme Court did not play the role accorded to it in this slumbering giant script. In the *Planned Parenthood v. Casey* decision of June 1992, the Court fooled both sides, upholding Pennsylvania's waiting period and informed consent requirements, while simultaneously refusing to reverse *Roe*, which had once been thought to forbid the very restrictions now upheld. It refused for three wildly unpersuasive reasons: (1) fidelity to precedent, (2) the belief that overruling a controversial decision like *Roe* would damage the credibility and legitimacy of the Court, and (3) the supposed political turmoil and chaos that would result from reversal. Of course, by studiously refusing to defend either the reasoning or the policy set forth in *Roe*, the Court did its intellectual integrity and therefore legitimacy no favor. But it did politicians an enormous favor: it removed abortion as an incendiary issue in 1992. Combined with the overwhelming focus on the economy, *Casey* served to defuse especially moderate voters who might have been mobilized by a more direct assault on *Roe*.[4]

As the election turned out, there was some slippage at the margin for pro-life forces. The general public was not, however, really in a pro-choice mood. Exit polling found that when those opposed to abortion in all cases were combined with those opposed to abortion in some cases, the result was a solid majority of 55 percent of the electorate. A CNN–USA Today poll, taken in the wake of the murder of a Florida abortion doctor in March 1993, found that 64 percent of the public was in the same position—rejecting the pro-choice position that abortion should be legal whenever it is desired by the woman. An absolute majority of 51 percent held that abortion should be legal "sometimes." The difference in these results may be partially attributable to the well-documented fact that minorities who have a low voter turnout have substantially higher pro-life attitudes than do white middle-class voters.[5]

The difficulty of mobilizing around the abortion issue in the 1992 cycle is nowhere better illustrated than in the fate of the federal "Freedom of Choice Act." This measure was originally conceived as a congressional response to the supposedly imminent demise of *Roe*. As first written it would have enshrined *Roe* in federal law and eliminated all state restriction such as parental notice or the waiting period upheld in *Casey*. When the Supreme Court did not reverse *Roe*, congressional Democrats thought of passing it anyway and forcing Bush to veto it, in September when the election campaign was just heating up. It failed of passage then, and even now, when it would not be vetoed, passage looks very doubtful. The fundamental dilemma is simple. Feminist groups such as the National Organization for Women and the National Abortion Rights Action League will not support a bill that includes parental notice or the *Casey* restrictions. But there may not be enough votes to pass a bill that overturns forty state laws on parental notice or the *Casey* restrictions now enacted in six states and surely coming in others. Democrats such as Senator Harris Wofford of Pennsylvania and Congressman Lee Hamilton of Indiana support the *Casey* restrictions, as do substantial majorities of the public. And it is just the votes of members like these that would be needed to pass a bill. Ninety senators are on record as supporting parental notice. NOW and NARAL cannot get what they want in a bill and they do not want a bill they might get if it approved of restrictions that they have spent years fighting in the states.[6]

Had Republicans been willing to think seriously about abortion policy, instead of indulging in red-meat rhetoric, they might have followed the lead of their greatest leader, Abraham Lincoln, who also had zealots clamoring for an immediate end to slavery. He fully shared their moral outrage. He knew, however, that short of war, the only way to end slavery was to undermine the perception that it was perfectly acceptable for one human being to own another. To change the practice of slavery, it was necessary first to undermine the theory of its rectitude. If Republicans had been really concerned about the most divisive issue of our time, they might have constructed a policy proposal that, by restricting abortion in a very modest degree (for example, with broadly worded "health of the mother" exceptions to a general prohibition), would have rejected the claim of an absolute private right set forth in *Roe*, while preserving, at least for some period, the practices legalized by *Roe* to which some Americans have grown attached.[7]

Such might have been leadership, even statesmanship, on an issue of grave concern and deep divisiveness. But the Republicans saw the passions unleashed by this issue and ran for cover behind slogans that pandered to the extremes. Not wanting to "waffle," they confused principle with practice and wound up publicly wedded to an inflexible position that offered little hope of translating their noble principles into substantive changes in practice. If Republicans and conservatives lose on this issue, they will have only themselves to blame. Zealous activists may be forgiven a measure of their ardor in behalf of a just cause. But those who aspire to political leadership ought to fashion policies that translate the goals of the activists into more than rhetorical winks and handshakes. Republicans have never done this on abortion and they may not now get another chance.

Health Care and the Liberal Understanding of Well-Being

On most polls of voter concern health care finished second only to the economy in the election cycle of 1992. Americans are clearly worried that many are unable to afford any health care, that their insurance benefits will be cut drastically, or that they personally will be bankrupted by a prolonged illness. Thus appear the twin problems with which citizens and legislators have been consumed in recent years: how to provide some minimum level of access to the millions who are now shut out of the health care system while controlling the escalation of health care costs so that millions more do not lose their insurance because either they or their employer can no longer afford it. Since the Perot campaign offered no serious health care proposals—indeed nothing beyond the absurd claim that he could fix the problem "without breaking a sweat"—our discussion here will be limited to proposals coming from President George Bush and then-Governor Bill Clinton.[8]

To some extent the public's response to health care concerns is a version of the "waste, fraud, and abuse" solution to the federal deficit. If doctors, hospitals, and insurance companies were not so greedy, if wasteful tests were eliminated, and if paperwork were drastically reduced, the money would be found to fix the system painlessly. Though politicians of every stripe have recited the mantra of "waste" over the years, no serious analyst of health care policy regards the policies that might be enacted in its name as sufficient to achieve the ends desired by proponents of universal access. Serious analysts know that the amount of gross domestic product spent on health care is going up in Western welfare states primarily as a function of increasing demand from consumers. Simple economics then leads to this conclusion: if you want to find to money to increase access, you must first control costs by attacking rising demand.

In order to limit the demand for health care in any serious way, however, it is necessary to limit use. This will mean placing limits on the things that might be done to secure the life and comfort of the human body. To limit use is to limit our ability to preserve ourselves as bodies. At bottom, what makes the health care debate so intractable is that limits on use require the very judgments about the meaning of human life and the proper limits of bodily existence that liberalism regards as only matters of personal opinion. As merely private opinion, such quasi-religious beliefs are impermissible as the grounds of public policy in liberal societies.

Liberal regimes of the contemporary West have found that they cannot bite this bullet very easily, if at all. So they have avoided setting forth the rational grounds of limits to health care use in publicly funded health care systems and have opted instead for patently irrational means for apportioning health care, e.g., waiting lists for surgical procedures like coronary bypass or age limits on the utilization of expensive technology like respirators or dialysis. These are the hidden realities of the Canadian and British systems, which are often touted in America as models for emulation.

The resort to such informal rationing is perhaps necessary because the liberal polity may be incapable of doing better. Lacking any publicly available means of determining which lives are worthwhile, even scorning the classical philosophic and religious traditions that pointed to the grounds of such a judgment, liberalism is a regime of the body incapable of announcing that some bodies, as bodies, aren't worth being alive. In adopting such rationing schemes liberal societies even violate the principles of economic rationality that they otherwise proudly support. Schemes that in practice deny care to the most productive citizens and offer it to the less, simply because of age or place in line, support the equality of bodily existence at the expense of economic rationality. Again, there are in liberalism either no limits or only irrational ones.

Without limits, publicly supported health care systems soon bankrupt public treasuries. We Americans have been fascinated by accounts of the supposedly "fairer," "universal" Canadian health care system for the past several years. But while we like what we hear about the Canadian system, we have hardly heard the whole truth. Would we like a system in which the average wait for coronary bypass operations is six months or the wait in some areas for pap smears is two to three months? Would we like a health care system that has powerfully contributed to a national debt that is 50 percent higher per capita than in the United States? Canadian interest rates have to be so high to finance this debt that over the past two years, as the result of a recession that was longer and steeper than the economic downturn in the United States, Canada lost between 100,000 and 200,000 jobs for good. Many companies went bankrupt or moved to the United States or Mexico. They, and the jobs they created, will not be returning.[9]

The difficulties that would attend the creation of any publicly supported health care plan in a fiscally sound and politically salable fashion deterred the Bush administration from offering any proposals for comprehensive health care reform, until the winter of 1991–92. It did so then patently only under political duress. The administration obviously thought that it must appear to be doing something, even if it did not really believe in what it was doing. The obviously political character of this move—which seemed to confirm the perception of many that Bush was insensitive to the plight of ordinary Americans— meant that Clinton and other Democratic candidates could harvest votes with campaign promises of health care reform guaranteeing universal access, to be paid for by wringing "waste, fraud, and abuse" out of the present system. Such pandering to fears about access and suspicions about wealthy physicians and greedy insurance companies was possible because the Bush administration made no attempt to educate the American people about necessary limits to health care use.

The Bush administration never made a sustained effort to sell the plan that it put forth in February 1992 to either the Congress or the

American people.[10] This is unfortunate because the administration had something useful to sell, at least as the starting point of reform efforts. Designed partially as a response to a plan put forward in 1991 by congressional Democrats, the Bush proposal at least seemed to play in the right ballpark. In general the administration sought to rely as much as possible on empowering individuals to make their own decisions about health care use. This individual empowerment was to be accomplished principally through a combination of tax credits and vouchers for the poor that would provide individuals with the resources to purchase insurance coverage that best met their personal needs and desires. Supposedly this would encourage competition among providers and insurance companies, competition which in every other area of economic enterprise has proved to be the only effective means of controlling costs and improving quality.

In theory the plan worked fine. In practice, however, it bowed to political reality in ways that dramatically undercut the power of its message. Genuflecting before the rhetoric of health care as an entitlement, a positive good, or "welfare right" to which all Americans must be provided access, the Bush proposal required the federal government to provide vouchers sufficient to allow recipients to purchase insurance coverage for some undefined "basic benefits" package. If other government benefit packages like worker's compensation and free medical care for veterans are any guide, this package would hardly remain "basic" for long. Able only to set a political, not a substantive, theoretical limit on benefits, the voucher system would inevitably find its benefit packages politically expanded, in this case (as in worker's compensation) by chiropractors, psychologists teaching stress management, and a plethora of other health care professionals. Furthermore, while the notion of individual empowerment is interesting, the "empowering" of the truly poor through Medicaid has been so sloppily organized, meagerly funded, and complicated by endless tinkering with the system that increasing numbers of private physicians simply will not participate. Medicaid is one of the fastest growing segments of state budgets, and among the chief causes of its growth is the explosive increase in benefits mandated by the federal government.

In terms of actual policy, the Bush proposal suffered from its own timidness. Wanting to avoid the political repercussions of massive change, the administration did not propose tampering with employer-paid health insurance in a manner that would have empowered their tens of millions of beneficiaries to become individual purchasers of health care. Nor did it propose voucherizing Medicare or Medicaid.

But without all of the people currently in the health care system acting as individuals in a free market, with cost-accountable purchasing decisions, it is difficult to conceive of any real effects on cost, which is the precondition of expanding access. If the government picked up the tab for vouchers, then access would increase for those who got the vouchers. But simply expanding Medicaid would do this without any real reforms.[11]

Comfortable middle-class, largely suburban, consumers with good first-dollar health coverage would not enjoy a transition to a truly free market in which they might have to save for some part of their health care bill and be responsible themselves for all of their insurance needs. The vast majority of these consumers now get their health care as an employment benefit. They do not "shop around" for coverage. That is done by the benefits "expert" of the employer. Realizing that these are the very voters on which Republicans have traditionally depended, the Bush administration did not propose the truly radical reforms such as those put forth by the Heritage Foundation or the National Center for Policy Analysis. Real reform will inevitably attack employer-provided, first-dollar coverage as a major culprit in escalating cost. When the consumer of health care is getting it with someone else's money, a market simply doesn't exist and the temptation for all parties in the transaction—patient, doctor, and hospital—to overspend is irresistible. The administration couldn't bring itself to propose real reform, which would have been politically risky, because it would have required these millions of consumers to create a real market by shopping for insurance coverage, and health care in general, themselves.[12]

During the campaign, Clinton did not spell out a detailed health care reform proposal, though he talked often about the need for serious reform and the twin goals that any reform must achieve: controlling cost increases and increasing access for the millions supposedly outside the present system. The main Clinton proposal—largely lifted from a much more detailed plan from Paul Tsongas—was for "managed competition," a seeming oxymoron that has several possible meanings depending on whether one emphasizes government management or free competition as the primary means of achieving the goals of cost containment and improved access.

The policy outlines that have come from Clinton—incorporated in the health care plan he submitted to Congress in 1993—have generally stressed government management and regulation to the detriment of free competition in health care. A national health board would establish a basic package of health care benefits to which every American will have access essentially as a right. This or companion boards would then establish global budgets for states and for networks of integrated health care providers. Through a combination of tax incentives and legal requirements on business, all Americans would be enrolled in one of these large conglomerates, known in the literature as "account-able health plans" (AHP) or in the Clinton plan as "health care alliances." Generally AHPs would compete for business by offering the benefit package defined by the national health board at a lower cost than their competitors. Broadly speaking, the basic idea is to get everyone into an HMO-style managed care system where the govern-ment will control the overall costs and level of benefits. In a health maintenance organization, the patient is charged one flat fee for all services and then must see the organization's physicians and follow their dictates on treatment, unless he wishes to pay for other treat-ments himself. Supposedly, this controls costs by encouraging early treatment and less hospitalization, though scant hard evidence exists for any such conclusion about cost savings.[13]

Some highly relevant recent data should be considered by all those thinking about fundamental health care reform at this juncture. In the period from 1982 to 1986, 75 percent of all Medicare funds spent during the last 90 days of a person's life went to hospital care. One study found that 46 percent of all Medicare expenditures during the last year of life went for care during the last 60 days of life. Yet it is indisputable that hospital care, frequently in an intensive care unit (ICU), does prolong life by some indefinite period. It is also indisputable that high-cost intensive care of terminally or gravely ill persons consumes a substantial amount of the resources devoted to health care in the United States. According to one study, 8 percent of ICU patients accounted for 92 percent of total billings. Finally, another study showed that the cost per year of life gained for patients admitted to the ICU with hematologic cancers, e.g., leukemia or the various lymphomas, both potentially treatable, was $450,000. The conclusion is inevitable. The money is currently available to bring most of the truly uninsured into the health care system if only we would restrict what technology some may use to prolong their lives so that other, less costly technologies may be used by others to prolong theirs.[14]

The difficulties of such a policy are enormous and varied but only one will be noted here. The resources to provide a minimum level of care to everyone must come from denying some types of care to some consumers. However, the proposal to use an inherently political process like the establishment of a national health board to set limits that are not properly within the purview of the founding principles of liberalism is bound to fail. The political character of such a board suggests that it simply would not be able to limit its judgments to questions of supposed "scientific validity," e.g., what evidence exists to show that acupuncture works to cure illness or relieve pain, and in what conditions? The politically charged character of supposedly scientific judgments by the Food and Drug Administration is well known and provides a useful comparison. A health board's much more complex judgments about drugs, therapies, surgeries, tests, etc., are likely to be even more manipulable in the face of political pressure, conflicting medical evidence, and consumer demand. An even more telling analogy is found in worker's compensation programs that are currently bankrupting state treasuries. Originally structured to provide carefully defined medical treatment for injuries received on the job and support during the period of recovery, these programs have, in many states, degenerated into scandal-plagued money pits that provide for chiropractic care, mental health services, stress reduction programs, and scores of other quasi-medical "therapies."[15]

This feature of expanding the list of covered care may be due to the well-known placebo effect. Patients who are given placebo treatment and told that it will "reduce your pain" or "make you feel better" report positive results 30 percent of the time, even though no physiological effect is possible. Hence any proposed treatment for an ailment like back pain or stress might find that it has a positive effect in 25 to 30 percent of the cases. Chemotherapy that is effective in only 30 percent of cancer cases surely will be approved for coverage by a national health board; why not, then, cover acupuncture or herbal medicine, with an equivalent reported success rate?[16]

That this is not an unrealistic budgetary problem for any form of publicly mandated and underwritten health care plan is evidenced by a study published in 1993. Researchers from Beth Israel Hospital in Boston and the Harvard Medical School found that in 1990 Americans paid more visits to so-called "alternative therapists," ranging from acupuncture to relaxation therapists, than they did to family physicians, pediatricians, and general internists combined. Those who sought out this care were largely well-educated, urban and suburban professionals. How can an admittedly political process conceivably say no to this demand? From veteran's benefits to worker's compensation the record of the liberal welfare state gives scant reason for optimism on this score.[17]

The basic difficulty of any proposal such as that of the Clinton administration is now obvious. At the micro level, a political process is precisely the worst means of making judgments about the relative medical merits of "tests" or "therapies." At the macro level, the judgment about the ends or purposes of human life that is required in order to set rational limits on the use of medical measures to prolong that life transcends the limits of liberalism itself. A political process within liberalism cannot be expected to set the limits which are required by managed care proposals because the limits themselves are not liberal limits.

Conclusion

On both of these topics, abortion and health care policy, liberalism's lack of a teaching about the ends or purposes of human existence leads to a profound absence of a moral voice that speaks of limits to liberty and of the duties of citizenship. Without a voice for the proper limits to the pursuit of private pleasure, desires become claims and claims become rights, proliferating without end. Lacking this public voice the modern welfare state wanders toward moral anarchy and financial collapse.

Liberalism began as a means of negotiating the terms of coexistence of moral and religious strangers who nevertheless had to live in proximity with one another. But the welfare-state liberalism of the late twentieth century, of which the problem of health care policy is symptomatic, presupposes that we are not complete strangers. True strangers cannot be coherently compelled to support one another with financial resources or moral energies. *Care* requires definition and in the defining comes a vision of what care is required and for what reason. To care for others requires not strangeness and isolation but community, the very community that liberalism originally denied could form the basis of political life. We have even taken on the Christian language of universal brotherhood to describe our actions. As Jean-Jacques Rousseau argued, this language of brotherhood makes all of us part of the same family and thus not strangers at all. Hence, denying health care to some becomes the moral equivalent of refusing to help one's kin get to the doctor.

The liberal welfare state is in trouble because it has tried to combine the language of care and brotherhood with the coercive power of government, while ignoring the shared purposes and convictions that, in real communities, render the language of care more than a vehicle for self-aggrandizement. Until we can reason publicly again about the proper limits of liberty and thus about the noble ends that true liberty will enable us to achieve, we will lack the capacity to comprehensively address issues such as abortion and health care.

Notes

1. For documentation see Los Angeles *Times*, Mar. 19, 1989; *New York Times*, Apr. 26, 1989; *Newsweek*, Apr. 23, 1989. Compare the remarkably similar figures from the *New York Times*, Apr. 24, 1966. For a review of all the relevant data see James Hunter, "What Americans Really Think About Abortion," *First Things* (June 24, 1992), pp. 13–21.

2. The serious pro-choice literature is enormous, reflecting various degrees of argumentative acumen. For some of the flavor of the popular case see Anna Bonavoglia, ed., *The Choices We Made* (New York: Random House, 1991); on the either/or character of the present debate see Laurence Tribe, *Abortion: A Clash of Absolutes* (New York: Norton, 1992); for the serious philosophic defense of abortion rights which concentrates heavily on the "hard cases" see Jane English, "Abortion and the Concept of a Person," *Canadian Journal of Philosophy* 5 (1975), pp. 10–26.

3. In 1988 and 1992 attempts were made to moderate the platform plank on abortion, without giving up the principle of opposition to abortion itself. Both times such attempts were rejected.

4. *Planned Parenthood of Southeastern Pennsylvania v. Casey,* Slip Opinion, 91–744, June 29, 1992.

5. *USA Today*, Mar. 18, 1993.

6. The difficulties of the recently reintroduced freedom of choice bill are discussed in some detail in Linda Feldman, "New Congress May Find Little Agreement on Abortion Rights Bill," *Christian Science Monitor*, Dec. 1, 1992.

7. For a fuller discussion of this point see Richard Sherlock et al., "Beyond *Roe*," *The World and I* (April 1993); Sherlock and Wilkins, "Mediating the Polar Extremes," *B.Y.U. Law Review* 1991:1, 403–88; and Chris Wolfe, "Abortion and Political Compromise," *First Things* (June 24, 1992), pp. 22–29. On the the prehistory of *Roe* see Stephen Krason, *Abortion: Politics, Morality and the Constitution* (Frederick, Md.: University Press of America, 1982).

8. This vagueness is evident in the discussion of health care in Perot's *United We Stand* (New York: Hyperion, 1992), pp. 87–90. Here he basically says "let's get a commmittee of experts together and get this thing fixed fast" with no detail whatsoever.

9. There is an extensive literature documenting rationing in Canadian health care. Recent studies which document the rationing in the Canadian

system include S. Globerman, *Waiting Your Turn: Hospital Waiting Lists in Canada* (Vancouver: Fraser Institute, 1990); Anderson et al., "Hospital Care for Elderly Patients with Diseases of the Circulatory System: A Comparison of the U.S. and Canada," *New England Journal of Medicine* 321 (1989), 1443–48; Roos et al., "Post-Surgical Mortality in Manitoba and New England," *Journal of American Medical Association* 263 (1990), 2453–58.

10. *The President's Comprehensive Health Reform Program,* Feb. 6, 1992.

11. Ibid., pp. 60–69.

12. For the NCPA proposal see *An Agenda for Solving America's Health Care Crisis,* a task force report for the National Center for Policy Analysis, 1990, and John Goodman and Gerald Musgrave, *Patient Power* (Washington, D.C.: CATO Institute, 1992). For the Heritage proposal see Stuart Butler and Ed Haislmaier, *A National Health Care System for America,* rev. ed. (Washington, D.C.: Heritage Foundation, 1989).

13. One version of what Clinton talked about favorably during the campaign is contained in Jeremy Rosner, "A Progressive Plan for Affordable, Universal Health Care," in Will Marshall, ed., *Mandate for Change* (New York: Berkeley Books, 1993), pp. 107–29. This volume is put out under the auspices of the Progressive Policy Institute, the "think tank" of Clinton's own Democratic Leadership Council, and has a foreword by Clinton himself. See also the report of the "Jackson Hole Group" (so named because of where it occasionally met) chaired by Paul Ellwood, of the Interstudy health care consulting group in Minneapolis, and Allen Einthoven of Stanford, formerly assistant secretary of Health, Education, and Welfare in the Nixon admininstration. These two are perhaps the leading experts in the country on managed competition, coming out of twenty years' work with and promotion of heath maintenance organizations.

14. The studies referred to are Schapira et al., "Intensive Care: Survival and Expense of Treating Critically Ill Cancer Patients," *Journal of the American Medical Association* 269 (1993), 783–86; Oye and Bellamy, "Patterns of Resource Consumption in Medical Intensive Care," *Chest* 99 (1991), 685–89; Gaumer and Stavins, "Medicare Use in the Last 90 Days of Life," *Health Services Research* 26 (1992), 725–42; Anderson et al., "Development of Clinical and Economic Prognoses from Medicare Claims Data," *Journal of the American Medical Association* 263 (1990), 967–92.

15. For some relevant data and discussion of the massive expanision of worker's compensation, see Charles Oliver, "No Pain, No Gain," *Reason* 24 (January 1993), 32–36, and Roger Thompson, "Workers' Comp. Costs Out of Control," *Nation's Business* 80 (July 1992), 22–25.

16. See, especially, Howard Spiro, *Doctors, Patients, and Placebos* (New Haven: Yale University Press, 1986).

17. Eisenberg et al., "Uncoventional Medicine in the United States: Prevalence, Costs, and Patterns of Use," *New England Journal of Medicine* 328 (1993), 246–52.

13

That Ozone Man:
Environmentalism and National Politics

Jeffrey J. Poelvoorde

On a pleasant evening in October in the midst of the presidential campaign, George Bush's train rolled into Spartanburg, S.C., a southern city of about eighty thousand inhabitants with comparatively low unemployment, a growing local economy, and a fairly conservative social fabric—in other words, solid Bush country. The crowd of fifteen thousand that had crammed into the train station thundered into applause and cheers when he finally appeared and ascended to the dais. His speech, short and formulaic, nevertheless generated wild enthusiasm among those gathered. They seemed to like his odd personal dialect blending elite Yalisms with pedestrian patter, and certainly had no trouble agreeing with his framing of the issues of the campaign as ones of character and prudence, nor with his claim that these characteristics clearly differentiated him from his opponents. When Bush ascribed to Bill Clinton a chameleon-like embrace of shifting and contradictory policy positions ("You can't turn the White House into the Waffle House!"), the crowd responded with laughter and shouts of approval. But when he moved on to Senator Al Gore and his environmentalism ("And what about . . . what about . . . *That Ozone Man!?*"), the people of Spartanburg could restrain themselves no longer: they exploded into howls and cheers that died down only when the president himself restored order. Bush had apparently struck a chord.

The issue of "environmentalism" is a strange lens through which to view the presidential election of 1992. It was, in reality, an issue that only floated in and out of the campaign, more like a "half-issue." First, it *was* an issue in the sense that one of the candidates, Senator Gore, had used it to hone out his national political identity, especially in his book *Earth in the Balance*.[1] (For, in truth, the vice-presidential candidates are running for the office of the presidency, and in two senses. They often stand as identifiable spokesmen for major planks of the party's platform, either reinforcing or complementing the main presidential candidate's embodiment of the party. Additionally, they, too, are "potential presidents." Therefore, they also must give some sense of their vision of the nation's good and potential direction and also what counts as an issue worthy of bringing before the American people as deserving national concern.) Gore was chosen to fill out the Democratic ticket partially for this reason: in addition to his relative youth, his Southern origins, and his overall appearance of moderate Democratic centrism, he could bring into the national electoral coalition those voters for whom environmental protection was paramount.

Yet, ironically, the environment was not a particularly visible theme in the Democratic campaign, as if the Democrats felt the necessity of dampening its visibility, of rendering the environment a factor in the election, but only a minor one. Gore, in other words, functioned more as a symbol than as a spokesman for environmentalism. Why? The above anecdote from Bush's campaign appearance suggests the explanation: the Democratic leadership sensed that most voters were (and are, to some degree) concerned about the environment, but not more than other issues, especially jobs and the economy. Furthermore, suspecting that the public spokesmen and organizations for environmentalism are viewed by the majority of American voters as drifting towards an imprudent extremism, the Democratic leadership strategically decided to allow Gore to include his environmental credentials on his resume, so to speak, but not to wave them too prominently.

Yet, if the president sensed that the Democratic ticket, or at least a major component of it, was vulnerable on this count, why was it not a sustained theme of offense in the Republican electoral strategy, other than a few pointed barbs offered on the stump toward the closing weeks of the campaign? Why did the Republicans not press harder to suggest that the Democratic ticket and platform embraced a form of extremist environmentalism which would arguably damage the national interest and undermine sound policy? The problem, of course, was that the president was suffering from his own vulnerability on the issue of the environment. One of Bush's rhetorical strategies during the 1988 presidential race and, to some extent, during his presidency, was to attempt to co-opt the criticisms of his opponents by adopting their rhetoric. In this way, he would appear to be reasonable and moderate, sharing the concerns of his harshest critics calling for more government action, especially in the areas of social services (a "kinder, gentler America"), education (the "education" president), and the environment (his campaign commercial on the edge of Boston Harbor attempting to head off Michael Dukakis's charge of environmental indifference). But especially in the area of the environment, Bush allowed himself continually to be backed into uncomfortable positions that appeared to be hasty and inconsistent compromises. This was especially evident at the Earth Summit in Rio de Janeiro in June 1992. Finally prodded into attending to show serious interest, but then trying to back away from commitments to the Summit's substantive conclusions, Bush sounded vague and trapped, occasionally contradicting himself and his subordinates and projecting to the world (and his political opponents) the specter of an embarrassing confusion. In other words, on the issue of the environment, Bush appeared to have his own "waffling" problem. Having never articulated a coherent and principled alternative to the kind of environmentalism espoused by Gore, the most that he could hope for was to carp on Gore's "extremism," while avoiding pointing too intensively at his own record.

So the environment hovered in the background of the predominant themes of the campaign. The issue is, nevertheless, worthy of attention. First, it is a study in how issues are included on the national agenda by being "presidentialized" as part of the national campaign for the presidency. Moreover, on its own merits, environmentalism deserves serious consideration from the standpoint of what effect prosecuting the agenda of environmentalists would have on our national policy and national political culture. We shall see that protecting the environment is not the same thing as "environmentalism," and that one of the tasks of presidential statesmanship in the coming decades will be to fashion a prudent synthesis of American political principles and environmental protection—a yet unfinished task.

Gore's Presidential Environmentalism

Before we consider *Earth in the Balance*,[2] Gore's presentation of a national policy based on his understanding of environmental preservation, it is useful to consider what counts, or *should* count, as a "presidential" issue. By a presidential issue, I mean an issue that deserves to become a major theme in a presidential contest. Beyond the general themes articulated by the parties supporting presidential candidates, a presidential campaign should focus on issues that a majority, or at least a substantial number, of citizens already experience, or could be persuaded to view, as critical to the nation's or their particular good. Second, a presidential issue should raise important questions about the powers and purposes of the federal government, so much so that we are forced to try to articulate them in terms of a philosophy of governance and even at times in terms of the Constitution. Last, a presidential candidate should be prepared to outline a responsible and feasible policy to attain the good desired, one that nevertheless is rooted in American political principles. Gore clearly is attempting to meet all three criteria in his book. *Earth in the Balance*, therefore, represents a major presidential candidate's attempt to transform environmentalism into a plank in a presidential platform.

Earth in the Balance contains three parts. Part I presents Gore's popular distillation of his understanding of the scientific evidence for impending global environmental collapse, especially in the areas of overpopulation, greenhouse gases leading to global warming, the planet's thinning ozone layer, disruption of global water systems, depletion of natural resources, and overproduction of nonrecycled garbage. Part II is Gore's diagnosis of the governmental, economic, cultural, and religious systems that have enabled us to wreak havoc on the world's ecology ("dysfunctional civilization") and his analysis of what healthy social and political principles would look like. Part III is an outline of a worldwide plan to reform humanity's ecological profligacy and reverse the damage already done—a "Global Marshall Plan" with the United States in the lead.

The overriding metaphor for the looming ecological crisis and its solution is war. In fact, Gore compares what is happening now with the period before the United States' entry into World War II. He constantly refers to Franklin Roosevelt's attempts to rouse an apathetic nation to the danger in Europe. The danger of Adolf Hitler was real, menacing, but invisible—only because the complacent and self-satisfied refused to look. So, too, the scientific and observational evidence for environmental destruction has been mounting up before our own eyes. But we, caught up in our shortsightedness, have willfully avoided looking. What has made us so? The "Four Horsemen" of environmental apocalypse: our fractionalized and interest-bound political system; our free-wheeling free market unleashing our relentless consumerism; our desperate addiction to the wizardry of Cartesian technology; and finally, our simple arrogance—of the American nation, of the developed world, of the human species.

Gore's image of a reformed society truly devoted to the most serious problem in human history also derives from war: the defeat of the Nazis and the waging of the Cold War. In order for our species to survive, it must adopt as its "central organizing principle" the preservation of the environment just as the nations of the West adopted as their "central organizing principle" Hitler's overthrow and the subsequent decades-long struggle against Soviet expansionism. If the free nations of the West were capable of such a sustained effort without destroying their social and political fabric, then it should be possible to engage in a worldwide effort to save the planet without radical transformation in our economic and political institutions.

The actual program consists of five "strategic goals": stabilizing the world's population (primarily through education and literacy); the creation and distribution of "environmentally appropriate technologies," especially to the poorer countries; the addition of ecological costs to market mechanisms so that the impact of economic activity on the environment can reasonably be figured into the costs of goods and services; a new generation of international agreements incorporating "regulatory frameworks, specific prohibitions, enforcement mechanisms, cooperative planning . . ."; and last, a worldwide system of conducting and disseminating environmental research that would "foster new patterns of thinking about the relationship of civilization to the global environment."[3]

It is difficult to communicate the book's sense of urgency and scope of subject. Gore constantly uses expressions such as "the most serious threat that we have ever faced,"[4] "Our ecological system is crumbling . . . ,"[5] let alone the book's title. This intensity of danger is presented as the nearly unanimous judgment of the scientific community, with only extremists or covert apologists for industry interests raising a barely audible dissent.[6] Given the extent of the emergency that he sees, it might be more accurate to say that the overall metaphor employed by the book in not "war," but "martial law." Moreover, as mentioned above, Gore envisions the nations of the world adopting as their "central organizing principle" the rescue of the environment. What does this mean? "Embarking on an all-out effort to use every policy and program, every law and institution, every treaty and alliance, every tactic and strategy, every plan and course of action—to use, in short, every means to halt the destruction of the environment."[7] In fact, Gore's analysis (including self-analysis) and prognosis suggest that he considers saving the planet not just an issue of survival, but of moral and political regeneration. The ecological crisis is a crisis, but is finally a great opportunity for humanity: to create a truly global civilization, to spread education and material resources among the poor masses of the species, to reform our culture of selfishness, to become *virtuous*.

We can see how Gore is attempting to meet the criteria for presenting a "presidential" issue. His rhetoric of alarm is necessary to persuade Americans of the danger which most of them do not actually experience in their daily lives. The analogy to the pre-World War II period is an attempt to describe the yet-unseen danger in terms that the majority of Americans can understand. His call for a "Global Marshall Plan" is an attempt to lay before the electorate a responsible and realistic policy to remake the world, carefully couched in an analogy to the first Marshall Plan. That first plan, too, was greeted by a skeptical or indifferent public (and Congress), but through active presidential leadership, it prevailed and eventually became one of the great American policy successes in the 1950s. What about the necessity of grounding a presidential policy in a larger view of governance or American political and constitutional principles? Here, Gore's book is most interesting—and most problematic. Like any Cold Warrior celebrating the victory of free government and economics over communism, Gore repeatedly attributes the victory of American institutions to their superiority. (Also to the willingness to stand firm in the Cold War.) Limited constitutionalism devoted to individual rights has led to the best and most democratic society in the world, while the free market has generated more freedom and prosperity than ever before imagined.

Here is the dilemma that points to the book's major flaws. On the one hand, it is a celebration of the essential dynamics of American politics and economics, so much so that it would appear to stand squarely in the mainstream of American opinion. On the other hand, for its larger ecological analysis to proceed, it must label those same institutions and the society shaped by them as "dysfunctional"—at the root, in other words, of environmental exploitation and degradation. The book's schizophrenic surface rhetoric (American institutions are fundamentally healthy versus American institutions are fundamentally dysfunctional) overlays the more fundamental policy analysis and prescriptions, with only one side of the surface truly being compatible with its core. It is important to grasp that a policy which has come to occupy the place of society's "central organizing principle" is hardly the same as "an important policy objective," or even "important national priority." "Central organizing principle" implies that ecological preservation has become our country's governing aim, with all other considerations deriving their relative importance from it. This deeper stratum of the book is the logical extension of its alarmist and critical stance, and suggests that the high praise that Gore has for American institutions and principles is a veneer that conceals environmentalist antipathy to American politics and gives the book a tone of mainstream acceptability.

Indeed, Gore's attempt to dress up an immoderate message in moderate language is not the most fundamental problem with his presidential environmentalism. Politics, even presidential politics, is partisan. Responsible partisanship attempts to retain a prudent grasp of the limits of its own view of reality, both for the purposes of *acting* prudently but also from the standpoint of *persuading* intelligent adversaries. But the author of *Earth in the Balance* is so contemptuous of disagreement that he imputes a moral or intellectual defect in those who do not agree. Gore assumes scientific unanimity and self-evidence for almost every major scenario of ecological catastrophe, when, in reality, the scientific community is far from agreement as to the likelihood or extent of environmental dangers.[8] In this sense, he uses science to advance an ideological agenda rather than to let scientific research—with all its attendant ambiguity—present a much more complex picture of the environment. In turn, the partisan character of Gore's scientific arguments points to his overall reversal of ends and means. As mentioned above, Gore hopes that a truly global and virtuous human culture will be generated by environmental policies. It is as if environmentalism is desired as a means to transform society rather than to restore ecological balance. Gore would argue, of course, that the program of individual and social transformation is necessary in order to save the planet. But his casting about for cultural and spiritual materials from Buddhism to Native American religions suggests the construction of a global civil religion rather than the curbing of pollution.

Other activist environmentalists are distinguished from Gore primarily by the absence of his laudatory rhetoric for American life and institutions. He himself is critical of the "deep ecologists" who would essentially shut down the engine of technological progress in order to dethrone American and Western civilization from its dominance in the human world, and to dethrone the human species from its tyranny over the global ecosystem.[9] Yet his framework of analysis is essentially the same as theirs, for his environmentalism and theirs share the same ideological underpinnings: the critique levied against the institutions and technology of the Enlightenment by Western Romanticism.[10] From Jean-Jacques Rousseau's philosophic salvos against science in the

1750s to the counterculture's protests against capitalistic society in the 1960s, modern life has inspired its own movements of rejection. Of these, the most powerful and enduring is the Romantic embrace of pristine nature as an alternative to the corruption of society in general and technological society in particular.

The Romantic Roots of Environmentalism

All of the major themes of the environmental movement of the past decades can be found in the seminal works of Rousseau, especially in *The First and Second Discourses* and *On the Social Contract*.[11] In these works, Rousseau articulated the major elements of Romanticism, especially its hostility to technology, to the free market, to notions of property, to inequalities of wealth and material enjoyment, and finally, to the ideas of individual rights and limited government that provide the basis for constitutionalism in the West. At its root, Rousseau's thought is particularly a rejection of the human as a "rational individual." For Rousseau, reason and individuality are artificial by-products of life in society, especially once the divisiveness of private property has snuffed out our original sense of oneness with each other and nature as a whole.[12] Because that sense—where our true happiness is experienced—exists before society, it is literally prerational or sentimental. Originally we were an intimate part of nature and felt that intimacy unreservedly.[13] We lived simply, according to our authentic needs; we lived happily, according to the dictates of our authentic sentiments.

What is especially ironic about Romanticism is that its recommendations for the design of government should culminate in such a radical concentration of authority, given its reliance on uncontaminated nature as the standard for human life. Two aspects of that standard explain Romanticism's statist tendencies: original authenticity, and equal and common enjoyment of nature. First, only with the concentration of authority—assuming the origin of that authority in the merged collective will of the people—can the alienated and artificially selfish individual overcome his isolation. In the radically intense community that generates and is generated by the concentrated authority of the state, individuals can experience a reflection of their original sense of unity with nature. Sentimental unity, in other words, overcomes rational selfishness. Second, with the properly founded and guided democratic will of the state, the people have a weapon against the exploitation and abuse of the elitist and self-serving property owners. The common and equal enjoyment of the earth's fruits, part of our original natural condition, is restored by the regulatory power of the state. In such a condition, "rights" are no longer experienced as the rationally discovered claims made by individuals against collective authority, but as collective standards for sharing the common ownership of the earth. If "virtue" means wanting and choosing the common good over one's own, then in such a condition, "authority" and "community" and "virtue" become almost synonymous.[14]

According to Romanticism, the institutions of liberal politics and economics only intensify the misery and exploitation of our denatured lives. The "market" becomes the arena where the powerful will press their advantage and the rest of us will sell ourselves or glut our appetites or both. Limited government with limited powers claims to prevent tyranny, but instead only protects the clever and fortunate from the regulatory power of the democratic masses. Individual rights become a handy rationale for the propertied to use their property without consequences, or to narrow the vision of the rest of us to our own little selfish spheres of private enjoyment, indifferent to the welfare of the whole. Last, technology comes to feed the appetites of the profit- and comfort-hungry, reveling in our rational and exploitative mastery over other humans, other animals, and the entire natural world.[15]

We can see the derivative remnants of these ideas in contemporary environmentalism, even in Gore's moderated version. On the domestic level, the regulatory state must assume an even greater role in society, forcing the market to add "cost" to products by calculating environmental damage incurred in production.[16] Also, to really ensure ecological outcomes in the economy, the government will have to direct investment into technology and products safe for the environment. On the international level, Gore's "Global Marshall Plan" and its call for the transfer of wealth to the less developed nations rest on a sort of "global egalitarianism," where the relevant political and moral unit of the human race is the whole species (natural and authentic) rather than the nation (artificial, self-serving, and divisive). The most extreme strand of contemporary environmentalism, the animal rights movement, attacks human superiority (founded on rationality) in the name of sentience. In the name of protecting the equal rights of other species to life and happiness (Can beings incapable of rational self-consciousness *have* "rights"?), this position prevents one from even identifying a human interest, let alone *asserting* a human interest. Yet, it has decisively affected national and international policy—in the name of protecting endangered species.[17]

Conclusion

Protection of the environment is, and should continue to be, important to the nation and to the globe. Yet, in the interests of preserving the *political* ecology of constitutional government and sound policy, we may want to view environmentalism with a cautious eye. Like any other important and potentially successful policy, environmental protection requires statesmanship. The statesmanly task is to place the practical challenges of specific policies *within* the political traditions of the republic—not the other way around. It is one thing to work within the framework of limited government and individual rights as opposed to using the issue of the environment (with the attendant manufactured panic) to call for a modification of these principles. But perhaps this is an example of the Constitution and the liberal tradition not keeping apace with the practical necessities of the American people, let alone the human race. Perhaps human survival *does* demand a curtailing of our economic and political traditions in the name of the good of the whole. Perhaps Gore is correct in his call to make environmental rescue our "central organizing principle." Reality makes us pause, however: the relevant science is too tentative, the passions of environmental advocates too unreflective and too intense, and the governmental solutions too authoritarian to tinker with the foundations of American society. Gore's "presidential environmentalism" is exactly the way *not* to transform environmental protection into a presidential or national issue. But neither is former President Bush's.

What would a prudent presidential environmentalism look like? Clearly, its predicate would not be apocalypse, nor its recommendation a "central organizing principle" of regulation and redistribution leading to economic and technological stagnation. It is certainly possible to separate out the critique of property and corporate capitalism from the legitimate concerns for environmental protection and to concentrate rationally on the latter. Even so, one need not leap to a laissez-faire view of pure market solutions to environment pollution and preservation of resources; some kind of governmental intervention into the economic realm is probably necessary. To address the problems of domestic pollution a reasonable policy of environmental protection could rely on clear legal standards grounded in cautious science, with the primary enforcement mechanism being judicial enforcement of damages rather than broad-based regulation. Also, it is surely possible to foster international cooperation on ecological problems generated by the actions of more than one nation and affecting the populations of other countries without resorting to collectivist principles inimical to national sovereignty, constitutional or limited government, and liberty and property.

Each presidential election is an education in the Constitution and in what the public should be willing to do in the name of policy and necessity. On the issue of the environment, our aspiring and actual presidents have not yet risen to the task. To refer to a truly relevant presidential precedent on how to build a prudential policy—Abraham Lincoln's handling of slavery—we see that environmentalism is the abolitionism of our day. Faced with ideological fervor that would undermine the Constitution and the nation's interests, while still not attaining its stated ends, Lincoln nevertheless repudiated the policy of passive drift of James Buchanan's administration, which also refused to articulate a clear principle as to the status of slavery. Somewhere between Gore's "environmental abolitionism" and Bush's passive eclecticism lies a consistent and moderate version of environmental protection. As with many other historical and current challenges to the American polity, we look to the office of the president to show us the way.

Notes

1. Al Gore, *Earth in the Balance: Ecology and the Human Spirit* (New York: Plume Books, 1992).

2. Of course, when Gore wrote *Earth in the Balance*, he was a senator running for vice president. As vice president, he has reissued the book, complete with a new foreword, therefore reaffirming its importance as a statement of potential national policy under the Clinton administration—or even perhaps under a future Gore administration.

3. Gore, pp. 305–6ff.

4. Ibid., p. 40.

5. Ibid., p. 42

6. Ibid., pp. 89–90.

7. Ibid., p. 274.

8. Ibid., p. xi. For sustained consideration of the debates within the scientific community regarding environmental catastrophe, see Ronald Bailey, *Ecoscam* (New York: St. Martin's Press, 1993), pp. 147–51; see also: Jay H.

Lehr, ed., *Rational Readings on Environmental Concerns* (New York: Van Nostrand Reinhold, 1992).

9. Gore, pp. 216–18.

10. This is most visible in Gore's explicit rejection of "Cartesian" science, with its "dualism" of body and soul culminating in the rule of soul over body and man over nature. *Earth in the Balance*, pp. 218, 230; see also: Michael M. Gemmell and Jay H. Lehr, "Ecology's Ancestry," and Richard F. Sanford, "Environmentalism and the Assault on Reason," in Lehr, ed., *Rational Readings*; also Christoper Manes, *Green Rage: Radical Environmentalism and the Unmaking of Civilization* (Boston: Little, Brown, 1990).

11. Jean-Jacques Rousseau, *The First and Second Discourses*, trans. Roger D. and Judith R. Masters (New York: St. Martin's Press, 1964); *On the Social Contract*, ed. Roger D. Masters (New York: St. Martin's Press, 1978).

12. *First and Second Discourses*, pp. 150–56.

13. Ibid, pp. 113–20.

14. *On the Social Contract*, pp. 52–55; 61–62; 68; 84–85.

15. One should note that the attitude of many environmentalists, Gore included, is somewhat schizophrenic. On the one hand, technology is the cause of the increase in our ability to destroy the planet. On the other hand, technology is necessary to monitor the damage and to prescribe remedies for it.

16. Gore, pp. 183–91; see also Richard L. Stroup and Jane S. Shaw, "The Free Market and the Environment," in Lehr, ed., *Rational Readings*.

17. Julian L. Simon, "Disappearing Species, Deforestation and Data," in Lehr, ed., *Rational Readings*.

14

The Year of the Woman

Delba Winthrop

Consider the following scenario for the Year of the Woman: The time
is right for change. Judging by appearances, public affairs are being
conducted by a bunch of unreformed spendaholics. Corrupt, incompetent politicians are elected, and when the rascals are periodically
thrown out, they are replaced by more of the same. As for the policies
they enact, their only constant is that each benefits one special interest
or another. If the electorate is unhappy about the situation, it isn't
unhappy enough to countenance any reform that might threaten either
its authority or its entitlements. Women, heretofore effectively disem-
powered, are about to claim a place in public life. Long having
managed their households and nurtured their children successfully,
and recently having honed their political skills, they conspire to take
over the government. Their promise is to rule honestly and efficiently,
though not necessarily disinterestedly.

So women come to power with a pledge to save the country. To this
task they bring sober judgment, proven microeconomic management
skills, discretion, generosity, and a spirit of cooperation. Men vote
them into office not so much because they are impressed by these
virtues as because gynecocracy is the one thing they haven't yet tried.
The women, professed conservatism notwithstanding, appear to be
emboldened by their electoral success and begin instituting sweeping
reforms. They will put an end to corruption and crime. In addition,
they will see to it that democracy's promise of equality is finally
fulfilled. To these ends they nationalize all property, establish a comprehensive welfare state, and protect by law the rights of all, especially
the geriatrically and cosmetically challenged. In effect, the whole
polity is to be transformed into one immense household. The much
overutilized law courts, along with other democratic political institu-

tions, are converted into communal banquet halls. On the whole, life will be sweet for both male and female citizens: most of the work will be done by slaves, and prostitution will be abolished.

Thus is depicted the first Year of the Woman—in 393 B.C. by the Athenian comic poet Aristophanes in his "Ecclesiazusae." It was thoroughly democratic in spirit—from its commitment to innovation and to equality, to its costs being borne by someone else (slaves), to its having been designed to benefit perhaps especially its leader, Praxagora (giving her, with others, the sexual freedom without scandal she craved). Whether the radical reforms initiated by Praxagora in the name of the gynecocracy would succeed even in Aristophanes' imaginary world is a question left unanswered at the play's end. The second Year of the Woman, with which we Americans are more familiar, began in the fall of 1991 with the Senate confirmation hearings of Supreme Court nominee Clarence Thomas. It culminated, but did not end, in the elections of 1992. The second Year having occurred in the real world, its meaning and therefore the measure of its success are even more complicated.

The what, as distinguished from the why and the so what, of our Year of the Woman is clear. Women did well, though not astonishingly well, in the November 1992 elections. The number of seats in the House of Representatives held by women increased from 28 to 47, and in the Senate from two to six. A seventh won a special election in 1993. Many more women had been nominated in primaries, especially Democratic. Most of the women elected won races in which there was no incumbent. Those who were victorious were qualified; they were not outsiders, but experienced politicians with established political careers and credentials. Moreover, their campaigns were very well financed by PAC money.

Among voters there were gender gaps. More women voted than men (54%). They voted for women candidates and, at the primary level, female candidates often agreed not to oppose one another. In the presidential vote, however, the gender gap turned out to be smaller than had been anticipated. George Bush fared equally well with men and women (38% and 37%), Ross Perot did slightly better with men (21% and 17%), and Bill Clinton did somewhat better with women (41% and 46%). He did best with women who were Independents and those who were unmarried. This gender gap was smaller than predicted probably for several reasons. Most obviously, Bush lost crucial support among the white males who had secured his victory in 1988, so his previous gender gap narrowed. Among the issues that might have induced women to support Clinton in even greater numbers, some cut both ways. Surely Bush's veto of a family leave bill in 1992 did not help him. But Clinton's emphatically pro-choice stance on abortion must have cost him the votes of pro-life women. The likelihood that the Gennifer Flowers affair would hurt Clinton badly was minimized when Hillary's *60 Minutes* appearance effectively made it a nonissue. If she could still live with Bill, maybe we could too.

The Year of the Woman can be said not to have ended with the November elections because Bill Clinton won. In the campaign he had promised that he would have a Cabinet that "looks like America." And so he does; or, as someone has quipped, it at least looks like Yale Law School. Though Clinton excoriated the "bean counters" and eschewed quotas, his Cabinet would not have looked much different had he used quotas. Indeed, his embarrassing search for an attorney general makes it even less clear that there were no quotas. In contrast, the fact that the Bush administration had filled 40 percent of top positions with women somehow never caught the public's attention. Finally, Clinton promised—or threatened, depending on your point of view—to give us "two for the price of one." Whatever one may think of Hillary Rodham Clinton's politics or of her husband's giving her a prominent place in his administration, and whatever her successes or failures, it is hard to imagine that the public's opinion about what a First Lady should be will not have been substantially, and perhaps permanently, changed by the end of Clinton's presidency. Cookie-baking skills may never again be highly esteemed.

Thus the Year of the Woman has established women, or at least some women, as political forces to be reckoned with. Were the gains of women spectacular and sudden enough to justify the designation of 1992 as the Year of the Woman? The label seems to have been attached when unprecedented numbers of women entered primary contests in the spring of 1992. Several important factors might explain this increase. Some could be termed accidental. Foremost among these was the House Bank scandal, which was widely perceived to be one more in an ever growing number of betrayals of public trust by politicians as usual. As a result, more incumbents than might have been expected chose not to seek reelection. Surprisingly, despite predictions that 1992 would be the Year of the Outsider, with "the ultimate outsider" role claimed by women, incumbents who ran were reelected. Some factors could be called long term, or background. Most important among these was that women had been making steady, if unspectacular, political progress for long enough so that there were now many more credible potential candidates, with respectable records as appointed and elected officeholders. Second was the not often enough discussed PAC money available to women candidates, primarily through Emily's List (Early Money Is Like Yeast). Emily's List contributes money to the campaigns of women who avow their support for federally funded abortions and an Equal Rights Amendment. It contributes early and often. By a procedure known as "bundling" it evades the $5,000 contribution limit per PAC to each candidate by merely collecting and passing along the contributions of individual donors. Thus it was able to pass along over half a million dollars to Lynn Yeakel's campaign against that bête mâle Arlen Spector and lesser, but highly effective, amounts to successful Senate candidates, Barbara Boxer, Dianne Feinstein, Carol Moseley-Braun, and Patty Murray. In previous years it had been Republican women who fared rather well. This year the gains were made almost exclusively by liberal Democratic women.

There were also unique factors that justify speaking of 1992 as the Year of the Woman. Most obvious is "Anita Hill." By this is meant, of course, the extraordinary Senate confirmation hearings of Clarence Thomas as an associate justice of the Supreme Court. We are not likely ever to know what really happened between Hill and Thomas when she worked as a lawyer under his authority, first at the Department of Education and then at the EEOC, and therefore, whether he was guilty as she charged of sexual harassment. Remarkably, however, except for the two individuals involved, the significance of the nationally televised Senate Judiciary Committee hearing over the weekend of October 12–14, 1991 lies elsewhere. Women, including senatorial candidates Yeakel and Moseley-Braun, said that their decisions to run were in large part responses to the mistreatment of Hill by the all-white, all-male Judiciary Committee. Men were unable or unwilling to "get it" when it came to the reality and psychic consequences of sexual harassment. Women would never attain justice until they were equally represented in politics and, for that matter, in all spheres of public life.

The incident and its aftermath are impressive for the success of feminist reasoning and rhetoric. In fact, the men on the Judiciary Committee did take Hill's charges seriously. They refrained from making them public earlier out of respect for Hill's own insistence first on anonymity and then on confidentiality. When the hearing finally was held, its outcome was not favorable to Hill. In public opinion polls taken immediately after the hearing, 24 percent said they believed Hill, while 40 percent believed Thomas. Women no less than men overwhelmingly doubted Hill. A year later 44 percent said they believed Hill, with only 34 percent still believing Thomas. Time, with the relentless assistance of the media, has won that which Hill could not win for herself, but from which she and others have greatly benefited. No new evidence supporting either Hill or Thomas has been revealed. The shift in opinion, as one observer has put it, makes about as much sense as the claim that a jury is better able to decide a case a year after having heard and evaluated the evidence than at the time of the trial.[1] Presumably, something like the following kind of reasoning caused the shift: We know that some women are sexually harassed at the workplace; therefore, this could in principle have happened to Anita Hill, too. Even if it didn't, we are going to take this opportunity to send a message, loud and clear, that no woman ever need tolerate it. If the greater good of womankind requires the sacrifice of one possibly innocent man's good name, the price is not too high for society to pay. Men can be made to "get it."

Thus women had captured the moral high ground long before the campaigns began. And, for better or worse, men are all too willing to believe that women are morally superior. Or, at least, they believe them to be less susceptible to the corrupting influences of public life. In fact, this belief has long posed a problem for feminists, who have reached no consensus on whether women are the same as or different from men. The high opinion of women's virtue was hardly diminished by the demagogic rhetoric of Ross Perot, who would have had us believe that democracy's only real problems are caused by corrupt political insiders.

The issues of the 1992 presidential campaign also helped both to energize and to elect women. Ever since pollsters and political scientists have been studying voting patterns, the only issue around which a persistent gender gap has emerged is that of foreign policy. Women have always been more reluctant than men to support wars or policies that risk war. This year, for the first time in recent memory, foreign policy was not an issue. Tough guys lost their issue on which to oppose women. It could seem that all we had to worry about was how to put people and their environment first. Our problems, we thought, would be—in addition to revitalizing the economy (stupid!)—health care, child care, and family leave, and making abortion rights secure from presidential vetoes and judicial dilutions. So this was the year not only of "women's issues," but of Democratic women's issues. The concern of more conservative women and men, namely "family values," never became an issue from which they could profit perhaps because of the unattractive way in which it was raised by Patrick Buchanan at the Republican convention. Murphy Brown remained triumphant.

Of course we were wrong to think that America would not face foreign policy decisions as difficult, if not as urgent or momentous, as at any time in our history. Nor did we take seriously the possibility that one of the first issues congresswomen and congressmen would have to consider was whether avowed homosexuals should be permitted to serve in the military. But even if we had merely reasoned that women's love for their own children made them any more or less capable than men of formulating national policy on health care, education, or even family leave and child care, then we would be as open to ridicule as Aristophanes' imaginary Athenians. Caring is not the same as governing.

At the Democratic convention in July much was made of the Year of the Woman. Arguably, the best and boldest speech of the convention was made by former Texas congresswoman and university lecturer Barbara Jordan. She concluded with her own tribute to the Year of the Woman, quoting the great nineteenth-century analyst of democracy, Alexis de Tocqueville. In a famous remark in *Democracy in America* Tocqueville goes so far as to credit America's prosperity to the superiority of its women.[2] Jordan chose the right authority on America and she got the quote right, but she may have missed the irony. While Tocqueville observes that Americans allow women to listen to political speeches, he in fact contends that America's women are superior because they stay out of public life. Jordan's misinterpretation deserves correction and comment because, in being so characteristic of our times, it sheds some light on what the Year of the Democratic Woman may portend.

In attributing America's prosperity and power to the superiority of its women, Tocqueville notes that the Americans of 1830 had made women the moral and intellectual equals of men while leaving them social inferiors. "In this," he says, "I think they have wonderfully understood the true conception of democratic progress."[3] Given that Tocqueville is even more famous for his praise of America's free political institutions and its active political participation than for his praise of her women, his acquiescence in women's exclusion from public life is problematic. Nor is it unimportant, because Tocqueville insists that he holds everything affecting the condition, habits, and opinions of women to be "of great political interest."[4]

When Tocqueville reflected on the attitudes of and toward American women a century and a half ago, he compared them favorably both to aristocratic paternalism and to the kind of democratic egalitarianism that immediately interprets difference in status as proof of unequal and, therefore, unjust and intolerable treatment. The American women for whom Tocqueville had such a high regard had been given remarkable freedom; they had been educated by exposure to all the charms and vices of society, that is, of men. Yet at some point street-smart, spunky maidens chose to become demure matrons, marrying and retiring to a cloistered household existence. While Tocqueville concedes that society required this of American women, he also presents it as an act of wisdom and courage, no less than of moderation, on the part of women. Moreover, it is a source of personal pride for them. These women gracefully accepted their lot in an imperfect world and made the best of it. Men, for their part, are said to have respected their wives' judgment. In his account of this transformation Tocqueville never says that this is natural *for women* in the sense that women's natures (e.g., as mothers) suit them, rather than men, to a private and apparently subordinate life. Because he does not, he suggests that women as homemakers play socially necessary gender roles which may or may not bring them happiness as individuals.

How could Tocqueville say that this situation reflects the true notion of democratic progress? Tocqueville proclaims himself to be a friend of democracy, and the proof of friendship he offers is his willingness to criticize democracy. He applauds the Americans for their attachment to free institutions, for their propensity to form voluntary associations, and for a level of political activity that, he says, must be seen to be believed. He praises these institutions, associations, and activities not only as bulwarks against tyranny, but as democracy's means of nurturing civilized human beings. He calls local political institutions—epitomized by the New England township—the "primary schools" of liberty and political associations like parties its "great free schools."[5] By participating in local government citizens acquire a taste for freedom and learn its habits. They meet frequently to discuss public business and serve for short tenures in numerous minor elective offices. Their ambitions are aroused, while tempered by affection and disciplined to respect the formalities of political order. The link between self-interest and a stable general good is made visible, as when citizens vote to tax themselves to pay for a school that benefits the children of all or, in truth, most. Political associations do not require a sacrifice of self-interest, nor do they suppose an identification of it with the interests of all. Hence they are "free schools"; they make neither onerous nor unreasonable demands. Rather, parties unite similarly interested selves to advance their common interest. Thus the self-interested ambition of individuals is enlarged to partisanship. At the same time, it is recognized as partisan, that is, partial. Political participants learn of the partisanship of democracy itself—the regime that first insists that all citizens are equal and similar, even if they are not, and then serves the interests of a majority, not all.

The interested, if disciplined ambition that finds its outlet in political association has as its purpose to further one politician's career at the expense of another's, but also to advance some political opinion. For Tocqueville, there is one substantive disagreement that lies at the base of all political partisanship. "One party want[s] to restrict popular [public] power and the other to extend it indefinitely.[6] Since the time of Thomas Jefferson's election in 1800, Tocqueville contends, proponents of the former opinion have lost their authority in American politics to partisans of the latter, democratic opinion. Many of the principles of these "aristocratic" partisans were established by the Constitution, some "were introduced under their adversaries' slogans," and others continued to be held only by people who eschewed politics altogether.[7] Thus what we see of America's partisan politics takes place within a fundamentally democratic horizon under which the greatest political dispute can usually be aired only indirectly.

Moreover, as Tocqueville well knew, all politics takes place in what we now call a political culture. Not only political opinions, but "habits of the heart," to use Tocqueville's own phrase, affect politics indirectly, but nonetheless powerfully. Tocqueville is far less willing to praise democratic opinions and mores, as distinguished from American political institutions and practices, which may be liberal and republican, but not necessarily democratic, in origin and spirit.

Several years ago someone jokingly gave to a male chauvinist I know a book entitled *The Feminization of America: How Women's Values Are Changing Our Public and Private Lives*.[8] Had the book been written 150 years earlier it would have been entitled *The Democratization of America*, or perhaps just *Democracy in America*. Virtually all of the transformations in American life described in the 1985 book and attributed to the increasing authority of women Tocqueville expects to be consequences of a gradual acceptance of democratic opinions and mores. This observation might lead us to ask whether one reassessment and redefinition of the Year of the Woman as the Century of Women does not go far enough.[9] However impressive the advances of 1992 for women may be, they may in fact be manifestations of an even more profound evolution of American political culture.

In *The Feminization of America*, Elinor Lenz and Barbara Myerhoff describe "women's culture" without seeking to determine whether the characteristics they attribute to women are natural or have been acquired through centuries of playing socially imposed gender roles. Women, they contend, are essentially concerned with the creation and preservation of life. It is women who have borne and nurtured children, who have cared for the sick and elderly, who have attended to the many little repetitive tasks whose completion makes everyday life livable. These concerns have engendered in women both a capacity to form intimate personal attachments and a readiness to empathize broadly. Women "connect." They prefer informal and adaptive cooperation to either subordination or leadership within rigid hierarchies. In general, they eschew form for substance, abstract principles for specific loyalties, respect for the transcendent for reverence for the immanent. They find "irresistible" "the vision of a nonsexist, nonracist, nonexploitative human family."[10] If they have their way, they will see to it that their sons, mates, and coworkers are "expressive, openminded, vulnerable, empathetic"[11] and make attending to human needs the national priority. They will face themselves, others, and the world with their "individual conscience [as their] ultimate authority, [and] a value system based on cooperation, compassion, and intimacy [as] an essential source of spiritual sustenance."[12]

These characteristics of women's culture the authors term "cooperative individualism," which they explicitly liken to the enlightened self-interest of *Democracy in America*. According to Tocqueville, however, individualism does not merely define women's culture; rather it is the foundation of American life as a whole. Enlightened self-interest is inevitably the democratic moral principle because it is the premise of democratic politics. "Providence has given each individual the amount of reason necessary for him to look after himself in matters of his own exclusive concern. That is the great maxim on which civil and political society in the United States rests."[13]

Yet for Tocqueville, our American doctrine of self-interest wellunderstood is as much a statement of a problem as it is a solution. Individualism is an opinion that each and every human being is capable of figuring out for himself everything he needs to know to live his life as he might wish. He need rely neither on his contemporaries for advice nor on custom or tradition as an authority embodying a collective wisdom. At the same time, since most people spend most of their time worrying about personal everyday problems that usually can be solved, it becomes easy to suppose that every problem is capable of rational resolution. Thus individual judgment becomes an immense intellectual and psychological burden. It is relieved in part by simplification. By relying on broad generalizations we can assume that similar facts and beings are actually identical or equal. The burden is even more effectively relieved by seeking refuge in public opinion. An individual looks around and sees many other people holding more or less similar opinions, thereby making them all the more credible. Yet he sees no particular person claiming responsibility for them, so no one's pride is hurt in subscribing to them. After the 1992 presidential debates, for example, television audiences were no longer told by political analysts who did well and why, but rather how other anonymous viewers like themselves reacted in instantaneous polls.

On the whole, Tocqueville shows, democratic public opinion holds to three dogmas: individualism, egalitarianism, and a sort of "decent materialism." Democrats not only make equality the presupposition of individualism, they make equality an end. After all, if individuals are equal in the most important respect, why should they not have equal results to show for equal exertions? The kind of equality that most recommends itself as a possible end is equal well-being or comfort. Enjoyment of well-being is individual, and we are all more or less equally capable of it. The Americans Tocqueville observed were "preoccupied caring for the slightest needs of the body and the trivial conveniences of life."[14] In their preoccupation they were not happy, but "grave and almost sad."[15] Because they had come to think that the happiness they sought consisted in experiencing the mortal body's pleasures, they fretted under the awareness that they had a limited time for such experiences. So while they methodically pursued desire after desire, they were saddened at the thought of not tasting all pleasures. Departing from Tocqueville's description, but not from his analysis, it is not too difficult to imagine that at some point these anxious Americans might come to value more the time in which to enjoy pleasures than the pleasures themselves, abandoning alcohol and tobacco in the hope of gaining an extra year or two to jog.

While Tocqueville loudly applauds the doctrine of self-interest well-understood for encouraging the American proclivity to associate, he more subtly faults it for the grounds on which it encourages association. The doctrine, he notes, is "wonderfully suited to human weaknesses," and it is the "best suited . . . to the needs of men in our time."[16] Despite its dictum that "what is useful is never wrong," it does, more or less successfully, persuade citizens to sacrifice some of their private interests for the sake of preserving the rest.[17] Why these remarks amount to criticisms becomes clear when one considers Tocqueville's account of the "habits of the heart" of democrats, and thus the particular ways in which they are inclined to associate.

When Tocqueville first observed America, he contrasted the "natural, frank, and open" manner of its social intercourse to that of still aristocratic Europe.[18] The Americans did not stand on ceremony; to the contrary, they despised formalities. In their everyday relations they tended to be gentle and sympathetic, and they came readily to the aid of their fellows in need. "Each instantaneously can judge the feelings of all the others; he just casts a rapid glance at himself, and that is enough. So there is no misery that he cannot readily understand. . . . It makes no difference if strangers or enemies are in question; his imagination at once puts him in their place."[19] In principle, the equality Americans recognize is equality of ability. In fact, however, the perceived or presumed equality that moves democratic citizens is an equality of need. Since each is all too aware of his own "misery," or neediness, "there is a sort of tacit and almost unintentional agreement between them which provides that each owes to the other a temporary assistance which he in turn can claim at need."[20] Thus underlying democracy's natural, frank, and open manners is not only a dogmatic assumption of equality but a preoccupation with need rather than ability. Similarly, the explicit and intentional agreements that articulate our democratic sense of justice tend to be constituted with a view to "the universal and permanent needs of mankind."[21] However necessary and desirable they may be, democracy's most just associations will never be humanly satisfying because they require us to disregard the peculiar needs and unequal abilities of each human being.

Worse, the sympathetic awareness of neediness that urges the utility of democratic associations may undermine their very possibility. Individuals need to associate because they are weak, and they will associate when they can anticipate that it will be in their self-interest to have assisted one another. But how can this calculation be relied on? And how can a collection of self-consciously weak individuals be supposed to be all that strong? Consequently,

the citizen of a democracy [develops] extremely contradictory instincts. He is full of confidence and pride in his independence among his equals, but from time to time his weakness makes him feel the need for some outside help which he cannot expect from any of his fellows . . . In this extremity he naturally turns his eyes toward that huge entity which alone stands out above the universal level of abasement [that is, the government]. . . . [H]e ends by regarding it as the sole and necessary support of his individual weakness.[22]

Thus Tocqueville's fear for democracy is that self-government in the broadest sense through associations will be subsumed by the benevolent despotism we now refer to as big government. This government will "care," and the obvious needs of all citizens will be met. But we as a people may well cease to cultivate the qualities of human beings that sustain their independence, liberty, and dignity.

To democracy's morality of sympathetic individualism Tocqueville opposes something like aristocratic honor or, in a form more appropriate to democracy, a concern for liberty and human dignity. Tocqueville's aristocrat ranks courage as the highest virtue. He will fight fiercely for his independence and liberty, although he is not an "individual." Rather, he respects hierarchical authority and tradition. His selfishness assumes the form of a passionate defense of his family and its good name. Adhering to formalities of all sorts, he conforms his behavior not to his "conscience" in the loose contemporary nonreligious sense, but to a fixed public code of mores. Keenly aware of his own distinctiveness, he is incapable of sympathy. But generosity and, when necessary, self-sacrifice and contempt for material comfort are obligations of duty.

The American woman Tocqueville deems superior might be said to combine the best of democracy and aristocracy. She reasons her own way to an acceptance of the forms that seem necessary to society and, arguably, to her own well-being. Moreover, it is she who effectively sustains what remains of resistance to the expansion of public power: she tends to be religious and attempts to make her home a respite from the life of anxious mediocrity encouraged by democracy's economic and social institutions. Throughout, she maintains her proud self-confidence in her character and judgment in the face of apparent subordination.

Today, American women are no longer content with moral and intellectual equality and social inferiority, and their dissatisfaction must now be indulged. But they, no less than men, might guard against being too much swayed by a public opinion that espouses democratic pieties. In Aristophanes' Year of the Woman, the women of Athens claim to replace polity with family while in truth destroying both. We can be more confident that their leader benefits herself than that she benefits the city. In our Year of the Woman, the women who have won political power have done so by blending their traditional images as care-providers with their new roles as successful career women. Yet many now seem poised to use their power to advance a radical, if democratic, political agenda. The feminization of America is coincident with the further democratization of America and a consequence of it. It may also become one more cause of it. It would be unfair and untrue to assert that American women have now consciously chosen to substitute for subordination to a particular man dependence on a paternalistic, if impersonal, government. But they may be tempted to do so. Contemporary women have been taught by democratic individualism to believe that they have been ill-served or even oppressed by traditional associations, especially the family. They may now determine to "change" government by giving to it unprecedented responsibilities, foreign as well as domestic, in the name of care and compassion.

Tocqueville advises Americans to pin their hopes for democracy on the sense of responsibility acquired by individuals in the practical activity of politics and on the confident restraint exerted by women. What women choose to do with their newly won public power will matter very much. In the speech in which Barbara Jordan invoked his authority, Tocqueville would have been pleased but not astonished to learn, she attacked her own party for its unthinking attachment to entitlements and to its "tax and spend" ways. All our women and men would do well to use the opportunity provided by the notice given to the Year of the Woman to reflect on what truly constitutes democratic progress.

Notes

1. David Brock, *The Real Anita Hill* (New York: Free Press, 1993), p. 17.
2. Alexis de Tocqueville, *Democracy in America*, ed. J. P. Mayer, trans. George Lawrence (Garden City, N.Y.: Doubleday, 1969), p. 603.
3. Ibid.
4. Ibid., p. 590.
5. Ibid., pp. 63, 522.
6. Ibid., p. 175 with p. 178.
7. Ibid., p. 177.
8. Elinor Lenz and Barbara Myerhoff, *The Feminization of America: How Women's Values Are Changing Our Public and Private Lives*, (Los Angeles: Tarcher, 1985).
9. P. Gaull Silberman, vice-chair EEOC, *Wall Street Journal*, Oct. 20, 1992.

15

The New Democratic Community: Clinton, Communitarianism, and the New Liberalism

Bruce Frohnen

"Now that we have changed the world, it's time to change America." These were Bill Clinton's confident words as he accepted his party's presidential nomination in 1992. America's victory in the Cold War, he argued, made it time for a new politics in this nation, to be ushered in by a new kind of Democrat. And then-Governor Clinton had reason to see himself as the fated new Democrat. For years he had participated in the Democratic Leadership Council, a group of self-styled moderates determined to rebuild their party's appeal to the middle class. For years he also had been a forceful advocate among America's governors for policies and rhetoric intended to bring forth a new vision of government's role in America's communities. Here was a Democrat who spoke of the need for personal responsibility. A Democrat who wanted to eliminate "welfare as we know it." A Democrat who wanted to increase police protection in the cities, institute enterprise zones, and eliminate excess bureaucracy. Surely this was a *new* Democrat?

Yes and no. Clinton's programs and even his rhetoric were much less revolutionary than he, his supporters or the press seemed to believe. From the start his proposals had much in common with those of his more overtly liberal rivals. But his proposed methods would extend liberal reasoning and policy-making beyond their traditional bounds. Where traditional liberals aimed to ensure human beings against the harms of life and the harmful results of their actions (for example through Social Security, welfare and unemployment insurance), Clinton aimed, where possible, to prevent the harmful events and acts themselves. His programs would educate us, and government, producing conduct and character that are safer and more in keeping with liberal goals.

As political scientist Theodore Lowi has argued, traditional liberalism has a problem; it undermines itself because its motivating idea—that government should not be in the business of judging private morality but should instead insure us against the harmful effects of private actions—makes everything a proper object of "neutral" government attention. All actions have potentially bad effects, and so liberal governments bankrupt themselves as they end up infringing on the very private sphere they were constructed to protect.

To their credit, Clinton and his advisers recognized liberalism's deeper problem: it encourages the very kinds of behavior against which it is supposed to protect us. Welfare programs promote dependence, permissive divorce laws promote family breakdown, and so on. Clinton's "new idea" was the realization that private acts have public consequences. Thus he sought to prevent harmful acts, in large part by utilizing families and local associations to produce the kinds of men who would not make demands on the already weakened liberal state. But Clinton did not trust private and social institutions to produce the kinds of human beings he liked—"tolerant" liberals. To produce these kinds of men would require that government "educate" families, churches, and local associations into the proper, egalitarian liberal mindset.

Much of Clinton's support and many of his ideas in this project came from a group of intellectuals, policy analysts, and activists calling themselves "communitarians." Communitarians took this label to show their conviction that individual rights, while important, must be balanced against the needs of the community. As Amitai Etzioni, editor of the communitarians' flagship journal, *The Responsive Community*, put it, "The essence of the communitarian position is that strong rights entail strong responsibilities."[1] In connecting rights with responsibilities, communitarians saw themselves as transcending traditional political divisions. In their view conservatives would violate the needy's right to public support and everyone's right to be free from "puritanical" social legislation. At the same time, liberals had come to see government as a provider of ever more public support to recipients owing nothing in return, and had forgotten the importance of families and the habits of moral responsibility taught therein. Communitarians meanwhile would use welfare programs as a means by which to teach responsibility (without resorting to "authoritarianism") and turn recipients into productive citizens.

Communitarian welfare reform, as Robert Shapiro put it, would "be . . . a basic plank in a new covenant of rights and responsibilities, governing the way Americans secure basic social goods."[2] Clinton claimed that this "new covenant" would produce "a government that offers more empowerment and less entitlement." There would be less bureaucracy and more economic opportunity because Americans would work together, having formed "a solemn agreement between the people and their government, based not simply on what each of us can take, but on what all of us must give to our nation."

Clinton made a number of specific policy proposals intended to enhance what he saw as a symbiotic relationship among liberal democratic values, rights, and responsibilities. College education would be made affordable to all by requiring aid recipients to engage in public works projects after graduation, presumably helping their communities and learning in the process. Government would guarantee universal health care, but keep costs low in part by stiffening requirements concerning preventive and prenatal health care. Training, education, and public spending programs would be beefed up to provide jobs for the habitually unemployed, but those receiving public assistance would be required to train, look for, and accept work where possible, or lose this support.

The accepted wisdom by the time of the convention was that such proposals made Clinton a new kind of Democrat. The story went that traditional leaders of the liberal wing of the party opposed Clinton's program because of its "centrist" leanings. New York Governor Mario Cuomo, it was reported, thought that Clinton's welfare proposals in essence "blamed the victims" of poverty and thus were tinged with racism. Yet Cuomo himself used communitarian language in his nominating speech at the convention. He praised Clinton for adhering to the "politics of inclusion," in which people "of whatever color, of whatever creed, of whatever sex, of whatever sexual orientation, all [are] equal members of the American family." Clinton, according to Cuomo, would "make the whole nation stronger by bringing people together, showing us our commonality, instructing us in cooperation, making us not a collection of competing special interests, but one great, special family—the family of America."

Cuomo's, and Clinton's, emphasis on the president's role as educator, as the man who will make Americans better by teaching them to cooperate (and that they can cooperate because they are essentially alike) lies at the core of communitarianism, as it lies at the core of liberal politics in general. Communitarianism is not, then, a "new" politics, but rather an extension of liberal politics. As for more traditional liberals, for communitarians politics is and should be the focus of public life and should be used to establish greater material equality. Government must not judge, let alone nurture, citizens' souls, but only maintain the peace so that the material pursuits of private life may continue, checked only by the political pursuit of equality.

Communitarians may be distinguished from more traditional liberals because they are eager to discuss the kind of character they feel is necessary to maintain liberal politics. Family and neighborhood "values" are important elements in forming this character. Yet this character, that of the tolerant pursuer of material well-being, is remarkably similar to that called for by traditional liberals. And this character is to be formed, not merely by the families, churches, and local associations of civil society, but by government "facilitators" and others educated in communitarian ideology. A return to traditional religious norms was explicitly rejected in favor of egalitarian structures such as "inclusive" families to be maintained by liberal state action, in the name of liberal goals.

Here I examine Clinton's communitarian program and its relationship to liberal democratic politics. I want to show that its "tough" technocratic and its "soft" values sides fit together to form a vision in which government retrains Americans into safer, more caring liberal citizens. I begin by examining proposals to reform bureaucracy and so "reinvent" government. I then discuss the communitarian approach to welfare reform and "family values." Finally, I examine the communitarian vision of just what, and how, government should teach us.

New Technocrats?

Often called the "Bible" of the Clinton administration, David Osborne and Ted Gaebler's *Reinventing Government* seems distinctly new and unliberal. In it Osborne and Gaebler gather together and systematize arguments they made both before and during the campaign. They favored privatizing a number of government activities, rearranging bureaucratic duties and attitudes to emphasize "client" service, and providing more discretion to administrative managers. Such reforms, according to their proponents, would make government cheaper, more responsive and thus more efficient. Yet these reforms would not aim to reduce the *role* of government in our lives; they explicitly aimed to make government *better* at reordering our lives. As the authors put it,

"Government is the mechanism we use to make communal decisions." The authors "believe deeply in government"—in its role in educating us, solving our "collective problems" and establishing "equity."[3]

One of Osborne and Gaebler's favorite notions was "anticipatory democracy," that is, government that tries to prevent problems rather than deal with them when they occur. Thus they endorsed preventive regulations such as bans on nonrecyclable packages, and favored government "futures commissions" and strategic planning. Such programs would reorient government, in their view, allowing it to transcend outmoded New Deal and Progressive structures in which the government attempted to do all the work itself. Now, they said, government would steer the ship, but leave others to do the rowing.

Such reforms clearly would entail change. But they hardly constitute a rejection of liberalism. Even the privatization Osborne and Gaebler recommended was far less than revolutionary. The sanitation and other basic services Osborne and Gaebler would privatize would not become the subjects of free competition, but of competition "managed" by the government—with wages, working conditions, and even specific employees mandated by that government. The state would give up direct control, but would continue to mandate who would do what, when, where, and how.

Other Clinton proposals to rationalize and limit government action also would leave government control intact. His "enterprize zones," supposedly market-oriented because they would entail tax breaks and a loosening of bureaucratic regulations, also would involve significant government oversight. Only businesses agreeing to employ a high quota of "disadvantaged" area residents and to reinvest in the locality would be eligible for these special dispensations. Government agents would have to approve detailed business and local government plans before any consideration would be forthcoming.

Osborne and Gaebler (and Clinton) sought "entrepreneurial government." What this meant, in effect, was that the problem Lowi sees in liberalism actually would be made worse by "reinvented" government. Bureaucrats would be further divorced from the consequences of their actions because they would have more power and less accountability. They would find it easier to regulate because regulation, now involving only "mandates" rather than detailed regulatory schemes, would seem more benign, fair, and easy. No longer saddled with the task of determining precisely *how* goals such as workplace safety and decreased pollution could be accomplished, bureaucrats would find it easier to dictate that companies and individuals do so. The liberal impulse to regulate everything actually would continue to rule. Government agents would be tempted to regulate everything and so would be unable to solve the problems of liberalism.

Only one thing would change: the increased emphasis on mandates would put the onus on companies and individuals to change their behavior more radically and with more initiative than would actual laws. Where specific laws require only acquiescence to government dictates, mandates require that "mandatees" determine exactly how they might obey the will of the state without going bankrupt. Reinvented government would require active participation rather than dependence and acquiescence. It would require citizens with cooperative, or at least active and inventive, characters.

Welfare

Communitarians' real contribution to liberalism was their recognition that private character produces public consequences. Communitarians recognized, and Clinton often emphasized, that unemployment, poverty, and other social ills come about in large part because individuals do not have the habits necessary for productive participation in public and especially economic life. To combat these social ills Clinton would reform welfare, rearranging economic incentives to make work more attractive.

Economic reforms would stem from a new and universal right. All Americans would be entitled to universal health care and pensions. But this new right would be linked to the responsibility to work. Clinton summed up his welfare reform program in his acceptance speech: "We will say to those on welfare, you will have and you deserve the opportunity through training and education, through child care and medical coverage, to liberate yourself. . . . But then, when you can, you must work, because welfare should be a second chance, not a way of life." Welfare recipients would have the right to have government provide the means—the education, training, and mandated health care—by which to liberate themselves from their dependency. But they also would have the responsibility to take advantage of these incentives, to get jobs and get off welfare whenever possible.

These proposals were at the heart of communitarianism's centrist appearance. A new, paternalistic government would instill habits of hard work and personal responsibility by demanding real effort on the part of aid recipients. Some called such proposals punitive or even "racist" because they would affect the poor (among whom minorities were overrepresented) rather than all Americans. But Clinton was not to be so criticized. He and his aides quickly pointed out that sanctions would apply only to those who "could" work, and that this category would be defined narrowly, leaving out the vast bulk of welfare recipients, including single mothers.

Because proposals such as "workfare" would affect few welfare recipients, they could be only a small part of any attempt to encourage work. Communitarians would have to look beyond a restructuring of work incentives to prevent dependence on government and so cure the ills of liberalism. They would have to look to an institution more natural and fundamental than government. They would have to look to the family.

As William Galston, now a Clinton domestic policy adviser, put it: "The core issue is a traditional one: the role of the family as a moral unit that transmits, or fails to transmit, the beliefs and dispositions needed to support oneself and to contribute to one's community."[4] Communitarians stood with tradition (and against traditional liberalism) by recognizing the family's essential role in forming character and by recognizing the individual's inherent responsibility to contribute to his community. Yet tradition was precisely what communitarians, and Clinton himself, were struggling against. For they sought to legitimate new "family values" and harness them to a liberal program. They sought to transcend traditional justifications for and even definitions of the family. The question was how such a new, "inclusive" family could be made to support the liberal system communitarians wished to preserve.

Family Values

One clear goal of Clinton's acceptance speech was to defuse the "family values" issue raised by his marital infidelities and by his Republican opponent. He told of his troubled childhood and of his mother's struggles in raising him with no husband. Clinton then declared that "Our families have values. But our government doesn't."

But what values do our families have, and what values does our government need? One value Clinton argued needed strengthening was that of supporting one's children. He called on parents (presumably absent fathers) to take responsibility for their offspring "or we will force you to do so." Thus Clinton showed his willingness to place political rhetoric, and perhaps sanction, behind at least one "family value." As throughout history, so today for Clinton we must take care of our own.

But Clinton's family values were intended to go beyond tradition. His family itself would be much more inclusive than his opponent's. Echoing Cuomo's earlier references to the American family, he called for "an America that includes every family: every traditional family and every extended family, every two-parent family, every single-parent family and every foster family. Every family."

Declining to be morally judgmental, government would fund whatever form of "family" individuals chose. Clinton's inclusive family values would "live in our actions, not just in our speeches." Government would support families by providing economic opportunity and jobs programs (as under traditional liberalism) and by mandating that employers finance universal health care and "family leave" to allow parents to spend more time with their offspring.

Clinton's "new" vision of family values was reflected in his choice of urban policy advisers. One chief adviser was William Julius Wilson, a black sociologist who had been much criticized by liberals for describing the declining importance of race in causing social breakdown in our inner cities. Wilson argued in his book *The Truly Disadvantaged* that high rates of illegitimacy (greater than 60 percent among blacks) were not caused by government programs which pay to support illegitimate children.[5] Instead, according to Wilson, the lack of truly "eligible" males kept women in ghettoes from getting married, even if pregnant. The problem, for Wilson, was that there were not enough jobs for which ghetto males were qualified. If only government would do its job of providing employment opportunities, families once again would form and cohere, ending many of our urban problems.

Government must support families. But there was more than this. As for Cuomo, so for Clinton the nation itself *was* a family. Throughout his career Cuomo, to many the leader of traditional liberalism, had spoken of the body politic as a family. As family members were duty-bound to help one another, so, for Cuomo, were more fortunate Americans duty-bound to help their less fortunate brethren. Indeed, in a speech at a New York church Cuomo had emphasized our duty "as a *government*" to be our brother's keeper.[6]

Cuomo, Clinton's rival but not his ideological enemy, had long spoken in "new" communitarian terms. He had emphasized the government's role as the keeper of the morals as well as the peace of the nation. He had emphasized politics as the proper sphere in which charity is to be done. He had, as a communitarian would, seen politics as the proper means by which to improve the moral as well as the material lot of Americans.

The government, as father, would take responsibility for those in need of assistance. But now the government also would seek to use families as one means by which to protect citizens from dangers like poverty. Through programs from Head Start and other preschool and day care mechanisms to prenatal health care to "values education," communitarians would foster a particular form of egalitarian, caring family in which children would be free from want and distress. Government programs would give them the character necessary to be independent of government programs.

Communitarians would seek to produce individuals with the means and character necessary to pursue their material wants and desires without fear of failure. Only in this way could liberal government cease producing welfare dependents and so remain viable. As Galston asserted, "a healthy liberal democracy, . . . is more than an artful arrangement of institutional devices and public policies. It requires, as well, the right kinds of citizens possessing the virtues appropriate to a liberal democratic community." And "stable, intact families make a vital contribution of such citizens." This was the source of the communitarian concern with the family. "Liberal democracy" requires a certain kind of citizen, and therefore should seek to produce such citizens.[7] Tolerant, egalitarian families should be encouraged and maintained so that they might raise children with appropriate, liberal democratic habits.

Once again asserting that communitarians transcend both liberals (who emphasize economic needs at the expense of moral issues) and conservatives (who "have harped on values while neglecting economic realities"), Galston argued for a "third way"—one in which responsibilities would attach to both government and family members. Government would have the responsibility to lower taxes on families, increase wages, and increase funding of supportive services available to families. Individuals would have the responsibility to support their children (whatever their relationship to the child's other parent); "to make every effort to get married and stay married . . . to refrain from activities such as substance abuse that harm their children and diminish their capacities as parents; and to involve themselves actively in their children's education and socialization."

This seems a rather spiritless vision of the role and responsibilities of family life. It rejects religious sanctity, tradition, and habitual affection as justifications and motivations for family unity. Yet the individual still is told to restrain his destructive urges as government provides material support in the name of family cohesion. But why support family cohesion? Why should we give up drugs and sexual and monetary freedom for the sake of the mere biological products of our sex drives? Galston answered: "We have known for some time about the economic consequences of family disintegration." And these consequences are simple to relate: the vast majority of children brought up in two-parent households never experience poverty while the vast majority of children who spend time in single-parent households *will* experience poverty.

Put succinctly, for Galston we should support families because "the best anti-poverty program for children is a stable, intact family."[8] Thus Galston continued the communitarian (and traditional liberal) emphasis upon the family as a unit of economic well-being. Government and individuals should support families because, statistically speaking, families are most likely to prevent the poverty we find painful to watch and the welfare dependency we find painful to support with our tax dollars.

Galston did point to other problems with family breakdown. "A mountain of research accumulated over the past two decades indicates that for the psychological development and educational achievement of children, as well as their economic well-being, the intact two-parent family is generally preferable to the alternatives."[9] Clinton refused such a "narrow" vision of the family's proper structure. Yet it was to the family's educative role that Clinton as well as Galston would look in rebuilding the character necessary for liberal democratic politics. Brought up in a stable environment, free from fear of hunger, failure, or criticism for being "different" on account of appearance, gender, sexual practices, or personal habits, children, communitarians claimed, would grow up to be happy, tolerant, and successful pursuers of material well-being.

Galston was careful to avoid making overtly moral arguments to support two-parent families. But he bowed to tradition more than once. He even took issue with Wilson's argument that families fail to form and cohere because of the lack of jobs. This argument was incomplete, Galston pointed out, noting that Wilson himself had come to accept that "signals of cultural approval and disapproval have autonomous effects on patterns of family life." Government must go beyond monetary support if families are to form and prosper. Galston even noted government's responsibility "to nurture rather than undermine the network of intermediary associations . . . within which families function best."[10]

Galston, like communitarians in general, recognized that families cannot survive on their own. They require support from neighborhood groups and local associations if they are to survive the hardships and temptations of modern life. But again, communitarians sought no return to traditional values. They rejected any overtly religious basis for the family, and saw civil associations as merely one more means by which government could foster "the psychological development and educational achievement of children, as well as their economic well-being." Communitarians sought to produce "well-adjusted" individuals who would not look to government for support. But how can liberal government bring this about?

The Politics of Community

Communitarians from the start were careful to distance themselves from any call for a return to traditional values or to a traditional form of family life. They feared being labeled conservative or "authoritarian." Thus communitarians spent much time and effort decrying conservatives as "moral majority types" and defending moderated forms of feminism, multicultural education, and affirmative action.[11] The 1950s in particular were a target of communitarian satire and charges of "authoritarian" inequality. Thus communitarians showed traditional liberals both their willingness to support liberal positions and their opposition to traditional "conservative" notions of the family's sanctity and its essential role as a social rather than a political institution.

For conservatives the family always had been separate from and more important than the political process. Government, in this view, should support traditional family roles and prerogatives, in large part by protecting them from political innovations. Communitarians, on the other hand, sought "to shore up social responsibilities by shoring up values education in the family and in the schools and by strengthening community bonds, which are the best carriers of moral commitments."[12]

Political means would be used to teach values in family and school and to "strengthen" the bonds of the local community. Communitarians did not trust religious organizations, let alone parents, to guide young people in their choices concerning, for example, marriage. Thus Etzioni called for laws "educating the young on ways to resolve conflicts and providing counseling sessions before marriage." Legally enforced waiting periods before marriage also would be used, not to "be punitive, but rather to signal society's concern for the preservation of the family."

The concern not to be seen as "punitive" ran deep among communitarians. Financial rewards to parents for keeping their children in school rather than fines for truancy, courses on tolerance or "interracial lunches" instead of legal sanctions to deal with so-called hate speech, and "carefully crafted" laws to prevent drug dealers from operating in public housing projects—all would, according to Etzioni, foster community. Some arbitrary acts would be necessary. For example, anyone dying without signing the appropriate form would be considered to have agreed to have his organs donated so that those in need of transplants could have them. But the new community would focus on counseling rather than coercion. The individual would remain master of his own destiny; he would merely receive helpful guidance and counseling from agents of the state.

Educators and other "facilitators" would teach tolerance, equality, and "moral reasoning." Thus, "schools should provide courses on human relations that teach people how to resolve conflicts and relate better to one another as spouses, co-workers, and fellow citizens."[13] We would be trained to discover for ourselves how best we might pursue our own ends without offending anyone and without surrendering to "authoritarian" moral strictures and structures. Families and local organizations would receive government support. But they would receive this support on condition that they submit to the ministrations of government educators so that they would be certain to further liberal goals.

To be sure, natural familial affections would continue to exist, but they would be made to further the political goals of liberalism. Bill Clinton and Al Gore themselves showed the nature of communitarian affection at the Democratic convention. Gore told the audience about his sister's death and his son's near-fatal car accident. Clinton spoke of his father's death and his mother's cancer. Each of these stories of personal tragedy was linked to a political argument—from calls for nationalized health care to criticisms of the incumbent's civil rights record. Sensitivity was a communitarian value, and one of electoral significance.

The family, as shown by both Clinton's and Gore's acceptance speeches, was the source of pain and lessons. It was a microcosm of political life, and its experiences were to be used in public forums and

even policy-making. Personal anecdotes replaced references to God
and tradition because, whereas personal stories involve a nonjudg-
mental sharing of spontaneous feelings, reference to more permanent
standards require that we accept moral norms based on a law higher
than ourselves or our political process. And the political process
remained for communitarians the proper locus of moral as well as
economic life.

Communitarians sought to reinvigorate families and civil associations as primarily *political* institutions. When discussing the moral
problems of our society, communitarians generally referred to the
need to reemphasize "people's political development—their capacity
to organize their common life." As for Osborne and Gaebler, so for
more value-oriented communitarians such as Etzioni and Berkeley
sociologist Robert Bellah, politics is the means and the forum of public
action. Families and civil associations, with the help of the state,
would train good citizens who would come together through political
means to distribute goods ranging from jobs to money to social status.[14]

Galston showed a more moderate side of the communitarian commitment to paternalistic government. Liberal governments, he insisted,
had to focus, not merely on substantive goals such as economic
equality, but also on teaching the habits necessary to sustain rights.
After all, Galston noted, liberal government itself was instituted to
guarantee these rights. Galston even recognized that most folk required religion, rather than merely government ideology, if they are to
act morally. According to Galston only a few intellectuals could
discern "philosophical reasons" for being good, tolerant liberals.
Thus, while school prayer and any public support for particular religions would be improper, the state had to foster an abstract religiosity,
recognizing the need for religious prejudices among the (presumably
ignorant and incorrect) masses.

Liberalism, according to Galston, was hostile to substantive religious life, yet depended on certain (mistaken) religious beliefs among
the masses. To solve this dilemma Galston would have government
tolerate traditional religious beliefs and practices when and to the
extent that they were consistent with the needs of liberalism. Arguments concerning religion and morality would be allowed into the
public arena to the extent that they were based on the functional utility
of moral norms. One acceptable argument: we should support families
because they help support children economically and are necessary
for children to grow up into tolerant, independent pursuers of material
well-being. But moral arguments condemning, or praising, given social

arrangements or personal behavior on the grounds that they are by nature good or bad would not be tolerated. According to Galston such arguments necessarily lead to intolerance. To argue, for example, that homosexuality is bad because unnatural or against God's law necessarily would lead to attempts to oppress homosexuals. Thus such arguments would not be allowed.[15]

Religion and traditional values are too confining in and of themselves. They are "illiberal" save to the extent they are useful in preserving liberalism itself—which cannot exist without the moral absolutes it by nature abhors. How, then, is liberalism, even with its communitarian face, to survive? Apparently through group therapy. Soon after taking office Clinton took his advisers with him to Camp David for a group counseling session. As reported in *Newsweek*, "Specially trained group leaders spent several hours teaching America's most powerful to open up and trust each other. The president started the ball rolling; he told a story about being teased as a fat child."[16]

Public policy itself now would find its moorings in the culture of consciousness-raising. As Clinton had learned to deal with his weight problem, so his administration would learn to deal with the difficulties of changing an intransigent Washington establishment. Decrying the "authoritarianism" of traditional community, but recognizing that community could not be dispensed with, communitarians sought to construct a "thin" community, based upon shared feelings of pain and inadequacy and instilled through the ministrations of professional facilitators.

Much has been said about the role of talk shows such as *Oprah* in American culture and politics. The 1992 elections brought the victory, not just of mass communications, but of mass "community." The ties that bind us were stretched thin as candidates sought to appear morally sincere while offending no one. The result, not surprisingly, was a shallow or thin morality based only on a very thin sense of common affection and purpose. But then the goal itself was morally thin—to make Americans more moderate in their selfishness and so allow the continuation of a "liberal democracy" devoted to the pursuit of physical and psychological comfort.

Notes

1. Amitai Etzioni, "The Communitarian Platform," *The New Democrat* 4 (July 1992), p. 23.

2. Robert Shapiro, "The End of Entitlement," in *The New Democrat* 4 (July 1992), p. 19.

3. David Osborne and Ted Gaebler, *Reinventing Government: How the Entrepreneurial Spirit is Transforming the Public Sector* (New York: Plume, 1993), pp. xviii–xix.

4. William A. Galston, "Family Matters," in *The New Democrat* 4 (July 1992), p. 19.

5. William Julius Wilson, *The Truly Disadvantaged* (Chicago: University of Chicago Press, 1987).

6. Mario Cuomo, "Speech at St. John the Divine," in *Diaries of Mario M. Cuomo: The Campaign for Governor* (New York: Random House, 1984), p. 214.

7. Galston, "Family Matters," p. 19.

8. Ibid., p. 20.

9. Ibid.

10. Ibid.

11. The most complete exposition of the communitarian platform is Amitai Etzioni's *The Spirit of Community* (New York: Crown, 1993), which was published soon after the Clinton inauguration and made much of the influence of communitarians in the new administration.

12. Etzioni in ibid., p. 23.

13. Ibid., pp. 24–25.

14. See Robert N. Bellah, Richard Madsen, William M. Sullivan, Ann Swidler and Steven M. Tipton, *Habits of the Heart: Individualism and Commitment in American Life* (Berkeley: University of California Press, 1985), especially pp. 217–18. I develop this argument more fully in "Robert Bellah and the Politics of 'Civil' Religion," *The Political Science Reviewer*, XXI (Spring 1992), p. 148.

15. See William A. Galston, *Liberal Purposes: Goods, Virtues, and Diversity in the Liberal State* (Cambridge: Cambridge University Press, 1991), Chap. 12.

16. *Newsweek*, Feb. 22, 1993, p. 44.

Conclusion

The 1992 Election and the Future of American Politics

Roger M. Barrus

The 1992 election was characterized by what Harvey Mansfield Jr. has called the "galloping informality" of contemporary American politics, the impatience of the people and their would-be rulers with the forms of constitutional, representative democracy.[1] This antiformalism was manifested, during the campaign, in both the candidates' methods and their rhetoric. It was reflected in the emphatic turn to populist campaign styles—bus and train tours, talk-show appearances, town-hall meetings, chatty infomercials, etc.—all of which were intended to establish a direct, personal relationship between the candidates and the people. It accounted for the almost exclusive emphasis in campaign rhetoric on the president's responsibility to care for the people and to meet their pressing needs. Finally, it was the cause of the candidates' virtual silence on the government institutions, in particular Congress, the courts, and the federal bureaucracy, that might come between the president and the people and interfere with the fulfillment of his personal responsibility to them. Bill Clinton's victory in the election ensures that the antiformalism of the campaign, the effects of which could already be felt in the early months of the new administration, will continue to influence American government and politics for the foreseeable future.

The antiformalist impulse did not, of course, first arise during the 1992 campaign. This has been an important element of American politics for some time, arguably from the very beginning. Popular resentment against the forms of representative government is essentially coeval with the establishment of constitutional democracy. Government forms constrain, indeed are meant to constrain, the majority will. Their purpose is to refine, enlarge, and elevate the opinions and interests of the majority. Periodically this resentment spills out in American politics, expressing itself in the form of popular discontent and demands for reform.[2] These protest and reform movements, which by no means occur only when times are hard, have as their general object the reduction of the formal distinctions between governors and governed. The 1992 campaign took place during what appears to have been the beginning of another period of popular discontent with the forms of representative government. This was the result of an event—the end of the Cold War—that should have been at the center of debate during the campaign, but amazingly went almost without comment, except for occasional boasting by the incumbent George Bush concerning his accomplishments during his term in office. In Bush's stump speeches, liberal democratic America's world-historic victory over Soviet communism was presented as on a par with the passage of the Americans with Disabilities Act and the so-called Civil Rights Restoration Act.

Victory in the long struggle with the Soviet Union had at least the indirect effect of unleashing the American people's deep-seated animosity to the forms of constitutional government. The end of the Cold War seemed to demonstrate the truthfulness of the claim, the slogan of so many popular leaders, that the people of the United States could accomplish anything, if they just put their minds to it. This political article of faith was further confirmed by the spectacular victory of American arms in the Gulf War. The dazzling hopes generated by victory in the two conflicts—hopes that Bush, basking in the warm glow of public opinion, did nothing to restrain—seemed to be confounded by continuing domestic problems, in particular the lingering recession of 1990. The recession, while not especially deep, nevertheless had profound political effects. Layoffs were largely from the middle-class, white-collar workers and middle-level management. It was thus more disruptive than previous recessions, the effects of which were largely confined to politically less vocal and active blue-collar workers. Ironically, the peculiar character of the recession was at least partially attributable to the end of the Cold War, which was already bringing about dislocations in the economy. The American people were not so much interested in the economic consequences of the peace, however, as they were in the cause of the failure of the promise represented by it.

This was popularly attributed to the failures of government, specifically to the "gridlock" between the Republican president and the Democratic Congress. The people were not at all careful to distinguish between political control of the institutions of government and the institutions themselves as the cause of these difficulties. In this way, the fantastic hopes and brooding fears generated by the end of the Cold War expressed themselves politically in the guise of popular frustration with the forms of constitutional government, and the essentially contentless demand for "change." It was this tide of popular passion that Clinton and Ross Perot, perhaps without fully understanding its causes, attempted to ride to power in 1992. They were unwittingly assisted by Bush, who did not perceive the danger lurking in his stratospheric poll numbers at the beginning of the campaign season. This was the cause of his apparent befuddlement throughout the campaign. He never could quite figure out what to say to the voters: whenever he would appeal for their support by pointing to his great achievements in office, he would be met with more insistent demands for change. The solution of Bush's rhetorical problem as incumbent president in a time of high hopes and deep fears, if indeed there was a solution to be found, required penetrating insight into the nature and essential problems of representative government. Here his vaunted pragmatism failed him. It was much easier for Clinton and Perot to take advantage of popular passion, by turning it against Bush, than for him to find a way to contain or redirect it. This is not to say that Clinton and Perot had any clearer idea of how to govern, given the popular frustration with the forms of constitutional democracy, than Bush.

Clinton's victory in the 1992 election transformed Bush's problem into his problem. From the beginning, he made it clear that he would govern in a very different manner from his predecessor. Bush erred on the side of inactivity; Clinton would err on the side of overactivity. This fit both what appeared to be the lesson of the 1992 election and Clinton's temperament as a child of the activist '60s. Just as "change" was the theme of his campaign, so it would be the theme of his administration. Clinton's inaugural address was a virtual paean to change:

When our founders boldly declared America's independence to the world and our purposes to the Almighty, they knew that America, to endure, would have to change. Not change for change's sake but change to preserve America's ideals—life, liberty, the pursuit of happiness. . . . Profound and powerful forces are shaking and remaking our world. And the urgent question of our time is whether we can make change our friend and not our enemy. . . . Thomas Jefferson believed that to preserve the very foundations of our nation we would need dramatic change from time to time. . . . Together with our friends and allies we will work to shape change lest it engulf us. . . . From this joyful mountaintop of celebration we hear a call to service in the valley. We have heard the trumpets, we have changed the guard. And now each in our own way, and with God's help, we must answer the call.[3]

Clinton in his own way was as pragmatic as Bush: he believed in sticking with what "worked." The effect of his pragmatism was apparently the same: no more than Bush did he seem to reflect on the practical problem of governing from the point of view of the nature and essential problems of representative democracy. In particular, he did not seem to consider whether his championing of change, while perhaps useful in getting elected to the presidency, by exciting the already excessive hopes and fears of the people, might make governing as president difficult if not impossible.

That there were problems with Clinton's approach to governing soon became only too apparent. Publicly committed to change, he found it impossible to resist public demands for change. He was forced to adopt as his own the proposed changes put forth by a host of different constituencies. The result was policy-making chaos, with the administration bringing out a flurry of major proposals, only to let many of them languish as it moved on to new issues. He was distracted from many of the issues that he had identified during the campaign as most pressing for the nation, in particular health care reform. Instead of submitting a reform plan within the first 100 days of taking office, as he had promised during the campaign, it was eight months before he had anything to present to Congress and the people. Soon the line on Clinton was that he had "too much on his plate" to really get anything accomplished. It was symptomatic of what was problematic about Clinton's approach to governing that the first great political battle of his administration was over a proposal to allow gays in the military. A distinctly peripheral issue to his agenda of domestic reform, it was brought forward only in response to pressure from gay and liberal activists. The result was an embarrassing defeat in his first encounter with Congress, and in an area—military affairs—in which the president absolutely must maintain his authority.

At the same time, as the agent of change—change as such—Clinton was reluctant to commit himself to any particular change. He was willing, even eager, to negotiate not just on the details but also on the substance of his policy proposals. An example of this was Clinton's abandonment of his proposal for a comprehensive energy tax, to be computed on the basis of the thermal (BTU) content of energy sources. This was a centerpiece of his first budget, and of his plans for a national energy policy. By dint of much legislative arm-twisting, Democratic leaders in the House managed to pass the complicated and unpopular BTU tax. When it came before the Senate, however, it was opposed by a small number of oil state Democrats. Rather than fighting them, Clinton almost immediately capitulated to their demand to substitute a hike in the federal gasoline tax. House Democrats were outraged at the president's surrender. Clinton managed somehow to stand for everything, and nothing. Soon the sobriquet by which he had been known by his critics in Arkansas, "Slick Willie," found its way into national politics. Clinton manifested an unseemly eagerness to compromise even on his proposal for health care reform, what was supposed to be the greatest monument of his (first) term in office. Almost before the ink was dry on the massive tome he submitted to Congress outlining his plan, the product of months of labor by over five hundred policy experts, he was saying that almost everything in it was negotiable, except for certain bedrock principles, including universal coverage. Democrats in Congress began to fear another sellout. It thus became necessary to assure them that this time he would stand firm. The nation was therefore treated to the absurd spectacle in the 1994 State of the Union address of Clinton pulling a pen from his pocket and, to the raucous cheers of congressional Democrats, threatening to use it to veto any health care bill that the Democratic Congress might pass that did not fulfill his requirement for universal coverage.

The result of Clinton's problems during his first months in office was an unprecedented decline in public support. His polls for a time were the lowest ever recorded for a president in his first year. This was potentially disastrous for a political leader who based his claim to rule on his personal relationship with the American people, his embodiment of their most powerful hopes and fears. Clinton's decline in the polls was turned around later in his first year, the result of an improving economy and legislative victories on the budget and the North American Free Trade Agreement (NAFTA). His big victories in Congress, however, testified more to his weakness than to his strength. He won the budget vote by the narrowest of margins, against solid Republican opposition, only when Democratic leaders raised the specter of a wrecked presidency. He owed his win on NAFTA to overwhelming support from congressional Republicans, who were ideologically committed free traders, and at the same time were averse to weakening even a Democratic president in the conduct of foreign affairs. All that could really be said about the improving economy was that the recovery from the recession, which actually began while Bush was still in office, was finally beginning to make itself felt. Even with his poll numbers back at about where they stood when he took office, Clinton was still politically vulnerable because of his approach to governing— vulnerable to the swirling passions of the American people and the people's contradictory demands for "change."

Clinton in effect brought his problems on himself, by attempting to govern as he had campaigned, as the people's agent for change. He continued to appear on morning talk-shows and in informal "town meetings." He set up campaign-style "war rooms" to push for congressional passage of the budget and NAFTA. He sent Vice President Al Gore to debate Perot on NAFTA, on *Larry King Live*. Clinton did not distinguish between campaigning and governing because he was insufficiently attentive to the need for government forms, and hence for formality in government, in the system of representative democracy. The need for the formalization or institutionalization of government was amply demonstrated in the most important political contests of his first year in office, although the point seemed to have been lost on him. To take only the example of NAFTA: the American people were not really capable of weighing reasonably the benefits and costs of the extremely complicated agreement, and hence to submit it to them for their judgment, as Clinton did in the public campaign he orchestrated from the White House, was to invite the manipulations of demagogues. Clinton did not, of course, create Perot as a political phenomenon; in the way he tried to govern, however, he gave Perot the opportunities he needed to stay politically alive. In his campaign for NAFTA, Clinton courted disaster, for himself and the nation. Defeat would have left the president seriously, perhaps fatally weakened, and Perot, who managed to promote himself as the leader of the opposition, as the principal arbiter of American government and politics. Clinton was rescued not by Gore, who by all accounts bested Perot in the meaningless *Larry King* debate, but by congressional Republicans, who delivered most of the votes needed for passage of the agreement. The net effect of Clinton's antiformalist strategy for governing was, then, to create openings for his most formidable enemy, while leaving his fate in the hands of his institutional opponents.

Clinton, in attempting to govern as he had campaigned, identified himself with the popular frustration with the forms of constitutional, representative democracy. After his narrow win on the budget, he declared that he had broken "gridlock" in Washington. There was never the slighest indication that he had considered whether there were important interests at stake for him, as president, in upholding the forms and formalities of government. There is an argument to be made, however, that the forms established by the Constitution have as their principal purpose the shielding of the president in the exercise of his legitimate authority. The Constitution charges the president with the responsibility of taking care that "the laws are faithfully executed." Since law is of no effect unless it is enforced, the vigorous exercise of presidential authority is essential to the establishment of the constitutional system of the rule of law. "Energy in the Executive," according to Alexander Hamilton, "is a leading character in the definition of good government," necessary not only for the "protection of the community against foreign attacks," but also for the "steady administration of the laws," the "protection of property," and the "security of liberty against the enterprises and assaults of ambition, of faction, and of anarchy." "A feeble execution" being "but another phrase for a bad execution," for Hamilton, "a government ill executed, whatever it may be in theory, must be, in practice, a bad government."[4]

While necessary, however, the vigorous exercise of executive power is a cause of fear for the people, who must be concerned how it might be used against them. There is, as Aristotle says, a certain "odium" that inevitably attaches to the executive magistracy.[5] The executive office must be properly constituted, then, in order to make it acceptable to the people. The Framers understood that the people would acquiesce in the vigorous exercise of presidential power, and hence in the effectual establishment of the rule of law, only if the president were hedged by suitable formal or institutional restraints. The presidency had to be embedded in a governmental structure that would ensure as far as possible the proper exercise of its powers. Presidential power is not only compatible with, but actually requires, the limitations embodied in the forms of the Constitution. More than this, it requires respect from the president for those forms. Presidential power is enhanced through its exercise in accordance with the forms and formalities of representative government. It is perhaps always tempting to presidents to go around the forms of the Constitution and govern by appealing directly to the people. Giving in to this temptation, however, by reminding the people of what they have to fear of the president, risks undermining the real power of the presidency.

The fundamental problem for Clinton—who at the end of his first year in office must have been at a loss to explain why, despite all that he had accomplished as agent of change for the people, he was mistrusted by many and abhorred by some—is that the American people, in accordance with the nature of peoples everywhere and always, are of two distinct minds. On the one hand, they are carried away by their hopes for, and fears of, the future. They want action, and they want it soon. They demand change from their political leaders. As a result they are impatient with the forms of constitutional, representative government, which seem to make all change painfully slow. On the other hand, the people are fearful and jealous of their leaders, who might abuse the trust placed in them. While not necessarily cherishing the forms of constitutional democracy, they do find something of a sense of security in them. They are fearful of political leaders who, even in pursuit of good ends, show themselves to be too ready to dispense with those forms. There is in this something of the legendary fickleness of democratic peoples.[6] President Bush, through his inactivity and rhetorical reticence, was impaled on one horn of the dilemma posed by the passions of the people. President Clinton, as a result of his hyperactivity and rhetorical excesses, risks being impaled on the other.

It is perhaps already possible to discern, for better or worse, the outlines of the 1996 presidential campaign. What is missing from contemporary American politics, as demonstrated by the 1992 campaign, is the statesmanlike understanding that the proper role for presidential leadership in a time of profound change is neither to ignore the irrational hopes and fears of the people nor to enlist blindly in their service, but rather to seek to educate or discipline them. This must begin with the promotion, by salutary example, of respect for the forms and formalities of constitutional, representative democracy.

Notes

1. Harvey C. Mansfield Jr., *America's Constitutional Soul* (Baltimore: Johns Hopkins University Press, 1991), p. ix.

2. See Samuel P. Huntington, *American Politics: The Promise of Disharmony* (Cambridge, Mass.: Belknap Press, 1981).

3. *Facts on File*, Jan. 21, 1993, p. 27.

4. Alexander Hamilton, John Jay, and James Madison, *The Federalist Papers* (New York: Mentor, 1961) 70, p. 423.

5. See Aristotle, *Politics* 1321b40–1322a7.

6. See the stories of Themistocles, Aristides, Cimon, and Pericles in Plutarch's *Lives of the Noble Greeks and Romans*.

Index

About the Contributors

John Agresto is president of St. Johns College, Santa Fe.

Roger M. Barrus is associate professor of political science at Hampden-Sydney College.

Daniel Casse is policy director for the Project for the Republican Future.

John H. Eastby is associate professor of political science at Hampden-Sydney College.

Bruce Frohnen is Bradley resident scholar at the Heritage Foundation.

Gary D. Glenn is associate professor of political science at Northern Illinois University.

Peter Augustine Lawler is professor of government at Berry College.

Harvey C. Mansfield Jr. is William Kenan Jr. professor of government at Harvard University.

David E. Marion is professor of political science at Hampden-Sydney College.

David M. Mason is director of the U.S. Congress Assessment Project at the Heritage Foundation.

Peter McNamara is assistant professor of political science at Utah State University.

Jeffrey J. Poelvoorde is associate professor of political science at Converse College.

James F. Pontuso is associate professor of political science at Hampden-Sydney College.

Ralph A. Rossum is Salvatori professor of American constitutionalism at Claremont McKenna College.

H. E. Scruggs is assistant professor of political science at Brigham Young University.

Richard Sherlock is professor of philosophy at Utah State University.

Delba Winthrop is lecturer in the extension program at Harvard University.